TOURNAMENTS OF POWER

Tournaments of Power

Honor and revenge in the contemporary world

Edited by
TOR AASE
University of Bergen Norway

Routledge
Taylor & Francis Group
LONDON AND NEW YORK

First published 2002 by Ashgate Publishing

2 Park Square, Milton Park, Abingdon, Oxon OX14 4RN
711 Third Avenue, New York, NY 10017, USA

Routledge is an imprint of the Taylor & Francis Group, an informa business

First issued in paperback 2017

British Library Cataloguing in Publication Data
Tournaments of power : honor and revenge in the
contemporary world
1. Honor 2. Revenge 3. Social interaction
I. Aase, Tor
303.3'72

Library of Congress Cataloging-in-Publication Data
Tournaments of power : honor and revenge in the contemporary world / edited by Tor Aase.
p. cm.
Includes bibliographical references.
ISBN 0-7546-3181-8 (alk. paper)
1. Honor. 2. Revenge. I. Aase, Tor, 1949-

BJ1533.H8 T68 2002
302'.1--dc21

2002066706

ISBN 13: 978-0-7546-3181-1 (hbk)
ISBN 13: 978-1-138-25846-4 (pbk)

Contents

List of Contributors

Tor Aase
Professor, Department of Geography, University of Bergen
e-mail: tor.aase@nhh.no

Haci Akman
Associate Professor, Department of Cultural Studies, University of Bergen
e-mail: haci.akman@ikk.uib.no

Joi Bay
Researcher, Institute of Legal Science, University of Copenhagen
e-mail: joi.bay@jur.ku.dk

Eldar Bråten
Associate Professor, Department of Anthropology, University of Bergen
e-mail: eldar.braten@sosantr.uib.no

Roy D'Andrade
Professor, Department of Anthropology, University of California San Diego
e-mail: rdandrade@ucsd.edu

Bruce Kapferer
Professor, Department of Anthropology, University of Bergen
e-mail; bruce.kapferer@sosantr.uib.no

Inger-Lise Lien
Senior Researcher, Norwegian Institute for Urban and Regional Research, Oslo
e-mail: inger-lise.lien@nibr.no

Marit Melhuus
Professor, Department of Anthropology, University of Oslo
e-mail: marit.melhuus@sai.uio.no

Leif Selstad
Associate Professor, Finnmark College Alta
e-mail: leif.selstad@hifm.no

Chapter 1

Introduction: Honor and Revenge in the Contemporary World[1]

Tor Aase

Europe has recently experienced a resurgence of honor as a topical theme in various realms of social life. It is invoked in court hearings; it is a recurrent theme in gang fights; and it is an integral part of identity formation in certain milieus. Commenting on violent gang fights in Oslo recently, a young man of Pakistani descent said, 'you cannot utter a critical remark to a Pakistani here without him feeling his honor threatened'. Such an obsession with honor runs counter to most Europeans' conception of modern living. Honor and revenge are out of place in modern European welfare states.

Theoretically as well, honor has no place in modernity. Honor and conflicts over violations of honor are thought to be phenomena belonging to the *ancien régime*, to be found in historical Europe and in traditional non-Western societies. Twenty five yeas ago, Americans who showed concern for their honor were perceived as suffering from a 'provincial mentality' and were sometimes labeled 'hopelessly European' (Berger et al. 1974). In the eyes of educated Americans, honor and chastity were, at best, seen as 'ideological leftovers in the consciousness of obsolete classes, such as military officers and ethnic grandmothers' (ibid. 78).

Peter Berger regards honor as one of the very hallmarks that distinguishes modernity from pre-modernity. In *ancien régimes*, honor is an integral part of hierarchical social formations where status is ascribed rather than achieved. Feudal Europe, with its clearly separated social strata into which chivalrous men and chaste women were born, is prototypical for this kind of social formation. In such societies, 'honor is a direct expression of status, a source of solidarity among social equals and a demarcation line against social inferiors' (ibid. 80). The person is intimately linked to the hierarchical order through his identity: 'In a world of honor, the individual discovers his true identity in his roles, and to turn away from the roles is to turn away from himself' (ibid. 84). Pre-modern man finds his identity in acting honorably according to institutionalized role expectations attached to his status. Thus, personal lives reflect the prevailing social order.

---

[1] I am grateful to my colleague Kjell Helge Sjöström for the layout of the book.

Berger believes that pre-modern society is transformed into modernity through the agency of technological innovations and concomitant changes in production relations. Parallel to these, he also observes a change in consciousness. Institutionalized ways of coping with everyday life are substituted by problem-solving inventiveness and a 'tinkering attitude'; many-stranded personal relations are substituted by anonymous social relations; and 'emotional management' and suppression of feelings become virtues.

In such a modern society, honor becomes obsolete. Since ascribed status and institutionalized role behavior have lost their social significance, there is no need to maintain group markers any more. The concern with honor is taken over by another moral enterprise, namely, the cultivation of one's dignity: 'Dignity, as against honor, always relates to the intrinsic humanity divested of all socially imposed roles and norms. It pertains to the self as such, to the individual regardless of his position in society' (ibid. 83).

Berger claims that the theoretical logic of modern functional rationality leaves no room for honor. The declining importance of honor in the modern world has also been argued empirically. In Norway, Christie used national figures of 'slander and libel' cases as an index of the social concern with honor (Christie 1985). A marked decline in the number of cases investigated by police since the Second World War until the 1970s, ties in neatly with Berger's theoretical assertions. In Sweden, however, there was a slight increase in cases during the late 1970s. Christie relates this increase to non-European immigration, suggesting that immigrants retain their sense of honor for a time after arriving in Sweden.

In Norway, it is also possible to detect correlations between immigration and allegations of slander and libel. Such cases – which are labeled 'violations of honor' in Norwegian – decreased from about 1100 cases investigated annually in the early 1960s, to a mere 500 annual cases in the mid 1980s, rising again to 800 cases a year in the 1990s (fig. 1.1). Parallel to this, the number of non-Western immigrants living in Norway has increased steadily since the early 1970s.

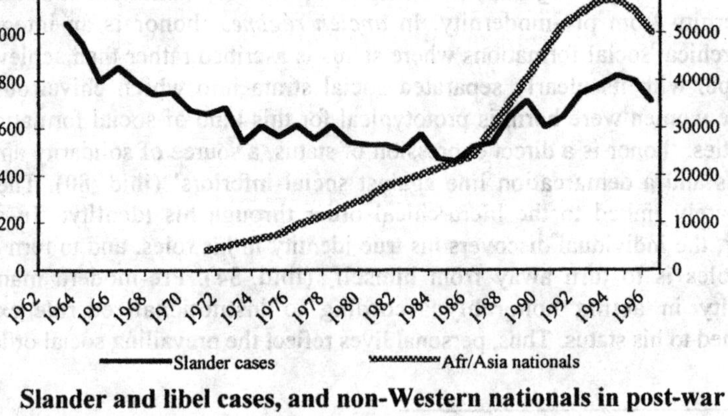

Figure 1.1 Slander and libel cases, and non-Western nationals in post-war Norway

The application of slander and libel cases as an index of the social importance of honor may, of course, be criticized. Firstly, there is a problem of validity. We do not know if the reported cases actually involve the kind of honor Berger is thinking about. Secondly, we do not know whether the recent increase in reported cases is produced by immigrants. If it is like Berger and Christie maintain, that honor is a cultural relict in modern society, it is also likely that immigrants will solve their disputes over honor outside the formal judicial apparatus.

1.1 The persistence of honor in modern democracies

However, if we turn to court proceedings involving immigrant residents to Europe, there is ample evidence that honor still matters in the modern context. Revenge killings in the name of honor have become a quite commonplace phenomenon in multi-cultural Europe. In cases where honor is claimed to be the motive of a homicide, the accused as well as the host society have a problem, since honor is not considered a relevant notion in the modern condition. France, for instance, abolished all articles concerning 'crimes of passion' from its penal code in 1975. The problem is illuminated by the following case.

A young Pakistani girl in Oslo wanted to marry a boy with whom she had fallen in love. Her father had other plans for her and opposed the love marriage, but the mother supported her daughter, and the two women left the family and went through with the marriage. Some time later the girl's brother, who continued to cohabit with their father, went to the young couple and shot both of them. He committed this heinous deed 'in order to save the honor of the family', he claimed in court. The Norwegian court, however, showed no understanding for such a defense argument. On the contrary, the boy was sentenced under 'especially aggravating circumstances' to maximum imprisonment, which is 21 years in Norway. In addition, he would be deported from the country once the imprisonment period had been completed (usually after 12-14 years if the prisoner has not misbehaved in any way).

The boy accepted imprisonment, but protested vehemently to deportation. Back in Pakistan, he expects to be persecuted by his former in-laws who are probably eager to avenge the killing of their son and brother. Thus, he would be punished doubly according to two legal codes: one in which honor does not matter as an argument of defense, and another where it certainly does. In Pakistan, he would hardly have been sentenced at all for defending the honor of his family. Now he will first have to endure imprisonment in Norway, and later he will face the continual risk of revenge killing in Pakistan.

In European countries where the prevalent ideology is immigrant integration rather than assimilation, the fact that honor matters to some citizens raises a moral dilemma: how far should the host society go in accepting alien notions of justice and crime? A recent controversy between two anthropologists over a homicide in a Turkish immigrant milieu in a Norwegian town illuminates the dilemma.

A Turkish teenage girl had a sexual relationship with a married Turkish man. The man was 13 years older than the girl, and he was a friend of the girl's family.

The girl later alleged that she had been forced into the affair unwillingly. When the encroachment was discovered, the girl's father and brothers decided to restore the honor of the family by killing the culprit. So they did, and hid the body. The body was found later by the police, and the case was brought to trial. The District Court requested an anthropologist, Reidar Gronhaug, to inform the court on the socio-cultural context of the case. Ultimately, the three accused men were given relatively mild sentences of 8 to 11 years imprisonment. The case was later appealed to High Court, who increased the sentences by adding 4 and 5 years imprisonment to the sentences previously reached by the District Court. In its apportioning of the sentences, High Court obviously disregarded the emphasis put on Turkish notions of family honor by the District Court.

Another anthropologist, Tordis Bochgrewink, is strongly critical to the kind of 'applied cultural relativism' as she calls it, that was allowed by the District Court. By defending the right to practice Turkish notions of honor in Norway, women are denied the right to sexuality and independence. Ascribing legitimacy to a 'collective motive' (Turkish notions of honor) implies accepting human rights violations in the name of cultural tolerance. Undermining Norwegian values and standards in this way is best described as 'generous treason' to Norwegian and Western culture (Bochgrewink 1997).

Gronhaug defends his participation in the District Court by inferring a core norm of Western judicial practice, that the accused party's premises of action should be understood by the court before verdict is reached. Revealing the 'cultural ecology' in which decisions are taken and actions performed makes it possible to find valid comparative cases from a cultural context that the court knows (Gronhaug 1997).

At the base of Bochgrewink's argument seems to be an assumption that honor is 'out of place' in Norway; it is practiced in a modern context where other standards should be applied in the valuation of actions – standards that may be subsumed under the label of individual dignity. Thus she argues from a 'modernist' position as described by Berger. Honor is out of place in the modern condition since it belongs to the *ancien régime*. But since cases like the above do come up from time to time, honor is obviously an aspect of contemporary Europe. Defenders of honor on the European scene are not only obsolete Don Quixotes combating imaginary enemies of the past, but social actors who are concerned with a cultural idea that is as real for them as dignity or individual freedom is to a 'modern' European. And what is more, honor is not only a concern of 'ethnic grandmothers'. Contrary to the predictions of 'delayed acculturation' theories, honor is a highly meaningful concept in the everyday lives of young second-generation immigrants, even more so than among their parents.

In chapter 2 in this book, Inger-Lise Lien observes that students at an Oslo highschool can be classified into four categories according to their concern with honor: Norwegian boys, Norwegian girls, boys of immigrant descent (mainly Somali and Pakistani), and girls of immigrant descent. In a social field where popularity and standing are the issues at stake, immigrant boys and Norwegian girls are the main actors. The point for immigrant boys is to seduce Norwegian girls and to protect their own ethnic sisters. A boy is honorable if he has

(Norwegian) girlfriends and if he succeeds in preventing other boys from getting near his own sisters. In this game, respect is won by creating fear. In the words of a Somali boy: 'They respect me because they are afraid of me'. Norwegian girls are fascinated by the willingness of their immigrant boyfriends to protect their honor. They accept the code of honor and act according to it, but at the same time they strive for equality with the boys and thus insist on a modern code of dignity.

Immigrant girls and Norwegian boys are kept out of the popularity game. The honor code is forced upon immigrant girls by the expectations that they must avoid bringing shame on their families by talking to boys, staying out late, or wearing Western clothes. Although Norwegian boys admire the honor and strength of immigrant boys, they withdraw from the game and seek girlfriends at pure Norwegian schools instead, where other attributes than honor are prized by the girls.

The result of such self-reinforcing, schismogenetic processes is a clear polarization of youths in Oslo, according to Lien. On the one hand, immigrant 'hyper-identities' in which honor and respect are core ingredients occasionally break out in violent gang fights with deadly outcomes. At the other extreme, the polarization nourishes nationalistic and neo-Nazi sentiments in some Norwegian milieus.

Early conceptions of modernity predicted that phenomena like ethnicity and religion would be relocated from the public sphere to the private sphere, becoming a raw material for individual identity formation rather than a basis for political and social action (Beyer 1994). Just as these predictions have proved wrong, dignity has also not managed to wipe out honor in the modern world. Thus the question arises: is the continued existence of honor a kind of 'cultural luggage' – an internalized habitus structured by social processes at the place of origin – that is brought to Europe by immigrants? Berger locates the notion of dignity at the heart of modernity: 'The concept of the naked self, beyond institutions and roles, as the *ens realissimum* of human being, is at the very heart of modernity' (ibid. 190). Should we, then, understand the continued occurrence of honor in modern democracies as a kind of contamination from pre-modernity? Is honor a pre-modern weed in a modern garden of dignity?

The arguments of Berger (1970, 1974) and Christie (1985) are firmly rooted in perceptions of 'acculturation' that were predominant in sociology during the 1970s and 1980s, and which assumed that immigrants would absorb majority culture after some time in the host society. Fisher formulates the sociological stance thus: 'In the first generation of immigration, problems are communal and family-related; in later ones vestiges remain at the personal level, and they, too, will disappear' (Fischer 1986:231). According to the traditional sociological way of reasoning, it is just a matter of time before the weeds of honor and other imported cultural traits will fade away under the influence of modern conditions.

A description of multi-ethnic Europe as a dual society where non-European immigrants have added traditional honor to modern dignity is close to hand. However, the chapter in this book by Joi Bay (chapter 3) strongly questions the validity of such a description. Danish outlaw bikers are also concerned with honor! Clubs like Hells Angels and Bullshit MC have an idiom for honor, *stærk* (strong), which is shared collectively among the members of a club. A challenge from a rival club must be avenged, otherwise honor is lost. Challenge and revenge may result in feuds which are ultimately terminated by the mediation of a third club. And clubs mark their rank in the MC hierarchy by special vests and patches. If an attack on the honor of a club is not avenged, it runs the risk of being degraded from the highest rank of 'outlaw' to a 'touring' club, or worse still, to a mere 'family' club. Indeed, there are striking similarities between notions of honor among MC clubs in Denmark and a prototypical feuding society in Northern Pakistan as described by Aase in chapter 5.

It is reasonable to assume that members of Hells Angels and Bullshit MC have been brought up in ordinary Danish families and spent their childhoods in ordinary Danish neighborhoods. Honor is hardly part of their cultural heritage any more than it is for Danes who are not active in MC milieus. It follows that the 'cultural luggage' explanation for the continued concern with honor in the modern world does not hold. Honor is a meaningful concept not only to 'obsolete classes' and ethnic minorities, but also to actors in highly modern social formations like MC gangs.

How, then, should we understand the persistence of honor in the contemporary world?

A striking feature in publications on honor is that few writers venture into the concept and ask what it is all about. Berger, for example, claims that honor is a 'group marker' and a 'source of solidarity among social equals' (Berger 1974). But he does not explain *what* is a group marker or a source of solidarity beyond referring to honor. Another writer on honor, Maddox (1987), explicitly rejects any endeavor to explain what honor actually is. Instead of trying to define honor, he sets out to describe its strategic use by socially situated actors in historical Spain. Analysing honor in its historical context, like Maddox does, must be appreciated in its own right. But his avoidance of defining its semantic content poses serious problems for purposes of comparison. How do we know that the phenomenon he subsumes under the term 'honor' corresponds to the Pakistani term *izzat*, or the Algerian *hurma*, or the Danish MC notion of being *stærk*? The problem of comparison becomes even more pronounced when we take into account that many societies have various conceptions of honor. In Pakistan, the distinct semantic categories of *izzat* and *gheirat* are both lumped together and translated with the English category 'honor', even by Pakistani writers (Ahmed 1996). The Kabyle of Algeria use three terms that are all related to various aspects of honor: *essar*, *hurma*, and *nif* (Bourdieu 1979). Which one of these do we refer to when we use the English term?

The ambition of this book is to look into the phenomena of honor and vengeance as they are conceived and practiced in the contemporary world. This endeavor calls for an approach that permits comparisons. Since any meaningful comparison implies that we must be pretty sure that what we compare are identical or similar phenomena, a more substantial perception of honor than that applied by Maddox is needed. Let us, again, turn to empirical reality and see if it is possible to infer the meaning of honor by looking at the way it is actually practiced in a pre-modern context.

1.2 What is honor all about?

Aase's chapter on Tangir in the Hindu Kush mountains in Northern Pakistan may serve as an illuminating case (chapter 5). Tangir is in many ways a prototypical feuding society. The feud is institutionalized in the manner that there are rules that define when a conflict (*dushmani*) develops into a blood feud (*mar dushmani*), and when it can be terminated through the mediation of a third party (*jirga*).

A conflict turns into a blood feud when honor is at stake. Any issue may jeopardize the honor of a family, although nowadays most feuds are fought over the chastity of women. An extramarital romance, a flirt, or even village gossip about such relations, compels the insulted family to restore its honor (*gheirat*) by killing a male member of the alleged offender's family. Sexual shame is embodied in the woman, and if intercourse has taken place, the only way to get rid of the shame is to kill the woman along with the offender, irrespective of whether the incident was encouraged by her or whether she was raped. This is a quite universal reaction to extramarital sexual relations in the Middle East (Faqir 2001).

More illuminating of the meaning of honor are cases where a woman is approached by a man unwillingly and no embodied shame is inflicted upon her. In such cases, only the male offender or another male member of his family should be killed in order to restore honor. The crucial question to ask is why a revenge killing restores the honor of an insulted family. What is the cultural logic in the notion that killing the male culprit restores the chastity of an insulted woman? The point is that it does not! The core issue in cases of illegitimate sexual approaches is that the male relatives of the insulted woman have proved unable to protect her chastity. They have demonstrated weakness since outsiders have succeeded in penetrating their domain, that is, the female chastity of the family. Such signs of weakness can only be restored by a show of force, which means a revenge killing. In this manner, restoration of honor actually means that a family re-establishes its credibility as protector of female chastity.

Even if female chastity is the most recurrent theme in Tangiri blood feuds, feuds are also fought over disagreements concerning land rights, water rights, and other issues. Thus, male honor is not ontologically linked to women's chastity. Attacks on female chastity constitute just one type of challenge to male honor; infringements on a family's land and water resources constitute another. The ability of a Tangiri family to defend its interests – whether those interests are female chastity, land, or water rights – is, *ipso facto*, its honor. The blood feud is an occasion to show that ability publicly – a tournament of power.

Another aspect of Tangiri blood feuds that testifies to the contention that honor has primarily to do with the public show of power is found in the procedures for termination of the feud. Peace is negotiated by the *jirga*, a council of influential elders who is accepted by both parties in a feud. One task of the *jirga* is to establish an account of losses on both sides and suggest compensation to the party who has a negative balance of losses. But the crucial point to notice is that a *jirga* cannot be held until both parties in a conflict have had the opportunity to show their strength. At least one killing or a serious physical injury must be committed from both sides before mediation can take place. In case of an illegitimate approach to a woman, compensation cannot be mediated directly. Only after the insulted party has killed one male member of the insulting family, and the offenders on their part have retaliated by a revenge killing, can a *jirga* be summoned. When both parties have succeeded in killing one of the other side, an honorable peace can be negotiated. Again, we see that the core meaning of honor is power. The feud cannot be terminated until both involved parties have had the opportunity to demonstrate their ability of defense publicly.

The synonymity of honor and power is not confined to Tangir only. In the mid 1970s, Jacob Black-Michaud carried out a survey of numerous cases of feud in the Mediterranean and in the Middle East. Analyses of a comprehensive set of data revealed that the exercise of power or the threat of power is a salient and recurrent theme in conflicts over honor. Inferring from this observation, he nearly reduces honor to power. 'Acts of violence carried out in the name of honor may always ultimately be seen as moves in the struggle for power and dominance' (Black-Michaud 1975:179). This does not imply that honor can be seen as a cover term for power – that acts performed in the name of honor amount to nothing but the execution of power. Rather, power exercised in the guise of honor may be viewed as a culturally legitimate demonstration of power. When honor is at stake, action is called for and the use of power is justified. Since honor is nearly synonymous with power, 'it is almost identical to the ability to defend it' (ibid. 181). The ethnographic survey leads Black-Michaud to claim that honor actually means a person's or a group's ability of defense.

Akman's chapter in this volume about Kurdistan (chapter 6) supports the view that honor can be seen as synonymous with self-defense. In contrast to Tangir where honor is primarily a family matter, Kurds mainly refer honor to the tribe. If an insult against a tribal member is not avenged, the implied message to the social surroundings is that the entire tribe is weak and afraid and thereby devoid of honor. In Akman's account, honor is challenged in situations where domains perceived to belong to a tribe are penetrated by outsiders.

It seems valid therefore to equate honor with capability for defense in parts of the Middle East and the Mediterranean. The next question to ask is about the general validity of the insight that honor is an epiphenomenon of self-defense. Does it shed light on the phenomenon of honor in general, or is it regionally and culturally confined to the Middle East and the Mediterranean?

The notion of honor among Danish MC clubs has obvious connotations of power. Honor is denoted by the term *stærk*, which actually means 'strong'. According to Bay (chapter 3), honor/*stærk* is intimately linked to the ability to defend territories of influence, which are symbolic rather than real. Bay describes a conflict between two clubs, Hog Riders and Barons MC, where acts of revenge and counter-revenge take place before a third party, Hells Angels, mediates a termination to the feud. Similar to Tangir, the parties in the MC feud must demonstrate their power publicly before peace can be negotiated.

In Java, Bråten also relates honor to the ability to defend territory, in his case the local community (chapter 7). The most significant primary group in Javanese society is the local community, the *kampung*, which is a fragile construct located between the individual and the state. In order to keep the loosely knit *kampung* together, people strive to adhere to the *runkun* code of conduct which commands patience, acceptance, and emotional detachment in local everyday life. *Runkun* thus resembles the notion of dignity. But when the local community is threatened by outsiders, people resort to intense spontaneous violence. In the stories told after such incidents, the violence is legitimated by the invocation of *kapok* – that the culprits had to 'learn a lesson'. *Kapok* can be seen as a kind of deterrence, communicating to the outside world that, 'we are able to defend our interests, so don't fool with us'. Bråten maintains that the intensity and brutality with which communal honor is defended in Java results from the fear that the *kampung* will collapse, leaving the individual with no communal level of identity formation: 'Vulnerable community creates strong expressions,' he contends. This argument may also be valid for European MC clubs. Javanese *kampung* and European MC clubs are both arenas for identity formation, rituals, and sociability, but they lack the reinforcing base that is inherent in blood relations (family) or in corporate economic estates.

Blood ties are also lacking in the case of second generation immigrant youths in Oslo. There, fictive brotherhood is generated through peer group loyalty. A gang of fictive brothers obtain rank (vis à vis other gangs) and popularity (among girls) by adhering to the honor code, which creates respect through fear. Lien claims that, 'The boy with ambition to gain honor is therefore constantly fearful that others will see his fear, because that would be a signal of inferiority' (chapter 2). Again, we see that honor is closely related to power.

Evidence from Mexico, likewise, supports the contended link between honor and power, that is, when it comes to male honor. The proverb cited in the title of chapter 10, 'A house that lacks a man, lacks respect', refers to the male role of defending family interests materially as well as symbolically. Asking how honor is constituted in a Mexican village, Melhuus convincingly argues that notions and practices of honor can not be understood unless its gendered nature is looked into. A family is respectable if the husband provides for the children and if he has exclusive disposal of his wife's sexuality. Challenges to these male roles 'taint the honor' (*mancillar el honor*) of a man and would traditionally provoke acts of revenge. But fulfilment of the male (*macho*) role implies that a woman is unable to support the children as well as fend for her own virtue. A strict sexual division of labour and the denial of women's right to their own sexuality are preconditions of male honor. Thus, changes in labour division will produce concomitant changes in gender relations, and ultimately in notions of honor. The validity of this claim becomes evident in cases where women have been left by their husbands. Being forced to provide for the children themselves, destituted women (*abandonada*) challenge the prevailing moral order according to which men should be the 'keepers' and women should be the 'kept' (*mantenida*). Presently, there seems to be a schizma in Mexico between rural moralities that rest heavily on perceptions of male honor and female shame on the one hand, and 'modern' institutions like banks that do not distinguish between the genders when they issue loans to income-generating activities.

Concluding from this short ethnographic inquiry, it seems that equating honor with the ability to defend oneself is a credible understanding of the term not only in the Middle East and the Mediterranean, but in other contexts as well. This is a very intriguing discovery, since it avoids the impasse of relativism and makes it possible to compare various expressions of honor. The comparative questions to ask are therefore: under what circumstances can power be exercised in a socially acceptable way, and in what situations will the parties involved in a conflict fall into disgrace if their case is not actively defended? Black-Michaud performs a comparative analysis according to these questions himself, and finds that apart from violations of women's sexual chastity there rarely exist any prescribed norms according to which honorable vengeance must be taken. In some cases an event results in blood feud; in another case a similar event does not.

With the important exception of female chastity, it is not possible to predict a feud in any society, according to Black-Michaud's findings. But on a higher level it is relevant to ask whether honorable behavior – the legitimate use of power in order to protect one's interests – occurs in certain political formations and in certain social situations.

1.3 Political contexts of honor and revenge

Let us return to Tangir for a moment. The Tangiri political structure is acephalous (literally, headless), which means that there exists no centralized political authority in the form of a chief, a king, or a bureaucracy. The only political institution is the *jirga*, whose function is limited to mediation only. If the verdict of a *jirga* is not accepted by the parties in a conflict, the *jirga* has no sanctions at hand to enforce its decision. In such a political system the individual family is in the last instance the architect of its own fortune. If it loses its ability to defend its interests, that is, the family honor, or if it even loses its reputation for having such an ability, its very existence is threatened by predatory neighbors. Under the acephalous political conditions in Tangir, honor is vital to the survival of the primary group, that is, the family.

Kurdish society does not qualify for the label 'acephalous', since it has centralized authority in the role of tribal chiefs. But on a higher level, the Kurdish nation is also 'headless' in the sense that there is no authority to regulate inter-tribal relations. The political rivalry between independent tribes is one of the main reasons why the Kurdish people have never managed to form their own state, according to Akman (chapter 6). The 'headless' tribal structure has been appreciated and exploited by regional states who vehemently oppose the idea of a united Kurdish nation. While the family is the primary political unit in Tangir, the tribe is the main level of political mobilization in Kurdistan. Interestingly, honor is related to the family in Tangir and to the tribe in Kurdistan, again signifying the close relationship between honor and politics, that is, power.

The Tangir and Kurdistan cases allow the following hypothesis to be put forward: Honor and vengeance are valid and legitimate expressions of power in groups and societies that are set, or that set themselves, outside the formal procedures of the state. The hypothesis challenges the stiff dichotomy of pre-modern honor versus modern dignity, since it allows us to regard honorable action in a modern context, not as an anomaly, but as an integral part of modernity.

Do the chapters of this book contain evidence to support the hypothesis? Roy D'Andrade grapples with the view argued by some writers that the Southern States of the USA are characterized by a 'culture of honor' which is not found in the Northern States (chapter 4). Extensive studies have documented that, compared with northerners, southerners become angrier and tend to be more aggressive on being insulted. However, in order to relate this difference in behavior to a code of honor, such a code must be argued for and demonstrated. In the words of D'Andrade, 'a society does not have an honor code if people just admire strong, aggressive men'. A code of honor must somehow be institutionalized; people must be expected to follow it or suffer the consequence of being disgraced.

In order to investigate the alleged difference between the American South and North, D'Andrade carries out a questionnaire survey where he confronts 350 undergraduate students with various constructed insult scenarios. Analysis of the data reveals no significant difference between southerners and northerners whatsoever. He concludes that there exists a strong common American culture with respect to the norms for response to insult, which he labels a 'code of decency'.

However, the observations that southerners more often react to insult with violence are robust and well documented, and cannot be rejected on the basis of a questionnaire survey. D'Andrade interprets the deviation between questionnaire results and actual behavior by suggesting that southerners hold two codes of conduct simultaneously. When confronted with the questionnaire scenarios, southern respondents refer to the common American code of decency. But when actually insulted or threatened, they act according to a code of self-defense. The moral correctness of using physical violence to defend oneself is still very much alive in the South: 'The use of violence in order to protect oneself is personally endorsed, institutionally supported, and collectively represented in a positive light throughout the South and West.' D'Andrade explains the continued survival of the self-defence code along with the decency code in the American South with the historical role of the state: 'Southern reliance on self-protective violence seems to have been the result of a lack of reliable state mechanisms for social control.'

D'Andrade prefers to apply the term 'self-defense code' to southerners' violent reactions to insult. But according to the argument put forward above, honor can be seen as more or less synonymous to self-defense. Since the distinction between the two terms thus becomes blurred, it can be contended that honor still matters in the American South, although not institutionalized in a specific code. The continued practice of honor – in the sense of self-defense – in the American South cannot be ascribed to the 'cultural luggage' explanation. The reason must be sought in the relationship between the individual and the state.

Moreover, the recent terrorist attacks on New York World Trade Center and the Pentagon have revealed a general American urge for violent response. It has been a unanimous claim in the USA (and in most of the remaining world) that those who supported the terrorists must be tracked down and punished. The logic of disrupting terrorist networks is of course to prevent future attacks. But in addition to such preventive measures, President Bush promised the American people that appropriate 'retaliation' should be taken. It can be questioned whether the rhetoric of retaliation was meant for the masses or whether it reflected the actual political strategy of the Bush Administration. But in either case, it had resonance with six out of ten Americans who wanted to declare war, according to a Gallup poll carried out by TIME Magazine and CNN immediately after the attacks. Even one of the world's most modern states calls for revenge when its ability of self-defense has been shattered.

Tangir does not have a state to regulate interpersonal relations; and the state in the American South leaves space for interpersonal regulations to the individual itself. Danish outlaw bikers also operate on the fringes of the state, but they do so by their own choice. For some reason, they do not accept the procedures for interpersonal relations offered by the state. The honorary term 'outlaw' which is given to the highest ranking clubs, indicates the value which is ascribed to operating outside mainstream norms and institutions. A salient aspect of outlaw activity is that police and official judiciary are kept out of internal conflicts. To be an informer is a great dishonor. Honor conflicts cannot be solved by the law, because that would offend against the very logic of honor, which is to be able to defend oneself. A club that goes to the police to complain about a wrongdoing committed against it, admits that it is not able to defend itself and thereby loses honor. It is not *stærk* (strong) any more.

Japan seems to be a special case in respect of the contextual practice of honor. In contradistinction to Tangir and Kurdistan, where honor is held jointly by family and tribe respectively, honor is ascribed to the individual person in Japan. Personhood is understood as a duality between an underlying or real self (*honne*) and an official front or 'face' (*tatemae*). Social relations are established on the front level where notions of honor are also located. In his analysis of local politics in a Tokyo neighborhood, Selstad finds that honor may be viewed as, 'a template through which local power and standing are negotiated' (chapter 9). Losing honor the Japanese way implies losing face, which is exactly what happens to one of the contenders for the position of community leader in the ward studied by Selstad. The candidate lost face since he was not able to predict the outcome of the local elections. He proved unable to defend his own image, and thus lost face. Since honor is ascribed to the individual person in Japan, a generous interpretation of the incident is that honor has to do with self-defense there as well, albeit in a symbolic manner. What is peculiar to Japan, though, is the apparent fact that face cannot be restored once it is lost. The looser in the local election was socially dead for the rest of his biological life; there was no way he could regain his face/honor.

The Japanese situation, then, differs from the other cases described in this book where lost honor can be regained through the medium of revenge. An aspect of honor that is not addressed by Selstad is the question of whether revenge is a valid reaction to loss of honor in the Japanese context as well, in the manner that it is directed inward towards oneself in the form of suicide. However, this line of inquiry will not be taken up here.

Neither does the Tokyo case seem to support the hypothesis of a social vacuum left open by the state, at least not on the surface of things. Although the neighborhood described by Selstad is a village-like relict in the metropolis, it is appropriately integrated in the urban and national structure, and so are the bearers of honor, the individual inhabitants. But it might be possible to account for the continued preoccupation with honor on a deeper level. Although regulating most aspects of civilian life, the state does not interfere with the real self (*honne*), but confines itself to the level on which social relations are negotiated, that is, the public person or 'face' (*tatemae*). Thus, even in modern Japan a space is left open by the state for the individual person to defend himself, that is, his real self.

In the remaining chapters of the book, the weak link between the state and groups who practice notions of honor can be discerned. Kurdistan exists on the fringes of four different states, geographically as well as politically. Among youths of immigrant background in Oslo, Lien observes that norm-breaking activity adds to a person's prestige. The Mexican example shows that extention of public services in the form of granting bank loans to women, challenges traditional notions of gender-based honor and shame. In Java, the eagerness with which the local community is defended can partly be explained as a resistance to local life-worlds being colonized by the system-world of changing state policies. Indeed, Braten contends that an understanding of the concern with honor in Java must be sought in the triadic relationship between local community, offender, and the state.

Looking at the ethnographies presented in this book, the hypothesis formulated above seems to have substantial empirical support. Honor is practiced in spaces of individual maneuver left open by the state (Tangir, Kurdistan, Japan, Java, Southern states of the US) or in social spaces gained by actors themselves (Danish outlaw bikers, second generation immigrants in Oslo). Honor is a valid expression in certain circumstances that may emerge in modern as well as in pre-modern societies. Indeed, the hypothesis put forward here dissolves the dichotomy between modern and pre-modern societies, at least on the level of the state.

The structuralist approach to the study of honor advocated so far stands in sharp contrast to the 'cultural luggage' position of Berger (1974) and Christie (1984). Writers who adhere to what is often called the 'post-structuralist' paradigm opt for a combination of the two by implying the habitual as well as the improvisational aspect of social processes. Rosemary Coombe, writing about honor and shame in the Mediterranean, puts it thus: 'An understanding of culture as constantly reproduced, modified, and transformed in the practices of social agents must be combined with a recognition that the motivations for such activities are also constrained and enabled by social traditions of cultural practice' (Coombe 1990:234). In order to understand the phenomena of honor and feuding, Coombe argues for a combined analysis of the strategic activities of actors, and the semantic limits within which such activities are carried out. It is not hard to agree with Coombe that people cannot practice honor unless they have some ideas about it. The chapters in this book reveal that honor is conceptualized in multiple ways: being strong (*stærk*), teaching a lesson (*kapok*), keeping face (*tatemae*), enjoying respect. In spite of semantic variation, all these constructs somehow have to do with power and the ability to defend oneself, thus they can be subsumed under the rubric of honor.

Even if a structuralist approach has considerable explanatory power in the effort to understand expressions of honor, it runs the risk of implying a behavioristic epistemology of human agency. Given the stimuli of certain structural conditions, actors simply respond by practicing honor and revenge. This is, of course, too simplistic. As is explicitly demonstrated by Akman (chapter 6) and Bråten (chapter 7) and implied in the remaining chapters, contests over honor are associated with strong emotions – fear, pride, distrust, senseless anger, and sorrow. Such emotions can be seen as the inevitable outcome of feuding, but they are also constitutive of the conflicts themselves. How, then, does the motivation to enter a destructive spiral of revenge and counter-revenge come about?

1.4 Revenge and emotions

When concerned to find the motivation of an honorable revenge, one possibility is to seek it in the habitus of the actors, in which the cultural semantics have been personally internalized. According to the logic of the habitus, a vengeful person does not even have to be explicit about the cultural values of honor, since the values have become part of his practical consciousness: 'The system of honor values are enacted rather than thought, and the grammar of honor can inform actions without having to be formulated' (Bourdieu 1979:128). Proponents of the 'cultural luggage' position will probably embrace the simplified habitus explanation, and so will some European populist political parties who equate immigration with import of social problems like gang fighting and killing in the name of honor.

Alternatively, the motivation of revenge can be viewed as relational rather than habitual, and we can look for it in the actors' network of social relations. This can be done on two levels.

In chapter 8 of this book, Bruce Kapferer wonders about the passionate hatred that is often implied in acts of revenge. By considering sorcery in Sri Lanka, as a gateway to the study of revenge, he contends that hatred erupts in concrete or imagined social relations. The hater projects the responsibility for her own mental state onto a real or imagined other, who must be destroyed in order to eliminate the very cause of the hatred. Revenge, in other words, becomes a means of self-purification.

The mechanism of self-purification through revenge is transparent is Sinhala sorcery where real persons are the targets. But since hatred establishes social relations as well as arising from them, the same mechanism can be seen at work in racist activity and in ethnic encounters, and even in resistance to the state when the state is anthropomorphized into an imagined person. In addition to the cases listed by Kapferer, I assume that elimination of hatred through revenge may also apply to situations where hate has been aroused by violations of honor.

Kapferer focuses on the dyadic relation between the hater and the hated in his effort to understand the psychology of revenge. But in addition to being a way of purifying the self through elimination of the source of hatred, revenge has a clear communicative side to it. Another aspect of revenge is therefore situated in the wider social network of the avenger – the audience, so to speak. The importance of communication pertains particularly to cases where loss of honor must be restored through revenge. Since honor is given by social others, those same others are the ones who must be persuaded to continue the ascription of honor. Indeed, the actual or expected evaluations of neighbors and friends are often the real agency of revenge. Propelled by the fear of being called a coward, a humiliated person is transformed into an avenger.

The mechanism of expected or real reactions of significant others in generating revenge is salient throughout this book. In one of the cases listed by Aase, a feud would hardly have developed at all were it not for the repeated teasing and gossip of neighbors (case 4 chapter 5). Bourdieu, in writing about the Kabyle of Algeria, also stresses the vital role played by social others in mobilizing revenge: 'A thief who enters an inhabited house, as opposed to a thief who steals cereals or animals left outside, lays himself open to blood vengeance; this is because people will be quick to insinuate that the honor of the womenfolk has not been respected' (Bourdieu 1979:114).

Looking for motivations of revenge in the social surroundings instead of in the personal habitus, allows for a contextual approach to the phenomena of honor and revenge. Since the motive is, partly at least, located in the social surroundings, it is reasonable to expect that practices of honor and revenge vary when those surroundings change. A person who is encouraged to avenge an insult in Pakistan may not feel obliged to do so in the UK unless he is strongly integrated into a Pakistani milieu there. The very conception of 'insult' is also different in a British and in a Pakistani social context. Approaching the question of motivation in this manner makes it possible to explain a meeting between two Kurds in a European city who belong to opposed families in an old feud still going on in Kurdistan, described by Akman in chapter 6. A habitual approach could hardly explain why the meeting in Europe follows a course of events which differs from the one it most probably would have followed in Kurdistan.

1.5 Tournaments of power

In sum, feuding in which the motive is to avenge violations of honor, may be viewed as *tournaments of power*, where the contestants are invited to prove their strength publicly. The actual challenge is extended by the insulting party, but the invitation to public show of strength is offered by the wider social surroundings, by actual encouragement, or by expected sanctions if the gauntlet is not taken up. Some tournaments may go on indefinitely, like the 110 year-old feud described by Akman, or they may be ended by mediation and mutual consent. Cases of feuds that are ended reveal that Black-Michaud was right in identifying power as the inner meaning of honor. When a feud over sexual misbehavior towards a woman is settled, it is not the chastity or honor of the woman that is restored; that can only be removed by killing her, the bearer of the shame, which is also often done in some societies (Faqir 2001). What is restored through a settlement is the public recognition of a family's or a group's ability to defend its interests – whether those interests are of a material or a symbolic character. The ability of a group to defend its interest is, *ipso facto*, its honor.

Execution of power in the guise of honor tends to be legitimate in social spaces left open by the state. Such spaces, or fields of activity, can be found in societies where no effective centralized political power exists, in centralized societies where the *Lebenswelt* of ordinary people has only partly been colonized by the *Systemwelt* of the state, and among groups within all-embracing state formations which for some reason have cleared their own spaces of maneuver.

The situational emergence of honor and revenge arises in certain social formations. But in the same manner as hatred erupts in personal relations and at the same time establishes and shapes those relations (Kapferer, chapter 8), the complex of honor and revenge affects the societies in which it occurs. Akman (chapter 6) contends that the stubborn concern with honor is one of the very reasons for the present Kurdish impasse, since the ongoing tournaments between rivaling tribes have been exploited by regional powers in a divide-and-rule manner. The high frequency of feuding over lost honor in Tangir kept the valley out of the flow of international development funds, for better or worse, until Norway built a hydroelectric power station there in 1996 (Aase 2000). The extreme preoccupation with honor and the formation of macho 'hyper-identities' in youth gangs of immigrant descent may on the one hand serve as a general male role model that breaks dramatically with the mainstream ideology of gender equality. On the other hand it propels the dichotomization of immigrants and nationals and adds fuel to racism and ethnic clashes (Lien, chapter 2). The sharp reactions to insult in the Southern and Western States of the US (D'Andrade, chapter 4) may be related to self-defense and the perpetuation of a liberal weapons policy, little understood and much resented by Europeans. Although not stated by Bay (chapter 3), it is a well-known fact that the closed milieus of outlaw bikers occasionally constitute environments for thriving organized crime. In Japan, legitimate efforts at 'keeping face' may conceal intentions of the real self and thus make room for the promotion of self-interest in the guise of common welfare (Selstad, chapter 9). And lastly, the passionate reactions to violations of local honor in Java are sometimes reflected by the state itself, and as such violent state campaigns are accepted and even appreciated by ordinary citizens (Bråten, chapter 7).

The ambition of the following chapters is threefold. Firstly, the intention is to demonstrate how honor and vengeance are articulated in various parts of the contemporary world. The point of departure is that notions of honor and vengeance are not put into practice in pre-modern societies alone, as maintained by Peter Berger (1974), and neither are they confined to the classical honor-shame region of the Mediterranean and the Middle East, where most studies of the phenomenon have been carried out. Secondly, the aim is to obtain a closer understanding of what honor is all about. In much of the literature on the topic, honor has been treated as a cover term with no substantial content; more often than not the concept stands out as a mysterious, unexplained residue in the analysis of social life. And lastly, an effort is made to identify social contexts in which honor and vengeance are possible and valid vehicles of expression.

My own approaches to these issues are expressed in this introduction. However, the reader is invited to draw her own conclusions from the various chapters that follow. All contributors to this volume have been asked to describe the practice of honor and revenge in its appropriate context. Thus, the texts allow the reader to comply with the insight offered by Good (1982), that comparison of social phenomena should be carried out on the level of systems, and not be limited to a few selected variables only.

References

Aase, T.H. (2000), *Clean Energy to Tangir*, Centre for Social Research, University of Bergen

Ahmed, A.S. (1996), *Pakistan Society. Islam, Ethnicity and Leadership in South Asia*, Oxford University Press, Oxford

Berger, P. (1970), 'On the obsolescence of the concept of honor', in *European Journal of Sociology*, vol. 11, pp. 339-347, Plon, Paris

Berger, P., Berger, B. and Kellner, H. (1974), *The Homeless Mind*, Penguin, Harmondsworth (UK)

Beyer, P. (1994), *Religion and Globalization*, Sage Publications, London

Black-Michaud, J. (1975), *Cohesive Force: Feud in the Mediterranean and the Middle East*, Basil Blackwell, Oxford

Bochgrewink, T. (1997), 'Anthropological uneasiness' (in Norwegian), in *Norsk Antropologisk Tidsskrift*, pp. 8: 26-36, Bergen – Oslo

Bourdieu, P. (1979), *Algeria 1960*, Cambridge University Press, Cambridge

Cristie, N. (1985), 'Hvor tett et samfunn?' ('How tight a community?' in Norwegian), Norwegian University Press, Oslo

Coombe, R. (1990), 'Barren ground: Re-conceiving honour and shame in the field of Mediterranean ethnography', in *Anthropologica XXXII*, pp. 221-238

Faqir, F. (2001), 'Intrafamily femicide in defence of honour: the case of Jordan', in *Third World Quarterly*, vol. 22, no. 1, pp. 65-82

Fischer, M.M.J. (1986), 'Ethnicity and the Post-Modern Art of Memory', in Clifford, J. and Marcus, G.E. (eds.), *Writing Culture. The Poetics and Politics of Ethnography*, University of California Press, Berkeley

Good, A. (1982), 'The Actor and the Act: Categories of prestation in South India', *Man vil* 17, pp. 23-41, Royal Anthropological Society, UK

Gronhaug, R. (1997), 'Civil Rights, the Multicultural, and Anthropology' (in Norwegian), in *Norsk Antropologisk Tidsskrift* (8) 3-4, pp. 256-272, Bergen – Oslo

Maddox, R. (1987), 'The Politics of Personhood in Early Modern Spain and the Question of Mediterranean Cultural Unity', paper pesented at the annual American Anthropological Association, November, pp. 18-22

Chapter 2

The Dynamics of Honor in Violence and Cultural Change

A case from an Oslo inner city district

Inger-Lise Lien

2.1 Honor as pride

Told by a Somali girl:

> It was in the music class. By accident, I pushed a Pakistani girl on my way from one side of the classroom to the other. She turned around, and shouted 'whore' at me. This was certainly an attack on my honor and it made me furious. I decided to show her who I am. Later, after school, I asked some Somali girls to help me. The Pakistani girl was standing alone, and my friends and I surrounded her, and I hit her hard. Then a lot of girls came running. They were her Pakistani friends. We all shouted at each other and fought until some teachers who were working late came running. The Pakistani girl was injured and had to be taken to the accident and emergency department. She only had some nail scratches so it wasn't serious. The next day, after school, the Pakistani girl asked her brothers and cousins to avenge her. Because they don't like fighting girls they attacked my brother instead, and all his friends got involved in this fight. Then the teachers came and stopped everything. Later, on another day my brother and his Somali friends were in Oslo City,[1] where they caught sight of the Pakistani brother and his cousin. So the Somalis attacked them. My brother told me that they would have killed the Pakistanis if the police had not turned up and parted them.

The human personality is a sacred thing; one dare not violate it nor infringe its bounds, while at the same time the greatest good is in communion with others (Durkheim 1953:37).

This sphere cannot be penetrated, unless the personality value of the individual is thereby destroyed. A sphere of this sort is placed around man by his honor (Simmel 1950:321).

In both Durkheim and Simmel's statements, there is a notion of people as vulnerable social beings who need to protect themselves by erecting a boundary. Honor is usually conceived of as that which gives a person his or her sense of pride

[1] Oslo City is the name of a shopping mall in the center of Oslo where young people tend to gather.

and autonomy. According to Peristiany (1974), honor relates to some supreme values that are specifically connected to the way sexual relations are controlled within the society, and how relations between men and women are organized. Complying with these values gives people a sense of pride, a reputation and public esteem that they strive for and usually talk about as respect. Honor is, according to Unni Wikan (1984), an experience-distant concept, while shame is experience-near, and she recommends the researcher to start her analysis with shame rather than with honor. But to my way of thinking, respect and pride are equally experience-near conceptualizations, and they are often used when talking about honor. To be put to shame is to be denied honor, and therefore amounts to a loss of pride. Honor can be seen as a specific form of pride, a relational form that can be read as a barometer for recognition given by others and conceived of as self-pride.

Pitt-Rivers (1965:21) defines honor as 'the value of a person in his own eyes, but also the acknowledgment of that claim, his excellence recognized by society, his right to pride.' He further argues that honor stands as a mediator between individual aspirations and the judgment of society. It has several facets, but theories of honor have until now varied greatly in the relative importance they accord to different qualities. Honor is both the internalization of the values of society by the individual, and that person's externalization of her self-image in the world. It is both a sentiment and a fact, and it seeks validation from an external authority that converts prestige into status (Pitt-Rivers 1968:504).

Honor and shame are so closely intertwined that many scholars have conceived the terms as two sides of the same coin. Wikan (1984: 636), however, argues that it is not simply a question of two categories of people, those endowed with honor and those endowed with shame. She holds that there is only one category – shameful people. I agree with her to the extent that shame will always be mentally present in everybody, it is always there as a threat to one's pride. And she is right in the sense that honor and shame are not always mutually exclusive, nor always a question of either/or. I would claim that honor can have both a quantitative dimension as well as a qualitative, situational and contextual dimension. A person can be more or less shameful and more or less honorable in different settings. This quantitative dimension is often overlooked by the different theories. The American psychologist David Nathanson (1992) claims that we should understand persons, personal motivation, and psychological problems in general more according to what gives pride and what gives shame within a given context. '[S]hame makes us long for invisibility,' says Nathanson (220). He argues that shame quite early in life becomes linked with the idea of an incompetent self, and the very idea of personal identity seems to be intimately involved with whatever we measure along the shame–pride axis. As disrespect or shame is very painful, we need strategies to deal with it, and Nathanson has described four different strategies that are commonly applied. The first is withdrawal, the second is to attack oneself, the third is avoidance, and the fourth is to attack others. To quote Nathanson again,

> If an attitude of withdrawal makes one appear somewhat depressed; if *attack self* tends to support deference and masochism; and if avoidance tends to favor narcissism,

> then *attack other* halts any tendency to look within the self and thus fosters systems of externalization, blame, and paranoia. A great deal happens to us when we decide to enter the world of attack other. (370)

We can understand in this sense our striving for pride as a universal phenomenon that is synonymous with our desire for recognition and our fear of shame, rejection and contempt. Every human being longs for recognition, but there are different behavioral standards in different cultural settings, and there are also individual differences in the way we handle shame and the strategies we choose for protecting the self. We may also have cultural ideas telling us which strategies and acts can justifiably be used in the different situations. While pride is a universal phenomenon and seeking it characteristic of social persons everywhere, the way in which it is experienced, talked about, sought, and the strategies used to guard it may produce a special form, a special system of thought, a syntax, a cultural form, a cultural schema or a script that can be described as a distinct value system which carries motivational force (D'Andrade 1995). Here, the system of thought will be described as a code of honor. It can be both conscious and unconscious and it can also have a specific geographical and historical extension. In this article both a cognitive and a processual perspective will be applied to show how the dynamics within a code of honor can create a violent social form and cultural change.

2.2 The code of honor and the code of dignity – two ways of obtaining moral pride

Berger, Berger and Kellner (1974) distinguish between two types of ideal-typical cultural moral codes (see Aase in the first chapter of this volume), and argue that a code of honor and a code of dignity are paradigmatically different from each other, and constitute logical and structural frames surrounding individuals wherein persons define their self, their role, and morals in diametrically opposite ways. The authors claim that in the West notions of honor have been influenced by medieval codes of chivalry, and are rooted in feudalism. If these concepts have survived up until the modern era it is mostly among groups that retain a hierarchical view of society, such as the military, and traditional professions such as law and medicine. The decline in the currency of honor in Western society is described as an outcome of a process of civilization. This development has led to the Declaration of Human Rights by the United Nations, where biological and historical differentiation among men is seen as irrelevant. It represents a development towards an individualistic and egalitarian ethos. While honor relates identity to the past, to membership of families, ethnic groups, to gender, and positions in a hierarchical society, dignity implies a true and lonely self, independent of social roles, and equal to others.

Larsen (1987) argues that the Idea of the Universal Man, developed during the Enlightenment, has led to the breakdown of moral spheres making humanity one rather than many. The move has gone from particularism to universalism. Moral standards for women should be the same as moral standards for men and standards for the rich should be the same as those for the poor. The Enlightenment changed our ways of thinking (Finkielkraut 1987), creating a paradigmatic shift in morals.

In his description of this detraditionalization process, Heelas (1996:2) argues that what we are basically seeing is a shift of moral authority from 'without' to 'within'. 'It entails the decline of the belief in pre-given or natural orders of things. Individual subjects are themselves called upon to exercise authority in the face of the disorder and contingency, which is thereby generated. 'Voice' is displaced from established sources, coming to rest with the self.' The categories of 'tradition' v. detradition or modernity bear a resemblance to our description of an honor v. dignity code. Heelas, however, argues against a pure periodizing of the evolution from tradition to modernity. He favors the co-existence thesis, holding that processes of traditionalization and detraditionalization operate simultaneously in different situations and contexts in the modern world. I would agree with him on this. Throughout history there have always been individuals who have been motivated by the authority within rather than the authority from without. Some of them are cultural heroes such as Copernicus, Jan Huus, Luther and others. So there was never a pure community determined by the 'honor code' alone, or a period of pure 'modernity' where everybody neglected the authority of external voices. But in spite of this lack of purity, 'honor' and 'dignity' signify paradigmatically different ways of thinking, and I would hold that we can identify periodical shifts, or geographical areas, where the one way of thinking dominates rather than the other. When anthropologists have described cultures of honor in certain areas of the world, their focus has generally been directed toward gender roles, and the ways sexuality has been controlled and codified (Peristiany 1974; Gilmore 1987; Delaney 1987; Mandelbaum 1988). For men specifically honor seems to be related to masculinity, power and material wealth (Davis 1987:6). Gilmore (1987) includes this material side of masculinity in what he labels 'fiscal sexuality'. In several anthropological accounts of Mediterranean and Middle Eastern countries the most important thing to control if a man is to obtain and retain honor is female sexuality. Melhuus (1993) distinguishes between a particularistic honor and shame codex that she labels 'gendered morality' in the sense that rules of conduct apply unequally to men and women, and a universalistic codex where ideas of equality and human worth are important ingredients for the concept of respect. She claims that these two moral codices are logically incompatible, though not necessarily empirically incompatible. Melhuus thus appears to comply with the coexistence thesis. But even though they may coexist as distinct forms, they cannot fuse into a logical whole that exists in the mind of the individual. Abiding simultaneously by both codes would put overwhelming contradictory pressures on the person involved. I believe, however, that people who in fact find themselves at the tense intersection between these two forms of moral code may solve the problem by switching between them, keeping situations where the one or other prevails apart to avoid moral clashes. We can illustrate the differences between the two ideal-types as follows:

Code of honor	Code of dignity
Basically 'traditional'	Basically 'modern' and 'postmodern'
Collectivist	Individualistic
Hierarchical	Egalitarian
Particularistic: Different moral standards for different categories of people	Universalistic: The same moral standards should be applicable to all
Outer directed morality: Subordination to external authority	Inner directed morality: Subordination to the authority within
Shame	Conscience
Gendered morality	Non-gendered morality
Stress on the social role	Stress on authenticity
Non-liberal ethic; loyalty, dependence and strong ties highly valued	Liberal ethics: freedom, independence and week ties highly valued
Mechanic solidarity	Abstract, organic solidarity
Control of female sexuality is a supreme value	Tolerance is a supreme value

As I see it, there are differences between these two codes that need to be mentioned specifically: while Berger, Berger and Kellner regard both as moral codes, to my thinking, the code of honor is more than a moral code. It includes guidelines for the institutional evaluation of people's positions on the social ladder along with their social reputation and popularity. These social evaluations have little to do with morality.

I have illustrated this non-moral aspect of the code of honor in my thesis on morality and emotion in Pakistani Punjab (Lien 1993), where I depict how a *chowdry*[2] from the Jat cast steals the savings of a man and his nineteen-year-old son. The *chowdry* managed to get hold of four hundred thousand rupees while the boy's father was away working in Saudi Arabia. After the incident the boy and his father were talked about within the community, shamed and ridiculed by the villagers for their naïvety and stupidity in trusting the man. The chowdry, on the other hand, was seen as a smart guy, and respected for his shrewdness. This shows that the code of honor in the Pakistani setting is blurred and unclear in its instructions and principles. It has a power dimension to it giving individuals unclear guidelines about where their respect should be directed – to the doer of good deeds, or to the person who can demonstrate power and do what he wants. This power dimension fits quite well with what Black-Michaud (1975) and Aase (this volume) argue, i.e., that honor and power are exactly the same thing, and that honor has to do with power and the 'ability to defend'. I still hold, however, that honor has to do both with morality and power, and that because the code is blurred in its levels and guidelines, it facilitates the development of a form of honor that I will designate here as hyperhonor, and that this hyperhonor can be traced in urban areas in the modern world. This extra quality of power and institutional status is not present in the dignity code, which is more normative and less of a socially descriptive code. This does not mean that persons who adopt the latter code do not engage in ranking others socially. They do rank others and are ranked by them in

[2] A chowdry is a respected landowner.

turn, but according to other descriptive codes in the social system. The dignity code is a moral code that specifically encourages people not to rank others but to regard them as equal.

Today, it is possible to find the two codes at work simultaneously in schools and the workplace. People may live within the precepts of a code of dignity at home, while at school they adopt another way of thinking, play a different game and follow the 'honor schema'. Immigrants from feudal areas that discover and learn about women's rights in the West – and the dignity code in general – may relate to it as a cliché (Spiro 1997) and pay lip service to it, but they may not necessarily believe in it, and in these cases the dignity code will not be fully internalized or held with any deep conviction even though it is talked about at school or in the workplace. Spiro (1997) argues that for a cultural system to be fully internalized it must be acquired at a level that has a powerful emotional attachment to it. The honor code can exist in society as a remnant of a tradition that has been reinvented in the city as a result of processes involved in modern life. But it can also be learnt on the meeting-ground between people from feudalistic societies and Westerners, and it gives them new ideas and new ways of defining themselves. These new ideas and norms can be internalized at different levels.

Anderson (1998), in a study of life in the streets of an inner city area in the USA, has found these two moral codes, though he gives them different names: 'the code of the street', which resembles an extreme form of what we have called 'the code of honor', and 'the code of the decent', which resembles what we call 'the code of dignity'. In urban areas, the 'honor code', or 'the code of the street', seems to be deeply internalized by gang members living there, who give it great credence and among whom it is a powerful activating force. Nisbett and Cohen (1996) say that a key aspect of what they call a culture of honor is the importance placed on the insult and the necessity to respond to it. An insult implies that the target is weak enough to be bullied. Since a reputation for physical strength is a necessity in a culture dominated by the code of honor, the individual who insults someone must be forced to retract; if he refuses, he must be punished or even killed. Because of the kind of logic that exists within a code of honor, Nisbett and Cohen argue that we ought to find more violence in parts of the world where it is dominant than where the code of dignity prevails. In cities with a high crime rate, Bourgois (1996) claims that a change of focus has transpired from respect to disrespect and an overwhelming fear of shame. 'The traditional search for respect has been radically transformed into a fear of disrespect.' The importance of fear for the code of honor is a topic to which I will return towards the end of this article.

So, what happens in situations where these two moral codes coexist? Is there a shift in morals, and if so, what direction does it take, and why? Is it the case that the hollowness and emptiness described by Berger, Berger and Kellner as a side effect of the code of dignity engender susceptibility to the code of honor? Ulrich Beck (1992) argues that retraditionalization can occur as a result of forces within modernity itself. We will look at the battles that take place between individuals complying with either a modern or traditional moral code to examine the direction this competition takes.

First I want to show the coexistence of two different systems of moral thinking in a secondary school in Oslo, corresponding to the moral codes described above. Then I will look at the tension caused by these two types of moral logic as we find it expressed at the school. I will also try to describe why an aggressive social form seems to be very attractive to the young. The school in question has become a jousting ground for opposing paradigms and strategies, and I will try to analyze, understand and present the kinds of social forms generated on this battlefield of morals and uncover the interactive processes and their outcome generated by youths striving to satisfy emotional needs and live up to moral precepts.

2.3 A presentation of a city school in Oslo: an atmosphere of profanation

I did fieldwork at a secondary school not far from the center of Oslo and in the surrounding neighborhood over several periods: two months in 1998; four months in 1999; and two months in 2000. I sat in on lessons and observed pupils in class, walked around in the breaks and talked informally with pupils. I also interviewed children individually in a separate room in the school and interviewed them at a hamburger bar outside the school. I also carried out focus-group interviews at the youth clubs in the area. In between fieldwork sessions at the school, I visited families to talk to parents, brothers and sisters. Switching contexts from the school to the youth club or the street provided a fresh environment for initiating a conversation, which gave the interviewees the freedom to talk more honestly about life at school and in other contexts. I discovered that these intervals in my study had a positive effect on the gathering of information. Taking a long pause after a period of intense interaction seemed to work very well for building trust. Pupils would come rushing to me to tell me what had just happened, while at the end of the first intensive period of data collection they seemed fed up by all my questions. This reinvigoration of contact made both them and me feel that we were meeting up again as old friends and acquaintances, and lots of old information was interpreted anew and discussed over and over, as new insights and news were added. I also interviewed teachers and some pupils in three other schools in the area. The qualitative study was supplemented with a questionnaire, which 140 ninth and tenth grade pupils completed. The pupils were aged from 12–15.

From 1987 to 1997 the number of children aged 7–15 in the area increased by 80 percent. Schools that had only a few pupils in the 1980s and were facing closure are now overextended. The numerical balance between Norwegian children and children from immigrant families has shifted and the immigrant children now predominate significantly. Among these, pupils whose parents come from villages in Punjab in Pakistan count for the largest group (almost 60 percent), with Somalis making up the second largest ethnic group. Norwegians counted only for 15 percent of the 400 pupils.

The main problem facing the school was the tough environment characterized by the frequent use of offensive words and insults. This was mentioned by many of the pupils that I interviewed, and was often discussed by the staff. The most commonly used obscenities were *hore* (whore), *ludder* (slut), *fitte* (cunt), and *felleshøl* (a neologism literally meaning 'an asshole available to everybody'). Children all over the city are familiar with these expletives, but it is the ease and the frequency with which they are used that astonishes newcomers most. 'I came to this school from another part of Oslo, and I was shocked by all the swearing. The most terrible words were said, and the teacher didn't seem to mind at all. It took me a long time to get used to it,' said one young pupil. Girls were often sworn at, either in Norwegian or Punjabi, Vietnamese, Somali, or Moroccan. Most of the youngsters knew these words in different languages too and they reacted strongly to them. If somebody who was being sworn at failed to react, his or her friends would try to get them to retaliate by saying: 'You shouldn't take that.' An insult could be parried with another insult, and at this level it could be said to resemble a verbal duel as described by Fleisher (1998) in his book on the Fremont Hustlers gang in Kansas City:

Boy-girl, girl-girl, and boy-boy relationships are built on verbal duels. Boys duel by calling each other bitch; girls call each other bitch; boys call girls *stink pussy*; girls call each other *stink pussy*; girls accuse each other of sleeping around; and both toss allegations of disloyalty at partners in previous relationships (45).

At the Oslo school, however, things could easily heat up far beyond the level of a fight between two pupils, growing into a schismogenetic process that could trigger massive violence between groups of girls or boys. A quite innocent quarrel between girls could result in a violent fight between boys that might only stop just short of murder, as the incident described in the introduction of this article shows.

During my research among Pakistanis in Oslo in the 1980s (Lien 1983, Lien 1997) I noted the ease with which the first immigrants picked up and used Norwegian swearwords. This can be explained as a compensatory effect for the lack of verbal mastery of the new language. The children at the school, who use an aggressive language, may find themselves in a similar situation as the early immigrants, and they use swearwords to compensate for a lack of Norwegian. Another explanation for this form of communication could be connected with learning and habit. The integration of immigrants started in a working-class environment where they lived alongside unskilled Norwegians. The first immigrants may have learned to swear at the workplace because they lacked sensitivity and an ear for the effect of the words early in their stay in Norway. They used them often, also in the family setting, thereby leading to the transmission of this form of language to their children.

The most insulting words for the schoolboys are *morapuler* (mother fucker), *homse* (homo), and *kjerring* (old woman), *ludder* (whore). The words used for girls are considered even more insulting when aimed at a boy, like saying *fitte* (cunt) to him for instance. The boys are also provoked by insults directed at their sisters and girlfriends and are prepared to fight for their honor as much as their own, as we saw above. It is not only the overt swearing that is a problem for the girls and the boys; there is also a lot of ill-natured gossip that is difficult to deal with. People could say things like: 'Fatima is in love with Ali,' or 'Eva has slept with Mohammed.' 'Your girlfriend enjoys group-sex. We've all had her.' The best way to provoke a fight is to say something insulting about a member of somebody's family, since the family is seen as an extension of oneself. Whether the accusations are true or false is not the point. An aggressive response makes it plain that people are not prepared to take insults lightly. Any discussion concerning potential truth-value is considered irrelevant by the offended party.

These verbal attacks create a climate of fear and distrust, with insults and counter-insults being thrown back and forth. During breaks and after school it was common for teachers to come running, calling to other staff members, to help break up a fight somewhere. The air was often full of tension, and teachers were often right when they suspected something was afoot. The police visited the school sometimes once a day in an effort to prevent or stop fights and defuse tension.

These types of arguments, or verbal duels, are the first of a series of steps that lead to the development of deep antagonisms, the creation of gangs, racism, and violence. The pattern is stereotypical. It starts with insults and swearing and ends in violence and the use of weapons. Popularity, honor, sexuality, and gender are important motivational factors in the development of violent gangs, and the attack strategy is the means used by both boys and girls to protect themselves in a contagious environment of disrespect.

Decker (1996) identifies seven steps in a violent process where gang violence escalates and ends with retaliation. It starts with loose bonds to a gang, then a collective identification of threat from a rival gang (through rumors, symbolic shows of force, cruising and mythic violence). Then something happens that galvanizes the gang, propelling it into action, before it de-escalates. The last step is retaliation. Decker's argument is that these seven stages reflect the gang's organizational and normative structure. He says that it is important to study gang norms to understand gang formation, and I agree with him. I argue, however, that the analyses of violent processes and gang formation should start at an earlier stage, i.e. before the formation of the loose bond between a number of young people forming a sort of nascent group. The first step in a general analysis should be an account of the total environment in which actors find themselves. From this description one can proceed to the group stage. The prevailing normative structures and the value hierarchies should be revealed through interactional analysis. This is a model for studying social change proposed by the Norwegian anthropologist Fredrik Barth (1966). It is particularly useful for understanding how groups are generated and the different forms that different groups can take within the same environment. It is important to see how the emotional climate, the normative system, and the opportunities that individuals face when they want to express their pride, or maximize their values, work together in constructing a social form. Will different normative systems create alternative courses of action? Is the code of dignity incompatible with gang formation, and adopting the code of honor more likely to lead to gang violence? Both qualitative and quantitative dimensions of the atmosphere are important to measure in the effort to reveal the kinds of social forms that are formed in an environment in which the two different codes are at work. Barth (op. cit.) argues that it is not enough to analyze norms alone in order to understand social systems, we need to look at all the constraints and incentives that canalize people's choices when interacting with each other. An explanation of a social form lies in the description of the processes that generate the form. 'Social forms, as I have tried to show, may be regarded as the results of processes - they are frequency distributions of behavior which may be explained as the outcome of social processes acting on a limited number of determinants' (Barth 1966:22). Here, we will try to identify the kinds of determinants that are involved in generating the processes that produce several social forms. I am also indebted to Gregory Bateson (1936, 1972) for his analysis of schismogenetic processes. Bateson (175) defines schismogenesis as a process of differentiation in the norms of individual behavior resulting from cumulative interaction between individuals. He identifies two processes: a complementary and a symmetrical process of schismogenesis. As we will see in the following, both processes are at work at the school, and the end result of these interactions can best be described as a social form.

2.4 The quantitative and the qualitative dimension – a tipping-point theory of cultural change

Both Barth (op. cit.) and Bateson (op. cit.) stress the importance of frequencies in generating changes in social processes to produce qualitatively different forms of outcome at the aggregate level. Malcolm Klein (1995) has also stressed the importance of both quantitative and qualitative factors in his efforts to define a gang. He distinguishes between juvenile groups and gangs and argues that while both are involved in more or less the same activities, the gangs are involved in crime and violence to such a degree that they tip over into a qualitatively different phenomenon. This tipping-point theory is especially useful for understanding change from one moral code to another.

Returning to the concept of honor, we could say that the significance of personal and collective honor in modern Western societies has decreased to such an extent that a tipping point has been reached. Modern society is qualitatively different from traditional society and while honor still plays a part, it is no longer the pivotal point it once was in personal relations. As honor is a hierarchical phenomenon, mediated through the language of respect, *not* speaking of it becomes important to safeguard egalitarian relations. In the dignity code there lies a moral imperative to avoid hierarchical thinking and especially talking about and ranking human beings. The ethos is: you must not mention your honor, but you must nevertheless strive to increase it, and distinction, fame, and glory will be your reward. Honor still has the power to bestow value on your name. All modern societies have systems for the bestowal of honor. When honor is formally awarded (for instance when books are published to honor a distinguished career), it boosts respect for the individual, as it does possibly his or her pride. This means that the switch to what appears at first sight to be a quite different mode of thinking is in fact *thinking and talking more about an idea to which one has already been exposed.*

Nevertheless, this mode of thinking and talking about honor can expand to such a degree that it engenders substantial changes in one's system of logic. This implies that the struggle for hierarchy would sideline the norm of egalitarian relations. Individuals would not feel the same commitment to equality as a norm, even though, at a superficial level, they might claim to adhere to it. What we then have is a change from a code of dignity to a code of honor. It is both a matter of qualitative and quantitative change. Historically the change has gone the other way around, but in a globalized world, the change can go in both directions.

At the school under study, however, the change has gone in the opposite direction. The Norwegian pupils recount that when they are at school, they switch over to a different way of thinking, what they call the 'foreigners' way'. They explain the switch by pointing to the importance of respect and honor. Some of the Norwegian pupils internalize this new way of thinking and become very concerned with their honor, talking constantly about it. There seems to be a revival of the idea of honor and respect especially among skinheads and neo-Nazi gangs (Bjørgo 1997; Fangen 1995, 1999), who read a lot of Saga literature in order to feed their masculine identity on tales of Viking warriors of yesteryear. The similarities between ideas of honor and some shared characteristics of ethnic gangs and nationalistic gangs are remarkable and I have mentioned them elsewhere (Lien 1991, Lien/Haaland 1998). But it seems that this revival of honor is not solely something that has emerged from the historical luggage of Norwegians and immigrants. It is also reproduced and transmitted within the interaction that takes place at the school, and it is reinforced by the amount of gangster videos and mafia films that these kids watch. Youngsters can develop a susceptibility (see Sperber 1984) to the code of honor on the basis of aspects of their local situation, and the processes that are at work there.

2.5 The overall moral framework of the school: the code of dignity

It is first of all the teachers who represent the dignity code. The code is represented in the curriculum, and is expressed through the role performance of both the male and female teachers. A male teacher said: 'I told the class that I had to hurry home every day to make dinner for me and my wife. You should have heard them. They laughed loudly and said that they found it unbelievable that my wife was superior to me, as I weigh a hundred kilos and could easily beat her up. She should make dinner for me and not the opposite, they said. Then I explained that in Norway we think in another way. That men and women should be equal.'

The teachers express a liberal ethic in which equality and tolerance are significant values, and they have a negative attitude to paternalistic behavior and threats of intimidation. 'I am afraid of using my position in a negative way, making pupils afraid of me. I try to be flexible and understanding,' says one teacher. In their educational thinking they stress subject–subject dialogs, rather than subject–object dialogs. The fear of violence, and the teacher's need to be seen as on an equal footing with his/her pupils, has led to the erosion of much of the school's external control mechanisms. Chewing gum is not really allowed, but is tolerated in class, and the teacher pretends not to notice. The children wear caps in the classroom, and the tolerance level for classroom noise is higher than before. Foreign pupils complain that the teachers are too soft and 60 per cent of the ninth and tenth grades want their teachers to be stricter with them. A Pakistani boy who had become a member of a gang said: '[When] I came to this school, everything was so easy-going, so soft. Nothing happened. I could do anything, and there was no reaction. I could look into the eyes of a teacher and swear at her, and she would look so unhappy, and ask me, why do you talk like this? The kindness has ruined me.' In several of the schools in the area teachers complain that the pupils refuse to come to class when the bell rings. Instead, they will sit and chat outside in the corridor during lessons. Some of the pupils in a neighboring secondary school told me that if they felt hungry they would go to buy chocolate in the middle of a lesson and the teachers did not seem to mind at all when they suddenly disappeared. The practice of this liberal and tolerant ethos together with the code of dignity has resulted in a situation in which aggressive and abusive forms of behavior have been allowed to develop more or less unchecked.

According to Berger, Berger and Kellner (op. cit.), intrinsic dignity is often seen as something that stands apart from and often against the institutional roles through which the individual expresses himself in society. The fact that roles are not important expressions of identity could lead to detachment and renunciation of responsibility. The teachers seem to express the dignity code by undercommunicating the authoritarian structures of the school. Their intention is to have an equal dialog with the pupils, more as their friends than as their superiors. So the dignity code, as expressed through the teachers' actions, may well contribute to a setting characterized by detachment, indifference, and avoidance. We see this avoidance strategy at work in the behavior of some of the Norwegian boys too. They retreat from the institutional definitions that the foreigners try to force on them at school. They decline to participate in activities with foreigners after school, and they refuse to fight for positions in the informal structure, which results in a loss in social value. They think of the girls as equals, not as weaker members of the human race in need of protection. They have the idea that everyone is responsible for himself, girls as well, and that a person should be morally guided by his inner will, and act in line with his conscience. What is more, some of their attitudes contradict the code of dignity, since the Norwegian boys nevertheless see themselves as better, more grown up and less childish than the foreign boys, who fight for respect in very childish ways, they say.

The dignity code is observed in the school by the Norwegian teachers, the Norwegian boys, and some of the Norwegian girls, as well as by some of the foreigners, especially the ones who see themselves as *modern*. However, in spite of this embrace of a more modern ethic, it can be difficult to live by the precepts and principles involved, especially for the foreign girls. Many of the foreign girls and boys at the school embrace in principle a 'modern' way of thinking. In their daily lives, however, their parents forbid them to practice 'modern living,' and parental control is strong. The honor code is forced upon them by the expectations of their family, which require them to avoid bringing shame on the family by talking to boys, staying out late, wearing Western clothes and doing things that would be conceived of as being Western. Several of the Norwegian girls ascribe to an egalitarian ethos and the idea of women's liberation, yet have to take into consideration the other moral code and act in opposition to the ethos they ascribe to in principle. Therefore, while a large number of the young students agree in principle with the dignity code, they nonetheless have to conform to the dominant rules and norms when at school by undercommunicating the dignity code and complying with the moral code of the 'foreigners', especially the elements of the dress code. In the words of one Norwegian girl: 'I no longer wear miniskirts or thin see-through summer dresses. I try to look decent because I know what the Muslim boys and girls will think.'

2.6 The code of honor – during breaks between classes

The code of honor is expressed in the informal structure of the school, and played out in breaks between classes and after school. It is expressed in the contest between pupils for popularity and standing, and it is especially expressed in the gender relations between boys and girls. In the newspaper *Dagsavisen* (18 January 1998) the journalist Tuva Gry Øyan reflects on a conversation she had with her sixteen-year-old Norwegian son. They live in the area where most of the material for this article was collected. Øyan writes: ''The most important thing is honor,' says the sixteen-year old, 'honor and respect.' We have started to talk about values round our kitchen table at Grunerløkka. A new phenomenon is emerging in the melting pot of east Oslo. A new and pluralistic shared culture is emerging, created by young people with family backgrounds from Norway, Pakistan, Morocco, Vietnam and other countries. This common culture influences also its Norwegian-Norwegian members, and will, I think, change Norway for ever.' This journalist has discovered that her son and his friends have embraced a new value system. Young boys and girls have become concerned with respect and honor, and, most importantly, they talk about it all the time.

Most of the Norwegian schoolboys that I interviewed are familiar with the new values but do not seem to have fully internalized them, even though they have to cope with them. They criticize heavily the concern of the foreign boys with honor and respect. It also appears that the Norwegian girl friends of Pakistani and Somali boys are concerned with honor to what these boys feel is an excessive degree, but not in the same way as the Pakistani and Somali girls. The foreign boys, with a background from non-Western societies, seem to lay greatest store by this value system and it is among them that the most serious competition for honor and respect takes place.

2.6.1 Popularity hierarchies among boys

There was evidence of several networks of boys with different backgrounds at the school. I will distinguish between three categories of boys: 1) *the hypermodern boys*; 2) *the moderate 'foreign' boys*; and 3) *the withdrawing Norwegian boys.*

Most of the boys in the hypermodern category can be described as half generation immigrants as most of them migrated to Norway as children. Their first years of socialization were spent in a traditional feudal society. But there are also some second-generation immigrants in the network of about 30 boys that we are dealing with here. They often watch American gangster videos, almost a film a day, and their role models in these films are the black Americans. Spergler and Curry (1993) describe the diffusion of gang culture in the USA as 'copy-cat gangs'. Miller (2001), in her study of girls in gangs in two American cities, found it striking that the girls gleaned their information about gangs from popular culture, and that they blurred the boundaries between their actual lives and the films they saw. It seems as if several of the boys and girls in the school have the same tendency to blur the distinction between reality and movie fiction since they find their aggressive role models among the heroes in the films. As many of the boys have broken loose from the control of their parents and their teachers, they conceive of themselves as different, as outstanding, as extramodern, as more adult, almost like the Americans they watch in the films. *Hyper* implies that their idea of being modern is more than being modern in a Norwegian way. It implies something more advanced, less childish, braver, involving more risks and being more masculine than their Norwegian counterparts, and having a larger network than 'the small kids at school'. They don't hang around with their brothers and cousins, their *biraderi*, as their Pakistani parents would have wished, but with kids and older boys they are not related to and who come from other ethnic backgrounds. In this sense they are breaking away from thc traditional expectations of their parents. Their striving for modernity is expressed in symbolic ways in fashion clothes and shoes, the latest model of a cellular phone, a Nokia or an Eriksson. To obtain these symbolic items of modernity several of the boys resorted to thieving from shops. They change cellulars and telephone numbers regularly as their bills come in, and have to steal a new cellular every three months or so. In his study of young people in four Norwegian cities, Haaland (2000) found a positive correlation between the amount of incoming and outgoing calls during a day, and the amount of violence committed by those who most frequently used their cellular. Talking and fighting seemed to be interlinked. In the hypermodern network we are studying, cellulars play an important role in mobilizing friends for a fight in addition to being a symbolic marker of modern identity. The expression 'the hypermodern boys' is based on the effects of the symbolic expression of a modern identity. When it comes to moral thinking, however, the mental schemas of these boys could just as well have been categorized as traditional since they reflect an honor-based mode of thought with its gender particularism and elements of hierarchical and collectivist thinking. But such collectivism is no longer based on blood ties or traditional family bonding but on peer group loyalty and a conception of fictive brotherhood. We can call this form a tradi-modern hybrid. It has a communicative-declarative form that I have used the term 'hyper' to connote. Several of the groups of boys have given themselves names such First Class Mafia, Gangster Brothers, Mafia Brothers, Black Gangsters etc.

There are many Somalis in the category I have called *hypermodern boys*. They are the most popular ethnic group at the school, especially in the eyes of the

Norwegian boys and girls. The Somali pupils were being taught in a separate introductory class. Some of them were exceptionally good athletes, excelling in running, football – they were the best at the school – and one of them was a famous hip-hop dancer. They had a reputation as war heroes with the courage and willingness to fight. As a Norwegian girl said: 'They are not willing to tolerate anything. They are so proud.' The Somali boys spoke a kind of pidgin Norwegian that was difficult to understand but they were popular because of their traditional masculine ways which forefronted physical strength, charm, and mobility, the ability to move around at will.

The hypermodern boys are 'loose in the streets', and require a lot of supervision, as they often are involved in 'spectacular' incidents involving fighting, quarrelling with teachers, stealing cars and driving around during breaks. Some of them have dyed their hair. They wear golden neck chains and American sports attire. They have Buffalo shoes, which the pupils regard as gangster shoes. They have many friends, both at school and elsewhere, because they move around in the streets. So their territory is more extensive than that of the other boys and girls, and they build alliances with different groups of youngsters in many places. They get a lot of attention at school from the teachers, but also the police, and they are constantly being talked about and talked to. This amount of attention may have a reinforcing feedback effect on their aggression. This has also been noted by Klein (1971) in an evaluation of a project in the USA: the amount of attention given to gang members increases delinquency.

A factor analysis[3] was run on the material gathered from interviews with ninth and tenth grade pupils. It showed that a factor called 'good grades' correlated negatively with membership of a Pakistani-dominated network, and even more negatively correlated with belonging to a multicultural network (i.e., having friends from a number of different foreign backgrounds). 'Multi-ethnic network' was positively correlated with weak ties to the school and other pupils. The multi-ethnic network factor was highly correlated with 'social dominance', an umbrella term for factors measuring masculinity, antagonistic relationships, use of violence, and fights. Boys in a Norwegian network correlated positively with 'good grades', feeling safe, non-dominance, and non-violence. The analysis confirms our other findings, that the group of boys from mixed ethnic backgrounds who are more violent than the rest do more badly at school, and are more ready to engage in violent behavior.

Robert Paine (1989) argues that in the Marry Baluch society in Pakistan there is a contradiction between 1) basic custom laws (the commandments of Islam, what is conceived to be one's duty); and 2) one's own willpower, one's resistance to the rules, and one's readiness to break them. By breaking the laws, one gains a reputation for fearlessness, showing the world that one is above the rules. He argues that such attitudes rest on a rebound mechanism by which norm-breaking activity adds to a person's prestige and gives him a 'heightened sense of self or of being' while at the same time increasing the status of the norms. Anderson in his

[3] This was done by my colleague Thomas Haaland.

description of manhood in inner city life shows that masculinity and respect are won by 'manifesting nerve'. 'True nerve expresses a lack of fear of dying' (Anderson 1998:9). Social norms can thus encourage people to commit acts that are simultaneously esteemed and condemned. In the case of the hypermodern boys they seem to be their own lawgivers and they try to give the impression that they are not afraid of anything.

The moderate 'foreign' boys tend to comply with the expectations of their parents and the community at large. They tend to be obedient and respect their parents' decisions, and avoid fights. They do not mix with Norwegian girls. Most of the foreign boys belong to this category. They hang around with their cousins and brothers in the evenings. Several of them (about 23 per cent) help their parents in the family shop after school and earn their own money by doing newspaper rounds in the morning. The moderate boys in this study consist of boys from different ethnic groups, and many of them still take lessons in the Qur'an at the Mosque. They observe Islamic or other religious norms while many of the hypermodern boys argue that they have distanced themselves from religious education. Nisbett and Cohen (1996) distinguish between two types of honor: honor as nobility of soul, magnanimity, and a scorn of meanness, and an honor that derives from virtuous conduct. The moderate foreign boys, of whom most are Muslim, tend to adhere to the latter version, a version implied in Islamic religious law, the Sharia. They do not visit the youth clubs, but they often sit with their friends in the rooms behind their parents' shops, or at home with friends watching videos. On Fridays and Saturdays they go out together with their parents and brothers to visit other families belonging to their ethnic community. They have a traditional conception of honor, and if their family is insulted they will fight for their family's honor.

It seems that the Pakistani boys, being a majority at school, could adopt a variety of roles without risking their popularity. Some of them were quiet and religious, others were aggressive and ready to fight for whatever reason (they belong to hypermodern category). Whatever their temperament and interests, however, they were all known for their readiness to get into a fight to protect a girl's honor whenever they felt it was under threat. For this reason Pakistanis were popular among the girls as boyfriends. They were seen as more responsible and trustworthy than the Somali boys, though not as much fun.

Norwegian boys represent a special category as they were at the unpopular end of the popularity scale both in the eyes of the foreign boys and girls and Norwegian girls. The Norwegian boys were known for backing out of conflicts and seen as boring and dull. They were unwilling to protect the girls or fight for their honor. They were unwilling to strike back when insulted, and were therefore considered to be weak, lacking in pride, and tolerant of everything. Norwegian boys were regarded as cowards and unmanly. As a Pakistani boy said: 'Pakistani girls can take a lot. A Pakistani boy will not tolerate anything. But the Norwegian boys are tolerant like the girls. They take a lot.' And in many ways the Norwegian boys were mute and invisible. They did not go to the youth clubs in the area; these were frequented instead by hypermodern Pakistani, Turkish, Moroccan, and Vietnamese boys. In spite of their invisibility and unpopularity, they did not seem to harbor feelings of hate or animosity toward the more popular 'foreign boys'. Rather the contrary. In interviews they expressed admiration, but also distance. Far from the absence of any directly expressed racism among the Norwegian boys and girls at the school, foreigners were at the top of the popularity list, and Norwegians at the bottom.[4] Some of the Norwegian boys complained that they had problems finding girlfriends in the area and were obliged to travel to the other side of the city where Norwegian boys were still in fashion.

In a neighboring school with a higher proportion of Norwegians (50 percent), some of the Norwegian boys had developed negative attitudes about the foreign boys, and Norwegian girls complained that Norwegian boys thought badly of them for having 'foreign boyfriends'. So the Norwegian girls regarded the Norwegian boys not only as unattractive, but as racists as well. This implies that a withdrawal strategy can lead to some kind of reaction where the blame for the ensuing invisibility and loss of status would be put on the 'foreign boys' turning them into enemies that needed to be fought. This could spark the formation of a violent nazi-gang with a return to an amplified version of the honor code as the ultimate outcome.

2.6.2 Popularity hierarchies among girls

As both of the moral codes were present at the school, there were two alternative ways of determining the girls' position. The Pakistani girls were regarded as superior and seen as pure, sacred, and chaste. The Somali girls did not have the same reputation for purity and innocence even though many of them were circumcised and under the strict control of their parents. It did seem as if they were freer to move around than the Pakistani girls. The popularity of the latter category must be understood against the background of their dominant position at school. Outside school, however, they were not to be seen, and were seldom observed in any of the youth clubs. Youth workers said that they had given up recruiting Pakistani girls as members.

These girls mostly used one main strategy to protect their reputation, and that was to be 'a good girl', which meant staying at home, not talking to boys, dressing modestly and secluding themselves as much as possible. This strategy of seclusion, or unreachability, was considered a 'Muslim' strategy by Norwegian girls, and was used mostly by the Pakistani, Moroccan, Turkish, and Somali girls. This strategy gave the girls a very high status and put them beyond the reach of boys who wanted to have intimate relations with them. A boy who dared to date this type of girl ran the risk of a beating from her older brothers. The mere effort to make contact with her would be seen as an insult in itself. A few Norwegian girls used this unreachability strategy to position themselves in the girls' status hierarchy, though they did not go to the same lengths as the foreign girls and lacked the same amount of brotherly protection. Nevertheless, being unobtainable, out of reach, increased the status of both the Norwegian and the foreign girls. I often heard

4 This was the general attitude among the pupils at the school, and even though the Norwegian boys resented this image, there was little they could do about it.

complaints by the foreign boys. 'We always get the bad girls,' they said, by which they meant a Norwegian girl or a foreign girl considered too modern and morally lax. Not being available was in itself a criterion for being good.

The parents of what I term the chaste girls were an important driving force behind the imposition of the unreachability strategy as they exercised extensive control over their daughters, so extensive that some of the Norwegian teachers felt sorry for the girls and sometimes helped them get round it. Most Pakistani girls had to go straight home after school and some were not allowed even to enter shops on the way or during breaks. Showing any interest in a boy was a risky business; a telephone call from the boy could result in the girl getting a beating from her father. The need to control the girls stems from the necessity to control sexual relations within a community structure that is heavily influenced by caste ideology, endogamy and the code of honor (Lien 1993, 1997). Some of the Pakistani girls tried to counter the unreachability structure by changing into Western clothes on the way to school. If they had boyfriends, they would lie to their parents, or keep it a secret. Their politics of everyday life (Ewing 1991) included trying to create leeway to follow their own interests within a framework dominated by the code of honor that demands obedience. Several Pakistani girls told me that they had been to youth clubs, though not where they could easily be recognized and talked about, which could result in a thrashing from their fathers and brothers. Instead, they had visited youth clubs on the other side of town were nobody knew them. The Pakistani girls who practiced the unreachability strategy paid for it with a lack of freedom, and sometimes a dull life, but they won a reputation for chasteness. Some Norwegian girls were envious of them. The Muslim boys considered Pakistani girls as the most pure and sacred. They have high status, and the Pakistani boys intend to marry them eventually. The Norwegian girls, on the other hand, are regarded as loose and promiscuous, almost as whores. One Norwegian girl said: 'We are useful as girlfriends, but not good enough to marry. It's tragic.' The position of the Pakistani girls and the Pakistani boys sometimes led to a Pakistani complex among some of the Norwegians. This was expressed in the interviews: 'I wish I was a virgin. But it is too late now. In my next life I want to be a Muslim, and behave like a Pakistani girl. Then they would respect me more.'

Another way of gaining popularity, especially among the hypermodern boys, was by acting in as modern, free, and mobile a way as possible. This involved joining the group of *hypermodern girls*, the counterparts of the hypermodern boys. In practice it meant dressing in a modern way, wearing jeans and buffalo boots instead of a scarf, openly having a boyfriend, going out with friends of whatever ethnic background. While hypermodern girls comply with a dignity code, as they want equality with boys, they also try to win respect by creating fear. To do this they draw on elements from both the code of honor and the code of dignity. The hypermodern girls consist of a network of girls who go to youth clubs in the afternoon and hang out with hypermodern boys on Friday and Saturday evenings. The hypermodern girls are mostly Norwegian but there are several Somali and Moroccan girls among them, too. There are no Pakistani girls in this network at this age.

In general, Norwegian girls come from families for whom the unreachability strategy is not considered a way to build a reputation or a basis for an identity. Chastity is not uppermost in the minds of these parents, but independence, personal responsibility, and tolerance. In this they subscribe to the dignity code in the same manner as the teachers. They allow their daughters to stay out after school, go to youth clubs, and have boyfriends. They regard this as natural behavior for young people – boys as well as girls. Girls are allowed to stay out until ten or eleven at night while several of the Pakistani girls had to be home at two or three in the afternoon.

In the event of a foreign boy becoming involved with a Norwegian girl, there were almost no risks of reprisals from the girl's family. Her brothers, if she had any, would not be inclined to give him a beating. Nonetheless, having a Norwegian girlfriend is not entirely risk-free. The boy could well become the object of insults, violent abuse, and fights. There was a great deal of competition among the boys in the hypermodern network with regard to dating and entering into close relationships with Norwegian girls, as the girls felt free to change partners whenever they wanted, dropping a boy and making him feel ridiculed and ashamed. In these situations, the boys tended to deride and shame each other, but also the girls whom they now found cheap and not worth their time, would use insults as a weapon. In the competition between boys for the attention of the girls, the loser would use verbal abuse to minimize his loss and stigmatize the girl he had failed to win over, or who had dropped him, and the person who had actually succeeded in winning the attentions of the girl would be similarly derided. This type of reaction could be seen among the foreign girls, too, whenever they agreed to become someone's girlfriend. They would be very secretive about the whole thing, however, because the risk they were taking in having a boyfriend was greater than if they had been Norwegian girls. Keeping their relationship a secret was thus a sensible ploy, but it also involved making concessions to the unreachability strategy. This was a source of considerable frustration and ambivalence to the Pakistani girls, not least when they saw the boys they were secretly in love with together with Norwegian girls. There was a tense atmosphere between Norwegian and Pakistani girls on the subject of boyfriends. The Pakistani girls were trapped in the all-inclusive system of control exercised by their parents and brothers, who were doing their utmost to force the girl to observe the unreachability strategy. It happened that older brothers, aged about eighteen to twenty, hung around near the school premises in an attempt to control their sisters. This would also send a message to any boys who might be thinking of trying to date their sisters or warn boys who had shamed their sister or insulted their brother at school. This tendency of the older brothers to loiter near school to deter younger boys from behaving disrespectfully to their family members was also a problem at some of the primary schools in the area.

2.6.3 *The strategies of the hypermodern girls – attacking and seeking protection from boyfriends*

Norwegian families have an average of two children. Quite often a girl will not have an older brother, or she may be an only child. It would be senseless in a Norwegian context to ask cousins to come and do battle for a girl's honor; it would simply not be understood as anything worth bothering about. A Norwegian girl is therefore left to her own devices to win or maintain respect in a climate where the code of honor prevails, and is obliged to find other ways to do so than enlisting the services of her family. One strategy is to fight for her honor herself, employing what I call the attack strategy. Another is to seek protection from the foreign boys, either by becoming somebody's girlfriend or by becoming a fictive sister. Often, the Norwegian girl will seek to combine these strategies; she will become a girlfriend, a fictive sister, and she will put up a fight to defend her honor. To enhance her fighting capacity, she gangs together with other girls, forming a group structure in which the dominant values are loyalty and group honor. The girls refuse to be abused, verbally or physically, and adopt aggressive forms to protect their honor. This leads to a double bind, especially for the girls, as they seem to lose their feminine virtue proper to the code of honor by exercising aggression. To find alternative respect, the girls draw on different resources: an aggressive behavioral form, the use of threats and weapons, developing friendships with aggressive boys, knowing a lot of dangerous and criminal people and gangs.

A Norwegian girl, the girlfriend of a Somali boy, said:

> My half-brother came [on a visit] from Mo i Rana, where he lives with my father. We went to Oslo City together and when he went into a tobacco shop. I stood outside, waiting. A group of Pakistani boys came by. They did not see me, but when my brother came out of the shop, I understood that they were going to rob him. There were four of them. So I hurried towards my brother, and I shouted to the Pakistani boys: 'Don't you know who I am. I am the girlfriend of … This boy is my brother, and you know who I'll get hold of if you mess with him.' Then they got scared. The Pakistanis understood, and they said: 'Sorry, we didn't see you and we didn't know he was your brother.' So, in a friendly manner, they patted him on his shoulder and left.

A strategy used by Norwegian girls to avoid intimidation is by entering into close relationships with boys from immigrant backgrounds, i.e. the hypermodern boys. When a girl is intimately involved with a boy, he develops a sense of attachment to her and sees her as his property. And as she has become a part of his domain, he will be willing to fight for her honor, even though she is a Norwegian girl and, as such, unchaste. However, what often happens is that when a relationship has broken off, or a girl has turned a boy down, the boy, instead of protecting the girl, will start to denounce her and do what he can to dishonor her name, proclaiming her a whore. If the boy has enemies or competitors, they will try to harm him and egg on a fight by calling his girlfriend a whore, or simply by having sex with her and boasting about it afterwards. Having a girlfriend thus makes a boy vulnerable to abuse, and if he finds out she wants somebody else, he really loses face, and risks ending in a fight with her new boyfriend. Thus, while girlfriends are highly desired, they are a risky proposition for the boys, involving them in a considerable number of fights. It is something of a catch 22 for both the boys and the girls.

A strategy used to guard against insults from the Norwegian girls and immigrant girls, is to develop more masculine ways of behaving, i.e. by assuming the attack strategy. Respect is won by creating fear. 'They respect me because they are afraid of me.' This is the first step in the development of criminal girl gangs.

Four of the schools at which I did fieldwork had girl gangs, which consisted of both Norwegian girls and girls with a foreign background: Latinos and Muslims. I call them gangs because they fulfill many of the criteria specified by Decker (1996) and Klein and Maxon (1985). They are involved in more violence and criminal activities than other young people, and compose closed and bonded groups with a high sense of identity. They had been in existence for a year or so and bore names such as Criminal Mafia Sisters, The Sisters of the Devil, Blood Sisters and the like. Their leadership is charismatic rather than formalistic. These hypermodern girls took their behavioral cue from the hypermodern boys and fought violently with other girls and boys. After a while they gained a reputation for being very dangerous. 'Nobody would call me a whore, because they know I can be dangerous and hurt them. They no longer dare to insult me.' 'A boy called me whore some time ago and I kicked his leg so that he couldn't walk properly for a whole week.' Several of these girls started their violent gang activities as a reaction to verbal abuse and to protect themselves from the whore stigma. They adopted the aggressive stance of the boys, establishing their own gangs, bearing weapons such as knives, and tried to build an image of themselves as dangerous people. At the same time they sought and achieved the protection of hypermodern boys, and were closely connected with them. At one of the schools, an established network of girls had sought the protection of the Somali boys. At another, a network of Latino girls had developed connections with some violent and criminal Vietnamese boys. At a third a multicultural group of antagonistic girls was in league with a gang dominated by Pakistanis and Latin Americans.

The violence, the willingness to commit crimes, the bonding, and loyalty represent the normative trappings they developed to combat verbal and physical abuse, and build up a form of respect based on an attack strategy and a reputation for violence, rather than sexual purity and unreachability. The girls in the Criminal Mafia Sisters were fourteen years old and had written statutes that they followed. Their gang had existed for more than a year. It seems that when chaste girls break out from under their parents' control and achieve greater freedom, they end up not as moderate girls but as hypermodern girls. The polarization of youth in Oslo seems to affect the whole city (Bakken 1998), and it may be said to be the result of a process of schismogenesis.

2.7 A schismogenetic process involving five parties at school

We may describe the amount of violence at the school as a product of several schismogenetic processes working together to produce the five social forms. The processes are enhanced or restricted by the overall existing normative codes. The code of honor seems to motivate and generate an aggressive and violent form of self-expression, in an atmosphere of intercode tension, producing a form of hyperhonor.

2.7.1 A complementary schismogenetic process between chaste girls and hypermodern girls

The chaste and hypermodern girls employ different strategies to obtain popularity – the one the withdrawal technique, the other the attack strategy. These distinct social forms are generated through the reciprocal exaggeration of behavior patterns, that is, through internal and external processes of differentiation that Bateson has termed complementary schismogenesis. Bateson (1958:176), defines the process as follows:

> If for example, one of the patterns of cultural behavior considered appropriate in individual A is culturally labeled as an assertive pattern, while B is expected to reply to this with what is culturally regarded as submission, it is likely that this submission will encourage a further assertion, and that this assertion will demand still further submission.

Although the chaste girls are numerically dominant, they are less assertive and more submissive than the hypermodern girls. The latter are fewer in number but very assertive and justify their assertive behavior by pointing to elements within both the code of honor and the code of dignity. As we have seen, the code of honor has different moral standards for men and women, and the hypermodern girls, rather than drawing on references to chastity in the code of honor, justify their assertive behavior by reference to standards for manly behavior in the code. This means that they reject the role of the submissive woman, and seek equality with boys by adopting the same behavioral standards. Their actions can be interpreted as a protest against submission and chastity. Their behavioral models are not the Norwegian boys but the hypermodern boys. Their behavior arises as a result of the interactional processes that take place with the latter group. The hypermodern girls seek recognition and respect by creating fear rather than demonstrating sexual purity. In spite of their adoption of an aggressive strategy they still carry images of purity with them though their ideals are indistinct, which in itself creates a lot of internal tension and confusion. The attack strategy can be seen as a protest against submission, which in turn can reinforce the withdrawal strategy of the chaste girls. The processes of differentiation engineer a split between the hypermodern and the chaste girls. The parents of the chaste girls loan argumentative elements from what they observe in the behavior of the hypermodern girls to justify a need for stricter control of the girls thus encouraging further withdrawal. The parents worry that freedom would lead to parental disrespect and to promiscuity, which they suspect of the hypermodern girls. But while parents concentrate all their energy on this task, they very often relax their control of moderate boys and hypermodern boys. The moderate boys are then put at a greater risk of more violent behavior and of tipping over and being recruited into the hypermodern category.

2.7.2 Symmetrical and complimentary schismogenesis among boys

There seems to be a process of *complimentary schismogenesis* between the Norwegian boys who adopt the avoidance strategy and the hypermodern boys of non-Norwegian descent. This avoidance strategy can tip over into open antagonism, spawning racism and violent behavior on both sides. Alternatively, it may result in a complete split between the various categories with a subsequent specialization in certain activities and a high degree of discomfort about the other categories. As Bateson says, '[s]ooner or later, the distortion of the personalities is likely to be accompanied by three effects: (a) a hostility in which each party resents the other as the cause of its own distortion, (b) at least in complementary schismogenesis an increasing inability to understand the emotional reactions of the other party, and (c) mutual jealousy' (op. cit. 187–188).

Complementary schismogenesis seems to have led to the development of neo-Nazi gangs in certain parts of Oslo. In the Manglerud area of Oslo a racist gang called the Vikings was established after a period of frequent visits by a Vietnamese gang, which resulted in violent episodes. And in the Bjoelsen area a violent racist gang called Boot Boys has operated and strengthened its position during the year 2000. It justifies its existence by referring to immigrant gangs. Their website gives one an impression of intense jealousy and hatred of 'foreign boys' and they express what they perceive as an urgent need to protect Norwegian girls from them.

There is also a kind of *symmetrical schismogenesis* between the hypermodern boys and the hypermodern girls. In their efforts to achieve dominance and masculinity the hypermodern boys cannot accept girls showing equal measures of aggression and fearlessness; this would involve them in a competitive process with girls. When girls strive to be equal, boys strive to remain on top. This competition in aggressiveness presses the process on, forcing the boys and girls to act more aggressively and criminally.

The hypermodern schoolboys steal cars, cellular phones, and clothes from shops. They have girlfriends and steal girlfriends from each other. This involves them in a process of symmetrical schismogenesis, i.e., a strategy of boosting honor through creating more fear and taking more risks and breaking more rules. Paine (1989) calls this 'living on high wire'.

Within this hierarchical system of thought there are only two positions in a relation between two antagonists, top or bottom. There is an emotional dimension to this dyadic relation, and this is the emotion of fear. The honor code contains instructions for the control of the emotion of fear. A man of honor must not show that he is afraid of anything, but he must strive to make others fear him. Schoolboys would say: 'I respect my father because I am afraid of him,' or 'I respect God, I fear him so much.' The person of honor should feel no fear himself but requires that others fear him. The necessity of inspiring fear in others has to do with the power dimension of the code. The moral is: you must represent a threat to those who do not take you seriously and who act against your will. They should be afraid of your willpower and readiness to act. Their fear, and your own lack of fear (nothing will stop you) should demonstrate who is the strong and dominant person and who is the inferior, weak and fearful one. The man with an ambition to gain honor is therefore constantly fearful that others will see his fear, because that would be a signal of inferiority.

The logic of emotions within the code of honor is obviously contradictory, placing the person in a double bind: you must fear your own fear and take care never to reveal that you are afraid, at the risk of ridicule and loss of status. At the same time, you must make sure that you yourself are feared. This dimension of fear, and the fear of fear, has not been sufficiently studied by those anthropologists that have developed theories of honor. The constant worry of falling into submission, of becoming subject to the Other, pervades this version of the code of honor, and the fear of being considered weak and timid forces the hypermodern boys into a competitive process with hypermodern girls, who have begun to become more assertive than the boys are used to in their ethnic communities. But as the hypermodern boys become more assertive to counter the girls' aggressiveness, this forces the hypermodern girls to follow suit. Despite abiding by both moral codes, what is uppermost in their minds is to be respected for assertiveness and spreading fear rather than chasteness. To quote Bateson once again,

> If for example, we find boasting as the cultural pattern of behavior in one group, and the other group replies to this with boasting, a competitive situation may develop in which boasting leads to more boasting and so on. This type of progressive change we may call symmetrical schismogenesis. (177)

It is the radiating communicative effect of aggression and violence that propels the process of symmetrical schismogenesis further, and drives the hypermodern boys to adopt ever more violent behavior. Violence is a very powerful communicative tool that can instantly turn one's position from inferiority to superiority, and stop any further verbal discussion on positions. When the enemy lies on the ground there is a feeling that the game has been won. The winner has been shown to have power. Violence has an effect of 'tactical pre-emption' (Riches 1986) by reducing the opportunity to retaliate by diminishing the power of the victim. It becomes obvious which of the two parties has power and which has lost it. Violence is therefore a powerful tool to force respect through creating fear. Making people fear you is an impressive feat, and withdrawal cannot compete with the splendor of violence as an expression of personal and group identity. The powerful symbolization of the attack strategy increases the readiness to use violence, giving the aggressive form a positive feedback effect on the social form. We have to be aware of the symbolic force that aggressive behavior can take, and the fact that when it reaches a certain level it can lead to cultural change. Escalating aggressive behavior produces thus a new morality and new behavioral norms – the code of honor in a hyper form.

Code of hyperhonor	Description
Hybrid form	Elements from traditional and modern thinking and living
Hierarchical	Fear of inferiority, and of expressing fear. Attack strategy preferred. Obsession with honor. My power should be supreme: 'I am above the law and the enemy'
Particularism	Different moral standards for different categories of people Situational blocking of empathy when robbing and fighting Blocking of communication and reception of information
Gendered morality from the boys' perspective	One moral standard for women, another for men 'Liberal sexuality for me'
Liberal thinking on ethnicity and blood family	Breaking away from pure ethnic networks, i.e., the caste system Establishing multicultural groupings, or cross-family groupings
Non-submission to external rules Individualistic and liberal ethics	Liberation from and distance to parents and teachers. Individualistic in relation to parents
Close ties	Loyalty to the peer group first – not the family Reconnection and submission to peer group control and authority 'Establishing fictive family or brotherhoods'
Non-tolerance	'I will not take (tolerate) anything'
Hypermodern American ghetto symbolism and expression admired	American and Italian clothes, golden chains, cars, newest technology; cellulars
Experimenting with crime and cultural taboos	Visiting discos, smoking, drugs, drinking alcohol, having sex at an early age, criminal activities and expensive habits

Violence and abuse creates mistrust, insecurity, and a need for trustworthy relations, and the method of establishing trust is to make alliances with others that are ready to fight with you. Through a network of alliances, a power base has been established. The need for bonding and loyalty becomes crucial, and the process of violent communication can be paralleled by the need to establish an organizational frame around the communicative process. Alliances through strategic connections to groups with a reputation for dangerous behavior become a form of armament. Tight-knit fictive brotherhoods and sisterhoods are created in an effort to construct relations that have a pre-emptive effect; an effect as communicative tools for obtaining respect based on the production of fear, and projection of fear on to outsiders. *The dyadic relation between individuals established within a code of hyperhonor, will always be a hierarchical relation*. The person on top has a sense of superiority and power and conceives of himself as a person unafraid of anything.

The person underneath is supposed to feel fear out of respect. These processes of creating fear to obtain honor have feedback effects on already established forms: the number of moderate boys and chaste girls would decline if they felt a need for protection, or they would withdraw completely leaving the field open for the hypermodern boys and girls, who would increase in numbers. Between these two hyper groups and the rest of society, there would be a deep gorge.

2.8 Conclusion

As we have seen, the code of dignity is losing its dominant position as a code for defining identities and roles in the multicultural schools I studied in the city of Oslo. Although it continues to exist at an abstract level it has lost much of its potency as a guide for action in practical life. The schismogenetic processes that have been described here and that take place in an atmosphere characterized by verbal abuse, intimidation, and moral tension, can lead to profound cultural and moral changes among youths in Oslo from all kinds of ethnic backgrounds. It can spark a widespread return to a code of honor, thus making it more likely for others to adopt its extreme form, all of which will involve considerable violence and abuse.

Some teachers have even begun to adopt the extreme form of this code of honor, seeking respect by creating a climate of fear. One teacher said: 'I once fought with a boy because he attacked me, and after this incident I got a reputation for being violent and dangerous. Do you know, this reputation is worth its weight in gold. When the boys see me now, they tremble and do whatever I ask them to. They respect me. It is good. Teachers must make themselves respected differently than before, so we can have peace at work.'

Teachers who oppose an authoritarian style and embrace the dignity code, have nonetheless become dependent on the authority of teachers with a reputation for violence. Whenever disciplinary problems crop up, these teachers are brought in as representatives of the institution to reinstate order and harmony by inciting fear.

Female teachers also have to deal with expressions of the code of honor during breaks. They often hear statements like: 'Why are you here? You should be at home with your children. A woman should stay at home.' A female teacher said: 'I often have to listen to the opinions of the foreign pupils at school, and you know, it strikes a chord inside me. It is as if some old deep guilt, a wound, is torn open.' So the code of honor influences not only the pupils, but many of the teachers as well.

But measures have been taken by the school to stop this process. An effort has been made to create order by strengthening the disciplinary system and finding acceptable and nonviolent ways of dealing with the youngsters. In many schools conflict arbitration programs have been introduced to teach children and delinquent youths how to solve conflicts through verbal negotiations, rather than through violence and fear.

In his analysis of schismogenesis in political and verbal contests, Ottar Brox (1997) argues that situations escalate because too few social scientists have taken the trouble to explain the processes at work to the people involved. Brox claims that some systems do not survive being understood. In the case of school violence and gang formation in Oslo, a lot of attention is being devoted to the problem these days. Experts talk to other experts, to teachers, to the police and the social workers, but perhaps what is needed is to explain the processes at work to the young themselves. This is what Giddens calls double hermeneutics, i.e., the interchange of frames of understanding between practical participants and those who study, analyze and publish accounts about them' (1984: 284, 374).

Maybe what is missing in the schools is a thorough discussion with the pupils on different ways of moral thinking, and an awareness of the consequences of an obsession with honor. An Iranian boy told me that he used to visit a psychologist once a week. This was a measure forced upon him by the authorities after he, a gang member, had been involved in several serious brawls with rather bad outcomes.

He said: 'The psychologist is training me to stop thinking about my honor. It is for my own good, he says. He is trying to remove the word from my mind, to make me free.'

References

Anderson, E. (1999), *Code of the Street – decency, violence, and the moral life of the inner city*, New York, W.W. Norton

Bakken, A. (1998), *Ungdomstid i storbyen*, NOVA-Rapport 7/98

Barth, F. (1966), *Models of Social Organization*, Royal Anthropological Institute Occasional Papers no. 23, Oxford, Basil Blackwell

Bateson, G. (1958), *Naven*, Stanford, Stanford University Press

Beck, U. (1992), *Risk Society: towards a new modernity*, London, Sage

Berger, P., Berger, B. and Kellner, H. (1974), *The Homeless Mind*, New York, Vintage Books

Bjørgo, T. and Carlsson, Y. (1999), *Vold, Rasisme og Ungdomsgjenger – Forebygging og bekjempelse*, Oslo, Tano Aschehoug

Bjørgo, T. (1997), *Racist and Right Wing Violence in Scandinavia*, Oslo, Tano Aschehoug

Bourgois, P. (1996), 'In Search of Masculinity: Violence, Respect and Sexuality among Puerto Rican Crack Dealers in East Harlem', *British Journal of Criminology*, vol. 36, no. 3

Broch-Due, V., Rudie, I., Bleie, T. (eds) (1993), *Carved Flesh: Cast Selves. Gendered Symbols and Social Practices*, Oxford, Berg

Brox, O. (1992), 'Schismogenetic Conflicts', in *Yearbook of Sociology*, University of Oslo

D'Andrade, R. (1995), *The Development of Cognitive Anthropology*, Cambridge, Cambridge University Press

Davis, J. (1987), 'Family and State in the Mediterranean', in Gilmore (ed.), *Honor and Shame and the Unity of the Mediterranean*, American Anthropological Association, Washington DC

Decker, S.H. (1996), 'Collective and Normative Features of Gang Violence', in *Justice Quarterly*, vol. 13, no. 2

Decker, S.H. and Van Winkle, B. (1996), *Life in the Gang*, Cambridge, Cambridge University Press

Durkheim, E. (1954), *The Elementary Forms of the Religious Life*, trans. J.W. Swain, Glencoe, Ill., Free Press

Ewing, K.P. (1991), 'Can Psychoanalytic Theories Explain the Pakistani Woman? Intrapsychic Autonomy and Interpersonal Engagement in the Extended Family', *Ethos*, June 1991, vol. 19, no. 2

Fangen, K. (1995), *Skinheads i rodt, hvitt og blatt.* En sosiologisk studie fra 'innsiden' Ungforskrapport 4: 1995

Fangen, K. (1999), *Pride and Power – A Sociological Interpretation of the Norwegian Radical Nationalist Underground Movement.* Ph.D. thesis published by the Department of Sociology and Human Geography, University of Oslo

Finkielkraut, A. (1987), *La defaite de la pensée*, Editions Gallimard

Fleisher, M.S. (1998), *Dead End Kids. Gang Girls and the Boys They Know*, Madison, University of Wisconsin Press

Giddens, A. (1984), *The Constitution of Society*, Cambridge, Polity Press

Gilmore, D.D. (1987), *Honor and Shame and the Unity of the Mediterranean*, Washington DC, American Anthropological Association

Haaland, T. (2000), *Vold - konflikt og gjengdannelse: En undersøkelse blant ungdom i fire byer*, Oslo, NIBR prosjektrapport 2000:14

Heelas, P. (1996), 'Introduction: Detraditionalization and its Rivals', in Heelas, Lash and Morris (eds), *Detraditionalization. Critical Reflection on Authority and Identity*, Cambridge, Mass., Blackwell

Klein, M. (1971), *Street Gangs and Street Workers,* Englewood Cliffs, NJ, Prentice Hall

Klein, M. (1995), *The American Street Gang. Its Nature, Prevalence and Control*, New York, Oxford University Press

Larsen, T. (1987), 'Action, Morality and Cultural translation', in *Journal of Anthropological Research*, vol. 43, no. 1

Lien, I.L. and Haaland, T. (1998), *Vold og gjengatferd*, NIBR - samarbeidsrapport

Lien, I.L. (1997), *Ordet som stempler djevlene*, Oslo, Aventura

Lien, I.L. (1993), *Moral og emosjoner i Pakistansk Punjab.* Unpublished doctoral thesis. University of Oslo, Department of Social Anthropology

Lien, I.L. (1991), 'En universalistisk og en partikularistisk moral', *Norsk Antropologisk Tidsskrift*, no. 3

Maxson, C. and Klein, M. (1985), 'Differences between Gang and Nongang Homicides', *Criminology*, vol. 23, pp. 209-222

Mandelbaum, D.G (1988), *Women's Seclusion and Men's Honor, Sex Roles in North India, Bangladesh and Pakistan*, Tucson, The University of Arizona Press

Melhuus, M. (1993), 'I want to Buy me a Baby! Some reflections on Gender and Change in Modem Society', in Broch Due, V., Rudie I. and Bleie, T. (eds), *Carved Flesh: Cast Selves. Gendered Symbols and Social Practices*, Oxford, Berg

Miller, J. (2001), *One of the Guys. Girls, Gangs and Gender*, New York, Oxford University Press

Nathanson, D. L. (1992), *Shame and Pride. Affect, Sex and the Birth of the Self*, New York, W.W. Norton & Company

Nisbett, R.E. and Cohen, D. (1996), *The Culture of Honor. The Psychology of Violence in the South*, Boulder, CO, Westview Press

Paine, R. (1989), 'High-wire culture': Comparing two agonistic systems of self esteem', in Man (N.S) 24 (657-72)

Peristiany, J.G (ed.) (1974), *Honour and Shame. The Values of Mediterranean Society*, London, Weidenfeldt

Pitt-Rivers, J. (1965), 'Honour and social status', in Peristiany J.G (ed.), *Honour and Shame. The Values of Mediterranean Society*, London, Weidenfeldt

Pitt-Rivers, J. (1968), 'Honor', in *International Encyclopedia of Social Sciences*

Riches, D. (1986), 'The phenomenon of Violence', in D. Riches (ed.), *The Anthropology of Violence*, Oxford, Basil Blackwell

Simmel, G. (1950), *The Sociology of Georg Simmel*, trans. and ed. Kurt Wolff, Glencoe, Ill., Free Press

Sperber, D. (1996), *Explaining Culture, A Naturalistic Approach*, Oxford, Blackwell

Spergel, I.A. and Curry, D.G (1993), 'The National Youth Gang Survey: A Research and Developmental Process', in Goldstein, A. and Huff, R.C. (eds), *The Gang Intervention Handbook*, Champaign, Ill., Research Press, pp. 359-400

Spiro, M. (1997), *Gender Ideology and Psychological Reality. An Essay on Cultural Reproduction*, New Haven, Yale University Press

Wikan, U. (1984), 'Shame and honour: A contestable pair', in Man 1984, no. 19

Chapter 3

Honor and Revenge in the Culture of Danish Outlaw Bikers

Joi Bay

The code of honor is fundamental to an understanding of the violence in the culture of outlaw bikers. A field study of outlaw bikers in Denmark[1] has evidenced how the culture's own concepts of honor and dignity are linked to the ability to defend personal and collective territories. Honor and the territories are continuously tested, challenged, infringed and defended in ritualized and symbolic ways. On the individual level these tests begin as either verbal or physical games and fights. On the collective level the honor contests start by deriding the predominant symbols of MC-clubs – their 'colors'. These honor conflicts can in either case provoke feuds.

3.1 Honor-based cultures

Cultures based on a code of honor can best be understood by a comparison with popular adventure games like *Dungeons & Dragons*, *Star Frontiers* or *Rolemaster*. In this kind of game each player is represented by a character, who is endowed with a certain amount of hit-points. As the characters move through the game they involve themselves in fights during which they can win or lose hit-points. The more hit-points a player earns, the higher he will rank in the game hierarchy; if he loses all his hit-points, however, the character will die and be forced to leave the game.

The code of honor can in many ways be compared to the rules of this kind of adventure game. In honor-based cultures, one does not collect hit-points but honor, which can be taken from or lost to the other participants in the contests of honor. the more honor collected, the higher one's rank in the status hierarchy. A loss of all honor leads to the forfeiture of further contests of honor.

Studies of codes of honor have dealt with Mediterranean cultures (Peristiany 1966, Safilios-Rothschild 1969, Knudsen 1989) or with Chicano subcultures (Horowitz 1983). In these cultures honor is of decisive importance for social relations, and forms the basis of their status systems. Such honor-based cultures differ from each other in many ways, but the code of honor seems to have several universal features:

1. Honor seems to be understood as an imaginary valuable resource. The resource is limited but constant, such that honor can only be acquired be capturing it from another. By doing so one will always inflict shame on the party who loses the honor. Honor and shame are complementary quantities.
2. It is a common characteristic of honor oriented cultures that honor is never accorded simply by birth, rank or wealth. Honor must be won or lost in competition with peers.
3. Contests of honor are ritualized games that consist of unending exchanges of challenges and replies, affronts and re-affronts, attacks and defenses. How one performs in such exchanges determines whether one acquires honor or shame and defines the participant's position in the status system.
4. To be an honorable man it is not sufficient to be capable of protecting honor when challenged. One must also be prepared to risk honor by challenging others.
5. Games of honor are always played in public. It is the public that assigns and deprives a man of his symbolic marks of honor by showing him respect or by expecting deference.
6. Both individuals and primary groups (families, clans, gangs and peer groups) participate in the honor contests. The honor of the individual and his primary group are reciprocally connected. If a member conducts himself in a shameful manner then the whole group is affected, and if a member of the group cannot protect his or her own honor (this applies primarily to women, the elderly and the dead) then the group will be responsible for restoring the collective honor.
7. Honor is closely associated with a man's sexual identity – his manhood. Women are also included in the code of honor, but they are not presumed capable of protecting their own honor. If a man cannot protect his women's honor he will experience a loss of manliness. In extreme cases the loss of honor and manliness will be so severe that the man will be regarded, and will look upon himself, as a socially dead person, as a man without social identity.

3.2 Bikers' concepts of honor

The code of honor is crucial to understanding the culture of outlaw bikers. Central events, traditions and values of the subculture can best be understood in the light of the code of honor – this applies to both the collective and the individual behavior of bikers.

Bikers' vernacular contains several concepts and expressions which are related to their code of honor.[2] A man or a club of honor is said to be 'strong' (*stærk*) or to possess 'class' (*stil*).[3] 'To be strong' has different connotations in the culture of outlaw bikers than in standard Danish. An outlaw bikers club can be 'strong' in spite of the fact that it has only few members and small assets. And a biker can in the same way be considered 'strong' even though he is small or physically frail. The crucial indication of a biker's or his club's 'strength' lies in the mode of comportment. To be ready to defend oneself, one's fellows in the club (called 'brothers' (*brødre*) in the bikers' vernacular) and the club's reputation enables one to gain 'strength'. 'Strength' is not a given quality or character but rather a property that can be won or lost like other possessions.

The other main concept of honor, 'class' or 'style' (*stil*), is used in a similar way. This expression involves a crucial honor-based value in the culture, which can be summarized thus: 'It is not what you do but how you do it.' The process of an act is more important than the result of the act. An example can illustrate this important principle of honorable behavior:

> In 1984, *Jønke*, a member of the original chapter of the Danish *Hell's Angels MC*, shot and killed the 'president' of a rival club, *Bullshit MC*. This incident initiated a three year long feud between the two clubs and their supporters. The feud resulted in nine killings and long prison sentences. The original killing of the president of *Bullshit MC* could not be regarded as an honorable act from any point of view. *Jønke* killed the rival president with a burst from a machine gun without giving his victim a chance. Nevertheless, *Jønke* gained a lot of honor from the subsequent events – not only in the culture of outlaw bikers but also in public opinion.
>
> Immediately following the murder, he was sought by the police but fled the country. While on the run, *Jønke* published his autobiography (Nielsen 1985; he was 25 years old at that time), which included a chapter on the shooting of the president of *Bullshit MC*. After three years living as a fugitive in Canada he went to the police. *Jønke* was sentenced to 16 years in prison, and during his trial gave several media interviews where he stood up for his right to kill.

Though most bikers will agree that the murder of the president of *Bullshit MC* was reprehensible and was done in a dishonorable way, they all characterize *Jønke* as a man of great honor. He succeeded in hiding from the police for three years, and he even wrote a book in which he expressed pride in his deed. His honor was emphasized when he later accepted his sentence of 16 years imprisonment 'like a man'. He had proved to be in control of the situation, and in this way he made a fool of the police and of society's legal system. He humiliated them, and deprived them of their right 'to have the last word'. 'To have the last word' in either a literal or figurative sense is the goal of any contest of honor.

The distinction between 'outlaw' and 'not outlaw' in the bikers' vernacular is a part of the subculture's honor-based classification system. To be *outlaw* (Danish bikers use the English word) is synonymous with being an honorable man or club. It means that the individual or his club is prepared to protect, by all available means, their reputation as being 'strong' and 'having class'. This will be done even if it involves acts which are considered criminal by the larger society.

Bikers' vernacular contains several expressions for contests of honor, i.e. the challenge of others' honor and the risking of one's own honor. 'To ask somebody to dance' (*at byde op til dans*), 'to sound somebody out' (*at føle hinanden på tænderne*), 'to whittle at each other' (*at småsnitte hinanden*), and 'to punk someone' (*at punke*) are all synonyms for the game of challenge.

3.3 The code of colors

Games and contests, both with and without the use of motorcycles, are important parts of the entertainment during 'runs' (*træf*) where different MC-clubs or different chapters of the same club meet during weekends 'in the riding season'. In tug-of-war competitions clubs or chapters compete for 'strength' and honor. Normally, the club with the strongest and heaviest members will win both the prize and the honor, but there are exceptions. A club that is about to lose can suddenly and synchronously drop the rope so that the other club's competitors fall to the ground. The winning club will end in the dirt and they will therefore win with shame, while the losing club will achieve the honor.

This way of splitting the prize and the honor between two clubs, which of course is especially popular when the ground is muddy, can also be seen in tug-or-war contests outside the culture of outlaw bikers. The winners of the competition end on their backs, a position which always connotes inferiority and humiliation. Yet this has a special meaning within bikers subculture because the colors of the winners thereby touch the ground. In this way the honor-winning club can bring about a situation where the club that loses honor has violated one of the rules in the culture's 'code of colors'. Colors or club patches are know in Danish as 'back badges' (*rygmærker*), because they are normally worn on the back of the biker's vest. Bikers' vests and club patches are parts of an international sign system – a grammar for the appearance of the 'patch' – and a 'code of colors', which governs the use and the functions of the patches. The same grammar and code is used by bikers throughout the world.

Vests and patches vary from club to club. In most outlaw bike clubs the 'patch' consists of the club's logo encircled by two stylized banners, called 'rockers'. The top banner shows the club's name, the lower the club's territory. On the front pieces of the vest one can normally find further information about the owner of the vest. The front patches will usually at least include the following: a metal badge with the club's logo (placed near the heart), small patches with the club's name and territory, the member's position if he holds office in the club, the member's street name, his seniority in the club (5, 10, 15 or more years), friendship patches (that indicate affiliations with both clubs). Besides these standard front patches you can find numerous individual adornments: patches in memory of lost 'brothers', Harley Davidson patches, patches from bikers'rights organizations and patches with letter abbreviations, which in some cases are internal and can only be understood by members of the same club. Other distinctive features in the grammar of the vest are the material (denim or leather) and its age.

To be a member of the subculture of outlaw bikers means being able to read the meanings of the vests. If two unknown bikers meet, they can, because of the vest, easily determine each others affiliations and positions in the subculture: Is he a 'clubman' or a 'freerider'? Which club does he ride with? Is it an 'outlaw', a 'touring' or a 'family' club? What is his status and seniority in the club and in the culture?

Just as one can determine the age of a vest from its patina and colors, one can also easily distinguish between new and old tattoos; the old ones have their own patina and lose the brilliance of a new tattoo. Old biker tattoos are signs of high status because they indicate long experience as a biker. Other body signs have a similar meaning. To have a large body volume – whether it is caused by well-developed fat deposits or muscles – is a sign of being a great and experienced man. It takes years to build a large body, whether done by drinking beer or building muscles. Long hair and beards have similar meanings, especially if gray. Large bodies and long body hair are signs of 'bikerwizdom' (sic!) – the American bikers' expression for experience within the subculture.[4]

For bikers who meet as strangers, the vest, the patches and the body signs provide essential information about each other. Information about their mutual status in the culture is vital when they interact: Who can expect to receive respect? Who will feel constrained to give respect? Will they match each other in a contest of honor? Contests of honor can only be played between equals. If the status difference between the competitors is too great, the contest will be dangerous for the subordinate while the superior will not be able to increase his honor in a contest with such an inferior competitor.

The sign system of vests and patches is similar to other signs of authority: the flag that represents the nation, the signature that represents the person, the uniform representing the institution, the logotype the firm, etc. Authority signs are marks of an authority's power to control rights, privileges, properties or territories, and they must therefore only be used by persons or institutions representing the authority. This rule is controlled by law, and offenses against the rules are sanctioned. These signs also function as distinctive markers that make it possible to identify the ruling authority and to distinguish between different authorities of the same type. They must therefore have an appearance that prevents them from being confused with other, similar signs.

Signs of authority are also symbols. They symbolize the collective or individual identity of the authority: the flag symbolizes the nation, the signature symbolizes the person etc. People who use such signs therefore have a close emotional connection to their signs. Hence, the signs must always be treated with proper respect and must be protected against insults, dishonor, and infringement, which are experienced as insults against the symbolized identity.

Bikers' club patches, signs and symbols are covered by the same rules as any other authority signs.[5] Their use is strictly controlled. They must only be used by club members, must be treated with the proper dignity, must be protected against misuse and dishonorable treatment.

3.4 Control of patches

The right to wear patches is heavily restricted and their use is controlled both in the individual club and in the subculture as such. Only full club members are allowed to wear the club's 'patch'. A biker who is a candidate for membership in an outlaw club usually has to undergo an initiation period. He will normally start as a '*hang around*' and in this period the back of his vest will only be marked with the two letters 'MC', which stand for Motorcycle Club. When he is promoted to the rank of '*prospect*' he will be allowed to add the bottom 'rocker' (the stylized banner) denoting the clubs territory to the back of his vest. The rest of the 'patch' (the logo and the club's name) will be presented to him at a ceremony after the club members have voted him into the club.[6]

If a new club wants to add club patches to their vests, then it has to pass through a similar trial period. There are no fixed rules or written bylaws in these cases, but the existing outlaw clubs in the area will not allow a new club to adopt a 'patch' unless the club has proven itself over several years to be worthy of the honor of a club 'patch'. During the waiting time, the club will be allowed to wear their logo as a small 'patch' on the front piece of the vest, and they will be exposed to a number of informal tests, which will give them the opportunity to prove that they are entitled to the club 'patch'. Such tests will normally be incidents where the new club is challenged by another club.

Admittance to the inner-circle of outlaw clubs, the 'patch holders', is thus restricted in accordance with the culture's code of honor. The whole club will not only be affected by, but will also be held responsible for, its members' conduct, and the club's honor depends on the reputation of its individual members. When the club members act jointly it is of crucial importance that every member is ready to defend the club's reputation. New members in a club must therefore be selected carefully; hence the long trial period.

The limitation of a new club's access to club patches is enforced on similar grounds. In spite of the fact that everyday life among outlaw bikers is characterized by frequent internal conflicts, they nevertheless regard themselves as a large 'brotherhood', and in fact consider themselves to be the aristocracy of the motorcycle fraternity. Only clubs that are willing to act in accordance with the traditions of this 'brotherhood' and who will not bring shame on this 'aristocracy of motorcyclists' are allowed to join the ranks of outlaw clubs.

This system of restricting the number of 'patch holders' is complicated by the large number of 'patch holding' clubs in Denmark. Most of these clubs are between 10 and 15 years old, and they adopted their patches in a period when the control of patches was much weaker than it is today. On the basis of their names, logos and patches, these clubs can be divided into two basic types: the grotesque and the awesome. The grotesque have laughable, absurd, crazy, and self-deprecating names and logos: *Dildo MC*, *Gonzo MC*, *Fat Rats MC*, *Stinkfoot MC*, and *Kosta Cow Riders MC* are examples of this type. The awesome clubs have powerful, formidable, and pompous names and logos: *Night Riders MC*, *Outsiders MC*, *Rebels MC*, *Tribesmen MC*, *Iron Wolfs MC*. Outlaw clubs are almost always of the awesome type, and they have been trying to limit the number of 'patch holding' clubs by fighting clubs with grotesque patches. The patches of the latter, and the way they are worn and treated by their clubs, do not accord with the ideals of the honorable outlaw.

> *Mental Midgets MC* attacked another local club, called *Rotterne MC* (The Rats) and they were forced to hand over their colors. They were told that they would only be allowed to wear colors again on the condition that they would change their logo to

something with more dignity. Their original logo was a rat having sex with a bit of cheese. They changed it – reluctantly – and their present logo is a rat's skull.

> For several years, *Hagar MC* – a small club from the town of *Kyng* on the island Funen – had Funen (Fyn) as their territory. When *Mental Midgets MC* moved to the island, they seized the colors of *Hagar MC*, which from that time on had to use their town as territory in their new colors while *Mental Midgets MC* has '*Island*' (spelled in English) as their territory.

Such incidents centering on the use of colors are by far the most common forms of conflicts between clubs. The right to wear a 'patch', to use certain motives and colors, and to state a territory on the 'patch' are challenged by an insult, and the way the club reacts to the insult is crucial for how the club is perceived within the culture, for its self-concept, and for its ranking in the hierarchy of bikers' clubs.

If a club is challenged then it has two options. It can either choose not to retaliate to the initial challenge and thereby accept the humiliation and dishonor that this lack of response inflicts upon the club, just like the clubs in the examples above did. Alternatively the club can 'take up the gauntlet', fight back by insulting the challenging club and in that way try to protect or gain honor but at the same time risk a feud where the club's future and the lives of its members are endangered.

> *Hog Riders MC* is a ten-year old club from Copenhagen, but they did not become 'patch holders' until a year ago. Shortly after adopting their colors a club member had a quarrel with a member from a local club – *Barons MC* – in a bar. It was not a serious quarrel, but for safety's sake the president of the *Barons MC* called upon the president of the *Hog Riders* to close the matter. *Hog Riders* chose to interpret this approach as a sign of weakness, and they responded by derogating *Barons*' colors and started questioning *Barons*' right to be 'patch holders'. *Barons* replied to this outrage on their pride by wrecking a car belonging to *Hog Riders*, who immediately retaliated by destroying the *Barons*' club house. Before this contest of honor developed into a serious fight between the clubs, the dominant club in the area – *Hell's Angels* – intervened. A peace conference was held and they agreed that each club should compensate for the material losses of the other. This course of events was the first test of the *Hog Riders*' capacity as a 'patch holding' club, and in this way they proved to the bikers' community that they should be regarded as an outlaw club.

3.5 Bikers' etiquette

On the individual level, greetings, gifts and invitations are the most important way of exchanging respect and marks of honor. The rules for exchanges of greetings and gifts are very similar to equivalent rules in other subcultures, but much more attention is given to the meaning of such exchanges.

The subculture's rules of greetings prescribe how different persons must be greeted. 'Brothers' hug each other, friends shake hands while acquaintances just say 'hallo' to each other. Concordant with bourgeois etiquette it is usually the highest ranking biker who takes the initiative in the greeting and who will determine what kind of greeting will be used. When two bikers who do not know each other meet, the higher ranking one will initiate the conversation by asking questions of the subordinate, and it is up to him to decide if and when an introduction is to be made, whether they will drink together, or even drink a couple of rounds together. 'Brothers' or friends drink in rounds, but it is usually up to the highest ranking biker to start the first round, the second round will be paid by the next in the hierarchy, and the rounds will not stop until the lowest ranking biker in the group has paid his round.[7]

These few examples of bikers' etiquette are sufficient to illustrate how such rules of good conduct contain innumerable possibilities for deliberate or unintended breaches, each of which might be interpreted as a sign of disrespect. They also reveal how a biker with high status can tie inferior bikers, or those who stand in his debt, to him or to his club just by dealing out greetings, rounds of beer or similar small favors and gifts. A man of honor cannot be in debt to another man of honor – an unpaid debt will always be regarded as dishonorable. This way of exerting power is the most common within the bikers' subculture, and is more prevalent than the use or threat of violence.

> *Mental Midgets MC* invited a neighbor club – *Gubsakkerne MC* – to a party in their club house, but the latter did not show up. To invite a club to a party is a way of showing the club respect – to demonstrate that the invited club enjoys the same status and belongs to the inner circle of the subculture. By staying away *Gubsakkerne* derogated the hosts of the party, who felt disgraced. They avenged the disrespect by invading the club house of *Gubsakkerne*, whose members were held up, forced to take off their vests, and told to turn up next time they were invited if they wanted to stay alive. Honor and respect cannot be forced through violence or threats of violence, however. The result was that bikers all over the country told stories about how the *Mental Midgets* had humiliated themselves.

3.6 Ritual insults

On the individual level, contests of honor are played in three different ways: practical jokes, ritual verbal insults and 'tall stories'.

> *Outsiders MC* had a party in their club house, which is an abandoned farm. As the participants at the party got drunk they went to sleep in their sleeping bags in the stable. At six o'clock in the morning they were all awakened by a violent noise. Some of the drunken club members had dragged a Harley Davidson motorcycle without mufflers into the stable and fired it up, laughing and shouting that 'this is how we wake people in our club – this is our alarm clock'. This practical joke was the occasion for a prolonged verbal competition. One of the sleeping guests grumbled about the brutal wake-up call and the early hour, but the owner of the motorized alarm clock responded by calling the dissatisfied guest a 'killjoy' (*hængehoved*). In this way a prolonged verbal contest was started. Accusations and insults were exchanged involving the whole spectrum of derogatory terms: 'nut, dickhead, cocksucker, queer etc' (*nød, Knold og Tot, dario, pikhoved, pikslikker, bøsse*, etc.). The verbal competition ended when one participant reverted to the ultimate insult among bikers,

> *rocker*.[8] The audience laughed when the loser could not respond and the winner gloried in their admiration.

Games such as these, practical jokes and the play with insolent terms, have many points of resemblance with practices such as 'sounding', or 'running a game on someone', which have been documented in other subcultures (Labov 1972, Folb 1980). The purpose of these games is always to make a fool of the other competitor and to win the admiration of the audience. Such games are not necessarily a token of hostility. It is normally a friendly and humorous form of interaction between club members or friends.

Every club has members who are experts in playing the roles of the ritualized games, the wag, the clown and the audience. The wag is the biker who has the largest repertoire of invective and is the most inventive and creative when it comes to practical jokes. The clown is the scapegoat, who always loses the verbal competitions and who is the most popular target for the wag's practical jokes. Both the wag and the clown are highly esteemed club roles, but they are not tied to certain persons. Because of the continuous competition involving honor and shame, different club members will be placed in the top and the bottom of the game hierarchy.

The best practical jokes occupy an important place in the history of the club, and become part of its repertoire of 'tall stories' (*løgnehistorier*). 'Tall stories' are neither lies nor truth. They are narratives about events in the history of the club; narratives that have been retold many times with the purpose of emphasizing certain themes, which always involve the distribution of honor and shame between the characters in the story. Though all the club members know these stories by heart, they all laugh every time the stories are told to newcomers.

The most common content of both verbal games, practical jokes and 'tall stories' are attempts to render one another unmanly. This is what happened, for example, when the *Hell's Angels* gave their rivals in *Bullshit* the nickname *Kolortene* (the cow's crap).[9]

To be unmanly is in itself a humiliation and the most effective way of labelling someone as unmanly is to assert that he is gay and to suggest that he plays the female part in a homosexual relationship. The most frequent verbal insults are slang for passive homosexuals and the best and most retold 'tall stories' belong to the same category:

There was a party in the club, and the club's clown was drunk under the table. He was in a coma and did not notice when he was stripped or when the club's wag poked an empty beer bottle into his anus. After several vain attempts they succeeded in waking the clown by pouring a bucket of water over his head. He did not notice the bottle in his anus until he tumbled to the ground and the bottle shattered.

Another popular theme of 'tall stories' is the feminization and consequent humiliation caused by the symbolic or actual castration of a biker:

> At a run there occurred a shooting contest between the clubs. Somehow one of the clowns succeeded in putting a bullet through his own penis. He was seriously hurt and

> they had to call an ambulance. Before the ambulance and the police arrived, they quickly got rid of the illegal guns. When the police interrogated them about the incident, they maintained that there had been no gun, and that the accident happened when they tossed some bullets into the campfire. The police believed this story, but the unlucky biker has been impotent ever since.

When games of verbal insults and practical jokes take place in the club or between friends, it is always interpreted as friendly high jinks. Honor and shame are distributed between the competitors, but it is very seldom that the games develop into conflicts where someone is seriously hurt, either physically or mentally. There are two reasons for this. First, everybody knows the rules of the game and that it is a ritual. Second, there exists a strongly enforced taboo against hostility and fights within the clubs. Members who cannot understand or cope with the ritual fights are fined a contribution to the club's cash box or are excluded in the case of a subsequent severe offence.

The distinction between the ritual insult and the personal insult is a fine one, especially when the game is played between bikers who are not in the same club or related in some other way. In these cases, harmless insults can easily escalate beyond the control of the competitors and result in a serious conflict. Most clubs have one or two members known to be (and who play the role of) troublemakers. The troublemaker is an 'image promoter' (Horowitz 1983); he is always looking for a contest, and has problems distinguishing between ritual and personal insults, especially when drunk. Such members represent a risk and a problem to clubs because their frequent external contests tend to involve the whole club in either fights or collective humiliation. The club's opinion of the troublemaker is mixed. On the one hand, he is able to bring honor to the club by his willingness to start honor contests and to protect the club's honor. On the other, his behavior can imperil not only the honor but also the very existence of the club. It is not unusual for a troublemaker to be expelled from a club if he cannot control his temper.

3.7 Concluding remarks

Contests of honor in the culture of outlaw bikers range from the most harmless and friendly verbal games or practical jokes to the most violent assaults. The actors in these contests are both individual bikers and clubs.

This comprehension of the bikers subculture as an honor-based culture influences our understanding of outlaw bikers in several ways:

1. Violent conflicts between clubs are not 'gang wars' but feuds, i.e. ritualized conflicts that are controlled by a logic known to all bikers: the code of honor.
2. The main causes for feuds in the culture of outlaw bikers are not, as claimed by the police and the mass media, conflicts concerning territories in the drug market. Some bikers and clubs *are* involved in drug trafficking and for that reason also involved in drug market conflicts, but all bikers – even law-abiding

bikers – participate in contests of honor. Such contests are frequently territorial, but the territories are symbolic rather than physical or financial.

3. The hypothesis of honor-based conflicts in the culture of outlaw bikers can explain why violence within the subculture is never or only very seldom reported to the police. Honor conflicts cannot be solved by the law because it is humiliating not to be able to return a challenge unaided.
4. This hypothesis can also account for the changeable allegiances within the bikers' subculture. Allied clubs or bikers become enemies and the other way around. It is not unusual for a feud to be concluded by a peace and for members of the losing club to be admitted as members in the winning club. This settlement of a violent conflict is an expression of the respect that old enemies in honor conflicts show each other.

Notes

1. Data for this paper was gathered during three years of intensive field research in the Danish subculture of outlaw bikers. The researcher has ridden with bikers from all parts of the subculture and has participated in different kinds of events: runs, motorcycle shows, motorcycle rodeos, meetings, parties and touring, in Scandinavia, Europe and the U.S. The research is funded by the Danish Research Council for the Humanities.
2. 'Righteousness', which is the main concept of honor among American bikers, has no equivalent in the vernacular of Danish bikers.
3. Words and expressions from the Danish bikers' vernacular are set in italics, while their American counterparts and translations of Danish words are in quotations. A considerable part of the subculturally specific vocabulary is imported from the culture of American bikers without translation.
4. Experience plays an important role in the status system of all subcultures, especially underground subcultures. The qualifications needed to manage within the subculture cannot be obtained in any other way than by experience. That is one explanation for the importance of the signs of 'bikerwizdom'. Moreover, these signs make it easy to distinguish between hard-core bikers and those with biker pretensions: weekend-bikers, wannabe's (want to be's) and RUBBI's (Rich UrBan BIkers).
5. Historically, the bikers' colors can be traced back to military emblems and to the start of the motorcycle culture in the last century. The original motorcycle sport clubs used emblems and banners, which can be traced back to the use of shields in the age of chivalry – cf. Bay 1987.
6. There are many variations in the initiation to an outlaw club. Some clubs do not have any trial period at all, while others can exempt candidates from the initiation rules if the candidate already has been a member in another club.
7. These rules apply only to situations where bikers 'drink together'. 'To buy someone a beer' is a quite different situation with its own rules. Such a situation is characterized by the subordinate showing his respect to a higher

ranking biker by buying him a beer. The subordinate will in this situation not expect to receive a beer in return.

8. 'Rocker' is the original Danish (and British) notion of an (outlaw) biker. The distinction between *bikers* and *rockers* is part of a classification system which bikers use to discriminate between in- and outsiders in the subculture; among bikers, *rocker* is now used only as a derogatory term.
9. This renaming was not only insulting because of the transformation from male to female, but also because of the transformation from an English to a Danish club name. Outlaw clubs tend not to have Danish names.

References

Bay, J. (1987), 'Vinden kalder – en afvigende historie om en afvigende kultur', in *Ungdom mot år 2000 – Et nordisk og europeisk perspektiv*, O. Stafseng & I. Frønes (eds), Oslo, Norsk Gyldendal

Folb, E.A. (1980), *Runnin'down some lines: the language and culture of black teenagers*, Cambridge, MA, Harvard University Press

Horowitz, R. (1983), *Honor and the American Dream: Culture and Identity in a Chicano Community*, New Brunswick, NJ, Rutgers University Press

Knudsen, A. (1989), 'Tavshed er magtens Tegn', *Årbog for Kvindeforskning*, Århus, Universitetsforlaget

Labov, W. (1972), 'Rules for ritual insults', in *Language in the Inner City*, pp. 297-353

Nielsen, J. (1985), *Jønke – mit liv*, Copenhagen, Tiderne Skifter

Peristiany, J.G (ed.) (1966), *Honour and Shame: The Values of Mediterranean Society*, Chicago, University of Chicago Press

Safilios-Rothschild, C. (1969), '"Honor" crimes in contemporary Greece', *British Journal of Sociology*, vol. 20, pp. 205-218

Chapter 4

Violence without Honor in the American South

Roy D'Andrade

4.1 The culture of honor hypothesis

In a series of publications, Cohen, Nisbett, Vandello, and their collaborators have argued that the American South is characterized by a *culture of honor* which legitimates physical violence as an appropriate response to insults and personal provocations. Cohen and his collaborators have presented an impressive body of evidence for this claim. They find on a range of measures, including ratings of expressive behavior, fantasied aggression in response to insult, and cortisol and testosterone levels, that southern undergraduates, compared to northern undergraduates, become angrier and tend to be more aggressive after being insulted. When faced with the problem of dealing with a persistently annoying person, southern undergraduates are likely to be more polite at first but become more openly angry and confrontational over time (Cohen, Vandello, Puente, and Rantilla, 1999). Cohen and his collaborators also find that the cultural representations and social polices of the South, compared to the North, excuse and sometimes actively support the use of violence as a response to insult or threat. Cohen, 1996, 1998; Cohen & Nisbett, 1994, 1997; Cohen, Nisbett, Bowdle & Schwarz, 1996; Cohen & Vandello, 1998; Cohen, Vandello & Rantilla, 1998; Nisbett & Cohen, 1996; Vandello & Cohen 2001,Vandello & Cohen n.d.).

4.2 Various cultural models of honor

In contrast to the detailed documentation of reactions to insult and attitudes towards violence, Cohen and collaborators have presented little direct ethnographic data on the current code of honor in the American South. Specific information about the southern concept of honor is necessary because honor codes vary considerably by society and historical period. Consider the following historical examples: At one extreme is the *tough guy* cultural model in which a man must act strong and be willing to be violent and reckless. Social rank is based on an established pecking order determined by agonistic encounters. Tough guys display their toughness and validate their rank by picking on those who are less tough. Insults, boasts, and blows are frequently exchanged between tough guys, sometimes resulting in serious, deadly, fights. Reputations for toughness are zealously maintained. Accounts of the tough guy model are found in Homer's *Illiad, El Cid*, the *Song of Roland*, and in ethnographies of inner city social life, such as Anderson's *Code of the Street*. The tough guy model appears to be common in societies or sub-societies in which men are required to be independent warriors.

Similar to the tough-guy model is the what Elser (1989), based on Pigetti's (1987), descriptions of the Mafia, describes as the *wise guy* code. The world of wise guys is divided into wolves and sheep. Wolves - the wise guys - use violence and deceit to take what they want from the sheep. Wise guys keep their commitments to each other, or they kill the person they are going to default before that person kills them. They do not warn their enemies, but attempt to kill them when they are not on guard. They demand respect from the sheep and from each other. Failure by one wise guy to show respect for another is tantamout to a declaration of war, making insults deadly. Wise guys are organized into families, with loyalty enforced by powerful sanctions. Much of wise guy behavior can be seen as a form of predatory business enterprise based on illegal violence.

Related to the tough guy model is the European model of nobility. The noble model emerged during the Middle Ages (Weber 1999). According to the code of European nobles, defeat in agonistic encounters no longer meant complete loss of status, at least not if one fought in the right manner and one had the right ancestors and political connections. In this model one could gain honor just by engaging in heroic battle or ritual combat. The noble was expected to be loyal to his lord, to reward those loyal to him, and to take his own life if he lost his honor. Society was divided into nobles - those with honor - and honor-less commoners. Nobles wore special clothes and emblems, ate special foods, and engaged in social activities forbidden to commoners. Commoners had to give respect and deferential behavior to Nobles. Nobles enjoyed a variety of rights not granted to commoners. It its chivalric form, the noble was expected to be virtuous, motivated by high loyalties to church and king, deferent to women of good birth, and concerned with religious questing.

A later, less caste restricted version of the noble model, the gentleman model, was common in Europe and the United States in the seventeenth, eighteenth and nineteenth centuries, lasting even into the twentieth (Weber 1999). The gentleman was a man of good birth and good manners. Gentlemen did no work except perhaps in the higher professions or better arts. Gentlemen kept their word, had feelings of the finer kind, and were discrete and well spoken. Gentlemen pursued a distinctive life-style of leisure, attending numerous ritual social occasions - salons, balls, games, theatre, etc. Given these life-style requirements, gentlemen were usually financially well off, normally because of inherited money and property. If insulted by slander or sexual trespass, the gentleman had the right to ritually insult the offender, who was then honor bound to agree to a duel with deadly weapons.

The present Middle Eastern Islamic model of honor, also found in similar form in southern Spain and southern Italy, has a central focus on the sexual purity of women of the family (Bourdieu 1966). Separation of women from men is marked by institutions such as the veil and the harem. Honor is a social matter, not just an individual matter; a man is responsible for and benefits from the honor of his family, his clan, his village, his tribe, and his nation. Maintaining honor requires constant vigilance in a world in which a gift can be as much a weapon as an insult or physical attack. A man of honor does not contest with those without honor because such contests are beneath him. Proper religious observance is an intrinsic part of having honor; great honor is bestowed in the Islamic world on those who visit Mecca and other pilgrimage sites.

Finally, officers in many of the world's militaries are expected to live by a well defined honor code requiring them to be scrupulously reliable and honest in their dealings with each other. They may not use their superior rank for personal gain or advantage. They must be strongly committed to their unit, follow orders without question, and be willing to face death in battle. In victory they are expected to be courteous to their vanquished enemy, while dignified and stoic in defeat. Special honor, acknowledged by medals and citations, is gained through battle and service, but regardless of length of service or combat experience, all officers are considered persons of honor. Failure to live up to the honor code is cause for dismissal from the service. The code for enlisted personnel - those who are not officers - is similar to the code for officers but less severe, except with respect to the issue of obedience to orders, which holds for all. Respect - salutes, standing in the presence of a superior, etc. - is given because of the person's rank, not individual characteristics. Honor, however, belongs to the individual and the unit.

The honor codes presented above are different in various ways, but they all share an important characteristic. These honor codes are *institutions*, not just shared attitudes (Pitt-Rivers 1966). For something to be institutionalized means that people in some group commonly and openly accept that certain persons, objects, or events must be treated in a special way (given special powers, obligations, esteem, or meanings) because of some property of that person, object, or event (Searle 1995). The special status of the person or object or event is typically displayed by symbolic markers. To say a group has an honor code means that the members of group not only define certain things as honorable and mark a person who has or does these things with special indicators, but also that they treat that person with respect and deference because he or she has this special status. In an honor code society, social rank is strongly influenced by degree of honor, which is treated as an objective fact about a person. A society does not have an honor code if people just admire strong, aggressive men.

Because an honor code, by definition, is an institutionalized part of a culture, it has a special kind of causal force that attitudes by themselves do not have. An honor code, as an institution, is a code people are expected to follow and must follow or suffer the consequences. Steward (1994), in a careful historical and ethnographic analysis, points out that in a full bodied honor code, honor is a *right*; a right to be treat with respect that can be gained, lost, and even pledged. Because honor is a right to respect, people who are honorable should be treated honorably, and people who are not honorable should be treated as dishonorable. To the extent that American southerners have a code of honor, this code acts as an imperative demand on them by society; a demand to act honorably or be stigmatized.

4.3 The question of the cultural code of honor in the South

How should the honor model of the American South be described? The ethnographic material presented by Cohen and collaborators is based primarily on eighteenth and nineteenth century historical accounts. The honor code they outline appears to be a version of the gentlemen's code. However, it is unlikely that gentlemanly honor is now the model for southern men; duels, ostentatious shows of good breeding, and a life of social leisure are things of the past. Even in the eighteenth and nineteenth century in the American South the European gentlemen's honor code was probably held by only a small percent of the population. Certainly the gentleman model is quite different than the conduct model described by Roebuck and Hickson (1982) for southern Red-Neck subculture. The Red-Neck model focuses on maintaining a style of life centered on hunting, fishing, drinking, and fighting. To an outsider, Red-Neck attitudes appear overtly sexist, patriarchal, racist, homophobic, and xenophobic. Norms of this subculture are marked by the use of physical violence as the appropriate response to many kinds of conflict, along with admiration for those who use violence effectively. While fighting is institutionalized as the best response in many situations, and men have reputations based on being fighters, reputations for violence are apparently not institutionalized, lacking symbolic markers and mandatory expressions of deference and respect. The code of the Red Neck appears to be a variety of the tough guy model, although not as fully institutionalized as it is in some street gangs, biker groups, etc. (Lien 2001).

The Red Neck code, like the code of the gentleman, is unlikely to be held in classic form by southern university students. The problem is to find a means of determining the actual code used by southern undergraduates. Cohen and his collaborators use response to insult as a major indicator of the presence of an honor code. In some honor codes, such as the code held by the Greek heroes or the knights of Arthur's court, insults do not affect honor and need not be responded to. In other codes, such as code expressed in Icelandic sagas, retaliation for insult is critical in maintaining honor (Stewart 1994). With respect to the American South, there seems to be consensus that, whether Red-Necks or Gentlemen, southerners feel that their honor is at stake when they are insulted. To investigate further the honor model of the American South, we developed a questionnaire asking respondents to rate how they would respond to various insult scenarios. For each scenario respondents made a series of ratings concerning:

1. (1) the *anger* aroused by the incident;
2. (2) the amount of *disrespectfulness* shown by the other person in the incident;
3. (3) the degree of *insult* involved in the incident;
4. (4) the degree to which *honor* would be at stake in such an incident;
5. (5) the strength of the *wish to do something back* aroused by such an incident;
6. (6) *what one would do* if this actually happened (nothing, walk away, etc.);
7. (7) if this happened, what one thinks *people would think* if one did nothing back.

The general expectation was that American southern men, and, to a lesser degree, women, in comparison to Californians or people from New York State, would give higher ratings for the scenarios having to do with *sexual trespass*, *physical provocation*, and *slander*, since these tend to be focal issues in honor codes. On the other hand, scenarios having to do with being scolded by a boss, or being asked to leave a party, or someone borrowing something and returning it broken, were expected to show little or no regional difference, since these irritations are not salient assaults on character or masculinity.

Most importantly, it was expected that across the relevant scenarios, southern men and women, compared to northerners or Californians, would give higher ratings on the anger scale, the honor scale, the scale for what one would do back, and the scale involving what people would think if one did nothing back. These predictions were made on the basis of an extrapolation of what it means to hold an honor code: if one has internalized an honor code one will invoke it frequently and saliently, breaches of the code will arouse anger, lead to physical violence, and one will expect to be judged on the basis of what one did back. Small or no regional differences were expected for the degree to which respondents felt the other person was being *disrespectful* or *insulting*, since these seem to be matters of standard American conventions which do not necessarily invoke an honor code. It was expected that southern women would show a profile of scores similar to the southern men, but would be less involved in feeling that their *honor* was a stake in the various incidents and less concerned about *what people would think* of them if they did nothing.

4.4 Method

The first step in the construction of the questionnaire was the construction and selection of insult scenarios. In an upper division course, undergraduates who had read *Culture of Honor* were asked to make up brief scenarios in which somebody did something insulting. Over four hundred scenarios were collected. A small group of undergraduates sorted these scenarios in general categories and selected the forty-five best scenarios with respect to clarity and representativeness. A pre-test questionnaire was constructed using these scenarios with five point rating scales for degree of insult, anger, disrespect, reputation damage, and feeling bad. For each scenario respondents were also asked to select from eighteen categories of behavior the behavior they would be most likely to do if this happened to them. A sample of thirty-five UCSD undergraduates were given the questionnaire and the results analyzed. Using a principal components analysis of the scenarios a further reduction to twenty-four scenarios was accomplished. The original eighteen categories of behavior reduced to twelve which showed reasonable scale properties. The rating scale for feeling bad was dropped because it lacked consistent correlations with other scales. The reputation damage scale was also dropped because it showed little variation across scenarios.

A second pre-test questionnaire was constructed with twenty-four scenarios and twelve categories of behavior which the respondent could select from as the most appropriate response to the scenario. For each scenario five scale ratings were requested; degree of insult, anger, disrespect, felt need to retaliate, and what others would think of one if this incident occurred and one did nothing back. A similar series of statistical analyses were performed and the final questionnaire constructed.

The final questionnaire contained fourteen scenarios, given below.

1. You are driving on the road and somebody cuts in front of you without signaling. You beep your horn and the person flips you off with an obscene gesture. (*driver flipoff*)
2. Somebody you know has been saying you are a liar and a cheat behind your back. (*called liar*)
3. A homeless man approaches you and asks you for money. You say no and he calls you a 'cheap bastard' in a loud voice. (*bag man*)
4. You are at a party with your friends and somebody from another group comes up and says you and your friends are not welcome and should get out. (*not welcome*)
5. You are waiting in line and some people cut in. You tell them to go to the end of the line and one of them pushes you. (*cut in and shove*)
6. You find out your lover has been cheating on you and lying about it. (*lover cheats*)
7. You are at a sports event and somebody you know grabs your camera and won't give it back to you. (*grabs camera*)
8. 8. You are at a party and you hear someone saying your spouse has loose morals. (*spouse loose*)
9. You are with your Japanese-American family on a trip. You stop at a restaurant and ask if your daughter can use the restroom. The waitress tells you the restroom is 'reserved for paying customers and red blooded Americans.' (*Americans only*)
10. You are having an argument with someone. This person starts saying obscene things about your mother. (*insults mother*)
11. You are walking down the hallway when somebody bumps into you, knocking you aside. The person turns and calls you an asshole. (*bump asshole*)
12. Your boss says in front of everyone in the office that you have been making a lot of stupid mistakes. (*boss criticism*)
13. You are on a date. Someone begins to put their hands on your date in a suggestive way. (*touch date*)
14. You let someone you know borrow something of yours but this person returns it broken and doesn't say anything to you about it. (*return broken*)

(The phrase in parenthesis after each scenario is the identifier used in tables and figures below.)

Five of the rating scales used the following format;

1. If this happened to me it would make me **angry**
(CIRCLE ONE)
    1. not at all
    2. a little
    3. somewhat
    4. a lot
    5. greatly

The scales that used this format were:

1. If this happened to me it would make me **angry**
2. If this happened to me I would think the other person was being **disrespectful**
3. If this happened to me I would feel **insulted**
4. If this happened to me I would feel my **honor** is at stake
5. If this happened to me I would **want to do something back**

Scale number six involved a selection from among a panel of behaviors.

6. If this happened to me I **would**
(CIRCLE ONE)
    1. do nothing
    2. walk away
    3. let the person know I noticed but do nothing else
    4. ask for an explanation
    5. ask for an apology
    6. tell the person off (using words or gestures)
    7. retaliate physically (hit, push, etc.)

The final scale was concerned with what others would think.

7. If this happened to me and people **knew about it**, and I did **nothing back**, the people I know would
(CIRCLE ONE)
    1. think better of me
    2. not change how they think of me
    3. think less of me

Also included with the questionnaire was a demographic background sheet, which requested information on age, gender, US citizenship, place of birth, language spoken in the home, parent's occupation, parent's place of birth, religion, city/state/county called home, urban/rural background, and several questions to ascertain where the respondent learned his or her ideas about what an insult its.

Five groups of respondents were given the questionnaire: 66 UCSD undergraduates; 84 Long Beach and Los Angeles high school students; 64 University of Alabama undergraduates; 97 University of Tennessee undergraduates, and 42 SUNY New Platz undergraduates. The undergraduates were primarily students in social science courses. The Los Angeles high school students came from a number of ethnic backgrounds. No problems were encountered with the administration of the questionnaire or obtaining human subject consents.

4.5 Results

The results by region for the *honor* scale are presented in Table 1. Results for the *anger* scale, the *what people would think of me if I did nothing back* scale, and the proportion of respondents saying they would use physical violence on the *what you would do* scale are presented in Tables 4.1 – 4.4. None of these scales, or any of the other scales, show significantly higher ratings for southerners for any of the scenarios. The southerners are not distinctive in their response on any of the scales with respect to the crucial scenarios of being insulted for one's race, one's lover cheating, someone insulting one's mother, one's date being touched in a suggestive way, being called a liar and a cheat, or having someone say that one's spouse has loose morals. The results for just men are the same, with southern men failing to show significantly higher ratings than non-southern men on any scale for any of the scenarios.

Table 4.1 Mean Ratings of Degree of Honor at Stake Reaction to 14 Scenarios by Region

If this happened to me I would feel my **honor** is at stake:
(1) not at all, (2) a little, (3) somewhat, (4) a lot, (5) greatly

Scenario	*Tennessee*	*Alabama*	*Total South*	*New York*	*Long Beach*	*UCSD*	*Total Non-South*	*South vs Non-South p<*
not American	3.9	3.6	3.8	3.8	3.8	4.0	3.8	n.s.
lover cheats	3.7	3.8	3.8	4.0	3.6	3.8	3.8	n.s.
critical boss	3.2	3.4	3.3	3.4	3.7	3.7	3.6	n.s.
mother insulted	3.1	3.1	3.1	3.3	3.2	3.8	3.5	n.s.
date touched	3.2	3.4	3.3	3.0	3.2	3.4	3.2	n.s.
called liar cheat	3.1	3.0	3.1	3.5	3.1	3.5	3.4	n.s.
said spouse loose	3.2	3.4	3.3	3.0	3.0	3.4	3.1	n.s.
cut in & pushed	2.7	2.8	2.7	2.5	2.6	2.8	2.6	n.s.
bumped	2.4	2.6	2.5	2.1	2.4	3.0	2.5	n.s.
not welcome	2.1	2.3	2.2	2.5	2.5	2.6	2.5	n.s.
grabbed camera	1.8	2.4	2.1	1.9	2.0	2.4	2.1	n.s.
borrow & broke	2.1	2.2	2.2	1.9	2.0	2.2	2.0	n.s.
bag man insult	1.3	1.4	1.4	1.6	1.4	1.4	1.5	n.s.
driver flip off	1.3	1.4	1.3	1.3	1.3	1.6	1.4	n.s.
region mean	2.6	2.8	2.7	2.7	2.7	3.0	2.8	

Table 4.2 Mean Ratings of Degree of Anger Reaction to 14 Scenarios by Region

If this happened to me it would make me **angry:**
(1) not at all, (2) a little, (3) somewhat, (4) a lot, (5) greatly

Scenario	*Tennessee*	*Alabama*	*Total South*	*New York*	*Long Beach*	*UCSD*	*Total Non-South*	*South vs Non-South p<*
lover cheats	4.8	4.8	4.8	4.8	4.7	4.8	4.7	n.s.
not American	4.6	4.5	4.6	4.7	4.8	4.7	4.7	n.s.
cut in & pushed	4.3	4.4	4.3	4.2	4.1	4.3	4.2	n.s.
said spouse loose	4.1	4.1	4.1	3.9	4.2	4.1	4.1	n.s.
date touched	4.2	4.2	4.2	4.0	3.9	4.0	4.0	n.s.
critical boss	3.9	3.9	3.9	3.9	3.9	4.1	4.0	n.s.
borrow & broke	4.0	3.9	4.0	4.3	3.9	3.9	4.1	n.s.
called liar cheat	3.8	4.0	3.9	4.3	4.1	4.1	4.1	n.s.
bumped	3.8	3.9	3.8	3.7	3.7	4.1	3.8	n.s.
grabbed camera	3.6	4.0	3.8	3.7	3.7	3.8	3.7	n.s.
not welcome	3.3	3.6	3.4	3.5	3.6	3.6	3.6	n.s.
mother insulted	3.8	4.0	3.9	4.0	3.8	4.4	4.1	n.s.
driver flip off	3.0	3.2	3.1	3.0	3.2	3.3	3.2	n.s.
bag man insult	2.1	2.6	2.3	2.0	2.6	2.2	2.3	n.s.
region mean	3.8	3.9	3.9	3.8	3.9	3.9	3.9	

Table 4.3 Mean Ratings of How People Would Respond if I Did Nothing Back across 14 Scenarios by Region

If this happened to me and people knew about it, and I did **nothing back,** the people I know would
(1) think better of me, (2) not change how they think of me, (3) think less of me

Scenario	*Tennessee*	*Alabama*	*Total South*	*New York*	*Long Beach*	*UCSD*	*Total Non-South*	*South vs Non-South p<*
lover cheats	2.4	2.5	2.4	2.6	2.4	2.3	2.4	n.s.
date touched	2.4	2.3	2.4	2.5	2.5	2.3	2.4	n.s.
said spouse loose	2.4	2.4	2.4	2.3	2.4	2.4	2.4	n.s.
not American	2.4	2.1	2.3	2.5	2.5	2.3	2.4	n.s.
grabbed camera	2.3	2.4	2.3	2.4	2.3	2.3	2.3	n.s.
mother insulted	2.3	2.2	2.2	2.5	2.3	2.3	2.4	n.s.
critical boss	2.2	2.1	2.2	2.3	2.3	2.3	2.3	n.s.
not welcome	2.1	2.1	2.1	2.3	2.3	2.1	2.2	n.s.
borrow & broke	2.1	2.1	2.1	2.3	2.2	2.1	2.2	n.s.
called liar cheat	2.1	1.9	2.0	2.2	2.2	2.2	2.2	n.s.
cut in & pushed	2.1	2.0	2.0	2.2	2.1	2.1	2.2	n.s.
bumped	2.0	2.1	2.0	2.1	2.0	2.1	2.1	n.s.
driver flip off	1.9	1.8	1.9	1.9	1.9	1.9	1.9	n.s.
bag man insult	1.8	1.9	1.8	1.9	2.0	1.9	1.9	n.s.
region mean	2.2	2.1	2.2	2.3	2.2	2.2	2.2	

Table 4.4 Proportion of total responses across all scenarios:

If this happened to me I would:
1. Do nothing, 2. Walk away 3. Let the person know I noticed but do nothing else,
4. Ask for an explanation, 5. Ask for an apology, 6. Tell the person off, 7. Retaliate physically.

	Categories						
Regions	do nothing	walk away	notice only	ask explain	ask apology	tell off	physical
Tennessee	0.07	0.12	0.09	0.28	0.14	0.21	0.08
Alabama	0.08	0.11	0.11	0.31	0.12	0.21	0.07
South	0.07	0.12	0.10	0.30	0.13	0.21	0.08
New York	0.07	0.10	0.10	0.36	0.11	0.20	0.07
Long Beach	0.08	0.11	0.10	0.32	0.12	0.19	0.08
UCSD	0.08	0.12	0.10	0.31	0.13	0.16	0.10
Non-South	0.08	0.11	0.10	0.33	0.12	0.18	0.08

In general, no systematic differences were found between regions. The remarkable similarity of all the regions can be seen in the correlations in Table 4.5 for mean rating of degree of honor by region.

Table 4.5 Correlation Matrix for Mean Ratings of Degree of Honor at Stake

Reaction across 14 Scenarios by Region

Regions	New York	Long Beach	UCSD	Tennessee	Alabama
New York					
Long Beach	0.97				
UCSD	0.94	0.97			
Tennessee	0.95	0.97	0.96		
Alabama	0.93	0.96	0.96	0.97	

Overall, these results show that there is a strong common American culture with respect to the norms for response to insults. These norms are quite similar across very different regions of the country. These results cannot be due a sampling bias based on using college students as respondents since the Long Beach high school students are equally and highly correlated with the four undergraduate groups.

All seven of the rating scales had similar correlational profiles of ratings across the fourteen scenarios. Table 4.6 presents the matrix for these correlations. These high levels of correlation indicate that, for Americans, being insulted, being treated with disrespect, and having one's honor at stake are semantically similar. It was expected that, especially in the South, there would be discrimination

Table 4.6 Correlation Matrix for Mean Ratings for Reactions across 14 Scenarios and 5 Regions

Reactions	angry	disrespect	insult	honor	do back	I would	people knew
make me angry	-						
other being disrespectful	0.93	-					
would feel insulted	0.89	0.83	-				
my honor is at stake	0.82	0.75	0.95	-			
want to do something back	0.90	0.90	0.77	0.75	-		
if this happened I would	0.83	0.77	0.66	0.61	0.93	-	
if I did nothing back and people knew	0.72	0.58	0.70	0.73	0.73	0.66	-

between matters of honor in contrast to events which are just aggravating. One might think that being called a liar and cheat is, for example, a more honor salient event than being criticized in a rude way by one's boss, although both might be equally aggravating. If this were the case, the ratings for honor would have a distinctive profile of scores across scenarios compared to the other scales. However, having one's honor at stake apparently means to Americans much the same thing as simply being insulted or being treated disrespectfully. Breaking the data into five separate regional tables resulted in no differences in the pattern of correlations.

While differences by region turned out to be small and insignificant, gender differences show significant patterning of moderate effect size. To summarize the data, ratings on each of the scales were transformed to z scores, and the differences between the male means and the female means computed. These results are presented in Table 4.7.

Women responded with more anger and felt more disrespected on all scenarios except the date scenario (someone puts their hands on your date in a suggestive way). Women also felt more insulted in eleven of fourteen scenarios. However, men said in ten of the fourteen scenarios that they would want more strongly to do something back, and in thirteen of the fourteen scenarios said they *would* do something more aggressive back. With respect to the degree of honor at stake, males were significantly more likely to give higher ratings for four scenarios (driver's flipoff, somebody cuts in line, somebody grabs one's camera, and somebody puts their hands on one's date). Women gave significantly higher ratings for the honor scale on the scenario in which one is told one is not welcome to a party. The scenarios which were most aggravating for men were someone putting hands on one's date, driver flipoffs, and having one's spouse's morals called loose. For women the most aggravating scenarios were having a lover that cheats, being told one is not welcome at a party, and someone saying obscene things about one's mother.

Table 4.7 Z scores for Male - Female Mean by Scenario by Rating Scale Negative Values indicate the Female Mean is greater than the Male Mean

	Rating Scales							
Scenario	angry	disrespectful	insulted	honor	want do back	I would	people think	scenario mean
flipoff	0.0	-0.1	0.0	0.4 **	0.4 **	0.2	0.1	1.0 *
liar cheat	-0.4 **	-0.2	-0.4 **	0.0	-0.2	0.2	-0.1	-1.1 *
bag man	-0.1	-0.1	-0.1	-0.1	0.3 **	0.4 **	0.1	0.4
not welcome	-0.6 **	-0.5 **	-0.6 **	-0.3 **	0.0	0.0	-0.1	-2.0 **
cut in	-0.2 *	-0.2 *	-0.1	0.4 **	0.3 *	0.3 **	0.1	0.5
lover cheat	-0.4 **	-0.4 **	-0.4 **	-0.1	-0.4 **	-0.4 **	-0.2	-2.3 **
grab camera	-0.2	-0.1	0.0	0.4 **	0.1	0.2	0.0	0.2
spouse loose	-0.1	-0.1	-0.1	0.2	0.2	0.7 **	0.2 *	1.0 **
American	-0.4 **	-0.3 **	-0.2	0.0	-0.1	0.3	-0.1	-0.8 *
mother	-0.5 **	-0.5 **	-0.4 **	-0.1	-0.2	0.1	-0.1	-1.8 *
bumped	-0.1	-0.3 **	-0.2	0.2	0.2	0.3 **	0.1	0.2
boss	-0.5 **	-0.5 **	-0.5 **	-0.2 *	0.0	0.1	0.0	-1.6 **
date	0.2	0.1	0.3 **	0.5 **	0.5 **	0.8 **	0.4 **	2.8 **
borrow	-0.4 **	-0.3 **	-0.1	0.0	0.0	0.1	-0.1	-0.7 *
Scale average	-0.3 **	-0.3 **	-0.2 *	0.1	0.1	0.2 **	0.0	-0.3 *

p values for t for male vs females * = p < .05, ** = p < .01

One might speculate that the reason women show a pattern of greater anger along with stronger feelings of being insulted and disrespected is that women expect more courtesy than men, and therefore find the same degree of violation more aggravating. That men are more likely to say they would respond more aggressively corresponds to the usual finding of greater male propensity to physical action and violence (Maccoby 1998).

Exploring the data with respect to differences between urban and rural, parental occupational class, birth order, and inner-city versus suburb categories for each of the scales and scenarios show few clear differences. The overall conclusion is that ideas about how one would respond to insulting events are widely shared cultural norms across regions and sub-groups in the United States. The strongest differences in the data are gender differences, with an average absolute mean difference across the fourteen scenarios by seven scales of .23 standard deviations (the absolute mean for Table 4.7).

4.6 Discussion

The immediate response to these findings was to wonder if the instrument used - ratings of how one would respond to verbal scenarios - was adequately measuring how respondents thought they would respond to insults. The results reported here seem to contradict the findings of Cohen and his collaborators, if not with respect to specific observations, at least with respect to their implications. The difference could not be due to the use of samples of undergraduates, since most of the studies have also used undergraduates. Both Alabama and Tennessee are Old South, and so the problem would not seem be one of regional sampling.

However, a good part of the worry about instrument adequacy has been dispelled by recent work by Vandello and Cohen (n.d.), using a variety of methods, which reports findings similar to ours. They describe a study they carried out in which northern and southern students were shown video tapes of person being insulted in a procedure similar to the procedure used in the Cohen *et al* study (1996) in which a confederate of the experimenter bumps into the participant as he walks down a hallway and calls the participant an 'asshole' In the videotapes the insulted subject either responded aggressively or shrugged off the incident and kept walking. Both northerners and southerners asked to rate their preference for the two preferred the less aggressive male, and no significant differences in preference between regions were found.

Vandello and Cohen (n.d.) also report a study in which questionnaires were administered which described five insult scenarios and respondents asked to rate the probability they would have punched the provoker in the same situation. Northern and southern men did not differ in their judgments of the likelihood they would punch the provoker (24.7% to 25.5%). Respondents were also asked to imagine a random sample of 100 males students at their university and predict how many of the them would have punched the provoker. Here the southerners did differ from northerners, with 44.5% expected to punch the provoker compared to 38.2% for the northerners ($p = .02$) Respondents also reported on how many fistfights they were in during high school, and how many fights the typical male at their university was in. southerners were slightly, but non-significantly more likely to have been in fights (1.46 to 1.03, $p = .20$), and to think that the typical male had been in more fights (2.96 to 2.33 $p < .04$). Respondents' estimates of peer fighting also correlated with their own self-reports of fights ($r = .49$, $p < .001$)

In a third study reported by Vandello and Cohen (n.d.), individual participants witnessed an event staged by three confederates. In this event a male confederate (the perpetrator) stepped on a case supposed to be holding the eyeglasses of the second male confederate (the victim), creating a loud cracking sound (actually dry pasta). When the victim complained and asked for an apology the perpetrator was rude and confrontational. When the perpetrator left the room the victim then asked the subject a series of questions. For half the subjects the victim asked questions about whether he should confront and attack the perpetrator. For the other half of the subjects the victim asked questions about whether he should apologize. When the victim left the room the third confederate, a woman, asked the subject open ended questions about the confederate who had

had his glasses broken. All responses of the subject were tape recorded and coded. Male subjects were rated as more endorsing of aggression by the victim. Both males and females responded in similar neutral ways to the apologetic confederate, but females were somewhat more discouraging of aggression to the hostile confederate. When asked whether they wished to be paired for further work with the perpetrator or victim, women preferred to be paired with the victim when he was apologetic, whereas men showed little preference between the hostile or apologetic victim.

Most strikingly, there were no significant differences between northern and southern subjects – either male or female. No significant interaction effects were observed. Nor did northern and southern participants differ in their choices for the pair-up partner in either the hostile or apologetic condition. Thus the results of recent work, using live experiments, video scenarios, and questionnaire scenarios, confirm the questionnaire findings reported above. The simplest way to put these finding is that (1) southerners do not differ from northerners and Californians in their judgments of what to do in the case of insult, and (2) these judgments are not the judgments one would expect from someone holding any of the honor codes described above. It should be noted that consistent gender differences are found with respect to response to insult, with women making more negative judgments about aggressive response.

How can one describe this widely shared code held by Americans? Anderson (1999) has used the term 'code of decency' to contrast with the 'code of the street.' This decency code can be described as a code in which one must be honest, respectable, and civil. If people are unpleasant, rude, or insulting, one should ignore them or tell them they are behaving improperly and perhaps ask them to explain or apologize, but one should not retaliate with verbal insult or physical force. Actually, the politeness aspect of this code is somewhat stronger in the south, as Cohen *et al* (1999) report in the study in which southern males were found initially to be more polite to an aggravating confederate than northerners.

Unlike honor codes, in which one needs to be concerned with how one is perceived because of the threat of loss of reputation, and in which one must counterattack those who infringe on one's honor, the code of decency stresses treating others civilly no matter how they act along with relative unconcern about one's own reputation or with 'getting even.' Stewart (1994) calls such codes *non-reflexive*, unlike those codes which one loses one's honor if one fails to retaliate to insults. Of course, at times decent individuals 'lose it' in the face of provocations and resort to bad language, violence, and attempts to retaliate. However, when this happens, the individual has broken the code and the normal response is shame, guilt, and apology. The degree to which individuals actually internalize this code of decency probably varies greatly, but not the understanding that this is how one should behave. In some areas of the country various aspects of the code are stronger or weaker, but the basic elements appear to be understood almost everywhere from High Schools in the inner city of Long Beach to Tuscaloosa and the SUNY campus at New Platz. One would guess even Red-Necks and Street Warriors understand the decency code, they just prefer to follow a different code.

The universality of the code of decency raises an interesting question: Why do southern males become angrier and more reckless than northern males when they are insulted? Then answer provided by Nisbett and Cohen (1996), that this anger and recklessness is caused by the code of honor held by southern males, while initially plausible in the light of various folk models of southern culture, now seems implausible in the face of the findings reported above. But the basic finding of Cohen and his collaborators that southerners experience greater anger in response to insult has proven robust, and the various indices of social demography show that when issues of insult or self-protection are involved, southerners are more violent than northerners (Nisbett and Cohen 1996). Attitude studies show that southerners are more likely than northerners to excuse and even condone such violence (Cohen and Nisbett 1997). Institutionally, southern and western states have less strict gun control and more permissive laws for the use of violence in self-defense (Cohen 1996). With respect to the collective representations, southerners and westerners subscribe to more violent magazines and view more violent TV shows than northerners (Cohen and Nisbett 1997).

4.7 Conclusions

The problem then, is to reconcile findings that on the surface appear contradictory. The South, it is argued here, has the same code of decency as the rest of the country. Southerners are not different from northerners in what say about how they would respond to various insults, or the degree to which they believe their honor is at stake in these insults, or what they think they would do about these insults, or in their preference for those who respond aggressively to insult compared to those who are not aggressive, or what they think people will think of them if they don't retaliate to insults. But they are different in that they become angrier and more aggressive in the face of *real* insult and aggravation.

One solution to this problem, presented by Vandello and Cohen (n.d.), is to say that while southerners do not actually hold a code of honor, they believe that others do. This is a *pluralistic ignorance* explanation. In support of this explanation Vandello and Cohen found in a series of studies that men believe that other men will be more aggressive than they are themselves, and this discrepancy is greater for southern men. And they found men who believed others were more aggressive tended to say they would be more aggressive themselves. They also found southern males were more likely to perceive others as promoting aggressive norms, especially in the case in which the signals were ambiguous.

Vandello and Cohen (n.d.) present two different mechanisms that might cause pluralistically ignorant perceptions to result in differing levels of violence. The first is that people are likely to do what they think others expect them to do and will approve of. Here the motivation is social approval or the avoidance of disapproval. The second mechanism is that if one anticipates that others will be violent, one must be violent to protect oneself. When many people think this it becomes a self-fulfilling prophecy.

The second mechanism described by Vandello and Cohen - that anticipation of others' violence increases the likelihood of being violent oneself - seems right. However, on the part of southerners, this expectation does not seem to be a matter of pluralistic ignorance. There are real cultural differences between the South and the North. Violence to protect oneself is personally endorsed, institutionally supported, and collectively represented in a positive light throughout the South and West. For example, the New York Times of March 12 2001 reports that the Charlie Condon, attorney general of South Carolina, has announced a policy that it is 'open season' on home invaders - 'invade a home and invite a bullet,' he said. 'I'm putting home invaders on notice that if an occupant chooses to use deadly force, there will be no prosecution.' Cohen and his collaborators have presented a wealth of examples of this kind. Southern reliance on self-protecting violence seems to have been the result of a lack of reliable state mechanisms of social control during both the pre- and post-bellum periods (Nisbett and Cohen 1996). In the South, anticipating that others are likely to be violent in agonistic encounters is not an ignorant assessment.

Why then should southern undergraduates show more anger and aggressiveness in response to insults but not differ from non-southerners in what they say about how angry such insults would make them? The social approval explanation is contradicted by the finding presented above that southerners do not differ from northerners in the degree to which the judge that others will think less of them if they do nothing back to an insult (Table 3). And southerners seem really angrier - they are not just expecting violence, they are angry about what the other person did. So there must be something in addition to the expectation of violence affecting these students.

Perhaps a deep sense of masculine pride, an uninstitutionalized narcissism, is at work here. Something like this has been said to be characteristic of southerners. Or it may be that greater use of physical punishment in early socialization has had an effect outside awareness on emotional responsiveness to any kind of aggression. Or it may be that just experiencing more physical violence in their lives sensitizes southerners to violence, making them more aroused in situations that involve violence, and whether this is experienced as anger, or fun, or fear, depends on context. In reading a scenario on paper or seeing a video, the threat to the self is not as vivid and salient as it is in an actual encounter, where much self-threat is likely to be experienced. *Perhaps under the conditions of an actual encounter, the southern culturally approved model involving the use of violence to protect the self becomes the contextual system of meaning that steers the emotional response rather than the decency meaning system.*

Thus, the speculation here is that the southerner has two cultural models. One is the decency model. The other is the self-protection using violence model. In the South both are institutionalized. In the case of an insult, the issue is which model will be invoked. On the face of it, the southerner should respond to an insult with the decency model since no 'real' threat to the self is involved. This is how they respond on a questionnaire. And, with respect to surface behavior, southern undergraduates do seem to follow the decency model. None of them, for example, are reported to have punched out the various confederate perpetrators or became verbally abusive. But when the insult actually happens to a southerner who is likely to have both greater expectations of surface civility and greater expectations of violence once aggression has begun, what is aroused is the self-protection/violence model. The result is real anger and readiness to fight.

In any case, whatever the proximal mechanism, the response of southerners to insult does not seem to be the result of a cultural code of *honor*. Like the wind, that code has gone.

References

Anderson, E. (1999), The Code of the Street. New York: Norton

Bourdieu, P. (1966), The Sentiment of Honor in Kabyle Society. In J. Peristiany (Ed.) Honor and Shame, Chicago: University of Chicago Press, pp. 191-241

Cohen, D. (1996), Law, social policy, and violence: The impact of regional cultures. Journal of Personality and Social Psychology 70, pp. 961-978

Cohen, D. (1998), Culture, social organization, and patterns of violence. Journal of Personality and Social Psychology 75, pp. 408-419

Cohen, D. and Nisbett, R. E. (1994), Self-protection and the culture of honor: Explaining southern homicide. Personality and Social Psychology Bulletin, 20, pp. 551-567

Cohen, D. and Nisbett, R. E. (1997), Field experiments examining the culture of honor: The role of institutions in perpetuating norms about violence. Personality and Social Psychology Bulletin, 20, pp. 551-567

Cohen, D., Nisbett, R., Bowdle, B., and Schwarz, N. (1996), Insult, aggression, and the southern culture of honor: An 'experimental ethnography.' Journal of Personality and Social Psychology, 70, pp. 945-960

Cohen, D. and Vandello, J. (1998), Meanings of violence. Journal of Legal Studies, 27, pp. 501-508

Cohen, D., Vandello, J., and Rantilla, A. K. (1998), The sacred and the social: Honor and Violence in Cultural Context. In P. Gilbert & B. Andrews (Eds.), Shame: Interpersonal Behavior, Psychopathology, and Culture, New York: Oxford University Press. pp. 261-282

Cohen, D., Vandello, J., Puente, S., and Rantilla, A. (1999), 'When you call me that, smile!' How norms for politeness, interaction styles, and aggression work together in southern culture. Social Psychology Quarterly, 62, pp. 257-275

Elster, J. (1989), The Cement of Society. Cambridge: Cambridge University Press

Lien, I.L. (2000), The Dynamics of Honor in Violence and Cultural Change: A Case from an Oslo Inner City School. Paper prepared for the Annual Meetings of the American Society of Ciminology. Norwegian Institute for Urban and Regional Research, Oslo

Maccoby, E. (1998), The Two Sexes. Cambridge: Harvard University Press

Nisbett, Richard & Cohen, Dov. (1996), Culture of Honor, Boulder: Westview

Pileggi, N. (1987), Wiseguy. New York: Pocket Books

Pitt-Rivers, J. (1966), Honor and Social Status. In J. Peristiany (Ed.) Honor and Shame, Chicago: University of Chicago Press, pp. 19-77

Roebuck, J. and Hickson, I. (1982), The Southern Redneck. New York: Praeger

Searle, J. (1995), The Construction of Social Reality. New York: The Free Press

Stewart, F. H. (1994), Honor. Chicago: University of Chicago Press

Vandello, J.A. and Cohen, D. (n.d.) Pluralistic Ignorance and the Perpetuation of Norms about Male Aggression. (under review Basic and Applied Social Psychology)

Weber, E. (1999), The ups and downs of honor. The American Scholar, Winder 1999

Chapter 5

The Prototypical Blood Feud

Tangir in the Hindu Kush Mountains

Tor Aase

The twin valleys of Tangir and Darel in the northern part of Pakistan have a long tradition of feuding. The few Western explorers who have visited the valleys have been struck by the frequency of violence and revenge.

> The history of the two valleys (Tangir and Darel) has been but a dreary tale of murder and blood feuds. So bad has it now become that there is no house without a vendetta, and life has become intolerable. Even murder appears to have lost its charm and the savages are sated with blood. (Schomberg 1935, p. 163)

Karl Jettmar, who made two short visits to the valleys in the 1950s, was also struck by the abundance of conflicts, most of which were 'triggered by adultery, deriving from a jealous husband or from the anger of the kinsmen of an unmarried young woman' (Jettmar 1994:5). Jettmar was surprised to find that the women were far from passive objects in such conflicts:

> *In this system of love, jealousy, and murder, preconditioned like a game and not devoid of sporting ambitions, the behaviour of the women was the most surprising phenomenon. Even after the legal regulations made it appropriate to kill them together with their partners, they risked their lives, often and without hesitation. (Jettmar/1994: 6)*

Between 1971 and 1988, the police station in Darel registered 128 homicides as 'feud killings' among a total population of some 25,000. There is no reason to assume that the rate of casualties was any less in neighboring Tangir, which this chapter is about.

The historical descriptions of Tangir and the scale of feuding indicate a place to be avoided by travelers. Indeed, no tourists visit Tangir on their way to picturesque Gilgit and Hunza further north. I find it proper to underline, however, that despite the negative impression conveyed by the above descriptions, I found Tangiri men particularly open-hearted, generous, and hospitable. The women I know nothing about. A male fieldworker has no opportunity to see women, not to mention talk to them.

Tangiri people have many qualities that are appreciated by Western visitors, but one of their qualities that should not be fooled with is their honor. The feud continues to be a salient feature of life in the valley. A substantial number of

Tangiri men carry guns wherever they go. Boys down to the age of twelve occasionally carry loaded automatic rifles over their shoulders. Here and there the landscape is broken by a fresh mound of stones, erected to commemorate a man killed at that particular spot. Even the settlements bear witness to the ongoing feuds. Several homesteads have fortified, three-storey stone towers that loom above the surrounding single-storey farm buildings, where families can spend the nights safely out of reach of hostile neighbors. Such homesteads are unique in Pakistan. Women, who are frequently the reason why feuds begin, are jealously kept out of the public gaze by their male custodians. The bazaar of the main village Juglot is strictly out of bounds for women and girls.

Conceptually as well, the feud is a significant element of Tangiri culture. Hostility is labeled *dushmani* in the local Shina language, and an enemy is a *dushman*, as in other Indo-Iranian languages (see Akman's chapter in this book). Under certain circumstances, a *dushmani* between two families can develop into *mar dushmani* (death hostility), which is the local term for the blood feud. The role of honor in transforming a hostile relationship (*dushmani*) into a lethal feud (*mar dushmani*), and the occasional settlement of such disputes, is the main theme of this chapter. What is at stake in a feud is somehow related to the honor of a family. For this reason, the feud cannot be understood without an appreciation of the phenomenon of honor.

In his ethnographic survey of feuding in the Mediterranean and the Middle East, Black-Michaud noticed 'the almost invariably violent reactions to offences involving the sexual honor of women' (Black-Michaud 1974:181). Tangiri men do not deviate from this norm. They are literally obsessed with the conduct of and towards their sisters, wives, and daughters. The men of the capital Islamabad are collectively belittled as *baghairatman* (men without honor) by Tangiris, since they permit their women to visit the bazaar unattended by male custodians, occasionally even without covering their hair.

In brief, blood feuds, or series of revenge killings, have a long history in Tangir, and they still recur on a substantial scale today. Culturally, concepts that relate directly to honor and revenge are highly meaningful to Tangiris. Thus, the 'semantic limits' of Tangiri culture permit the strategic pursuit of blood feud; such is Coombe's methodological claim in applying the term 'feud' to a series of killings (see Coombe 1990, and the introduction to this book).

Taking into account a) the longstanding tradition of feuding, b) the scale on which feuding takes place today, and c) the clear local vocabulary that relates to feuding, it is reasonable to regard Tangir as a prototypical feuding society, in the sense that it is a 'best example' (Lakoff 1990). As such, Tangir offers a good opportunity to study the complex of honor and revenge in its pure form, so to speak. Let us now turn to the feud itself, and see how it turns out in real life – and death!

Case 1

Number 1 of family A was married to no. 5 of family B. The couple had two sons and a daughter (A11, A12, A13). A1 managed a small shop in Tangir, and he used to lead a quiet and respectable life. Some years ago, a man from a distant village took up temporary residence in the neighborhood. The stranger was poor but handsome, and A1 got the idea that his wife had some romantic affair going on with him. A1 passed on his suspicions to the brothers of his wife in family B. The brothers agreed that if A1 killed the alleged lover, they would immediately kill their sister B5.

The suspected lover was, however, on the alert, and A1 did not manage to get close enough to kill him. Instead, A1 took his paternal cousin A6 for a second wife in order to punish his first wife. He moved to the house of his second wife and left the first wife and the children in the old house.

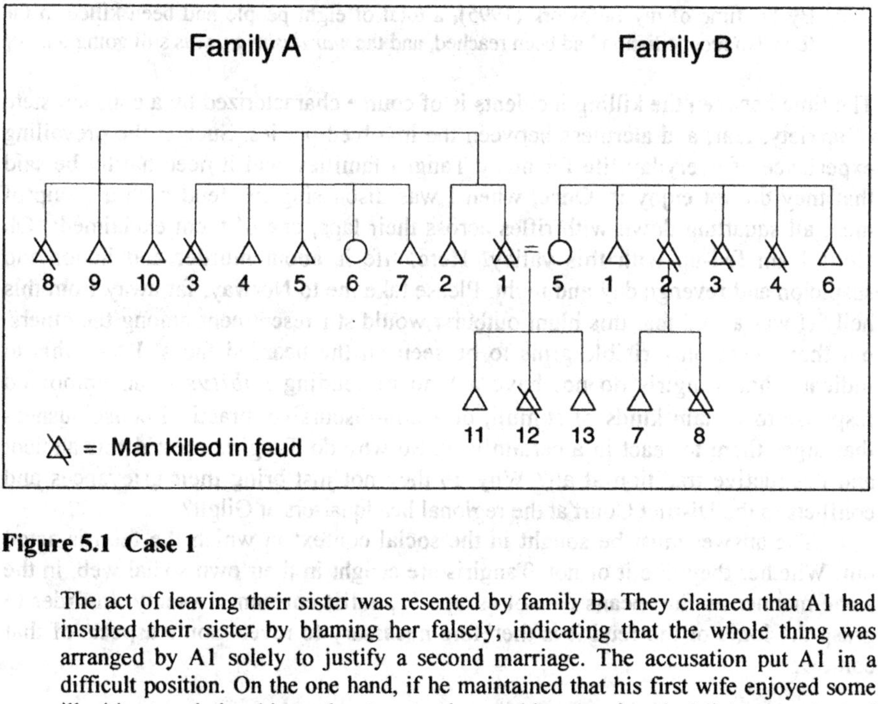

Figure 5.1 Case 1

The act of leaving their sister was resented by family B. They claimed that A1 had insulted their sister by blaming her falsely, indicating that the whole thing was arranged by A1 solely to justify a second marriage. The accusation put A1 in a difficult position. On the one hand, if he maintained that his first wife enjoyed some illegitimate relationship to the stranger, he would appear in a bad light since he had not avenged the insult. There was an immediate danger that he would be branded as *baghairatman* – a man without honor – a coward who could not defend his exclusive rights to a sexual relationship with his wife. On the other hand, if he dropped the accusation against his first wife, his act of taking a second wife would emerge in a bad light, effectively justifying the accusation of the B family.

The relationship between the two families deteriorated, and one day B4 killed A1. By this act, the *dushmani* (hostility) between the two families was converted into a *mar dushmani* (blood feud). The first wife moved with her children to her paternal family B, where the children were left in the custody of their maternal uncles.

Family A did not take any retaliatory action against family B. They preferred to wait until the two sons of the deceased A1 came of age and leave the decision about revenge to them.

> A few years after the initial homicide of A1, however, B2 killed A3, accusing him of planning to avenge the former killing of A1. Family A, now having suffered the loss of two of its members, could no longer stay calm. A9 killed B3.
>
> When the two sons of A1 reached adolescence, they decided to avenge their father. They left their maternal uncles with whom they had spent their childhood and moved into the house of the A family, their paternal home. Family A then killed B2 and B4. Later on B7 killed A12, his own maternal first-cousin with whom he had spent his childhood. Family A killed B8, and family B retaliated by killing A8.
>
> By the time of my fieldwork (1995), a total of eight people had been killed in the feud. No reconciliation had been reached, and the *mar dushmani* was still going on.

The time between the killing incidents is of course characterized by a constant state of anxiety, fear, and alertness between the involved parties. Such is the prevailing experience of everyday life for many Tangiri families, and it need hardly be said that they do not enjoy it. Once, when I was discussing the feud with a group of men, all squatting down with rifles across their laps, one of them exclaimed: 'Oh God! I am fed-up with this valley! Here, life is about murder and honor and suspicion and revenge day and night. Please take me to Norway, far away from this hell?' I was afraid that this blunt outburst would stir resentment among the others, but there were only risible grins to be seen on the bearded faces. I take this to indicate that Tangiris do not have a kind of feuding *habitus* – an embodied response to certain kinds of stimuli, or a non-discursive, practical consciousness that urges them to react in a certain way. So why do Tangiris uphold this ancient and destructive tradition at all? Why do they not just bring their grievances and conflicts to the District Court at the regional headquarters at Gilgit?

The answer must be sought in the social context in which the feud is acted out. Whether they like it or not, Tangiris are caught in their own social web, in the same manner as Europeans cannot escape capitalist consumer society. In order to grasp the logic of the feud it is therefore necessary to reveal some aspects of that context.

5.1 The social context of the feud

The population of Tangir at the time of my fieldwork was approximately 23,000, comprising 17 ethnic groups and 7 languages. The local word for ethnic group is *kaom*, which is variously translated by English speaking Pakistanis as 'caste' or 'nation'. There exists a local ranking of the groups, but they are not castes in a Sanskrit sense since the ranking is not religiously sanctioned. An exception may be the Sayeds, who claim direct descent from the Holy Prophet (*pbuh*) and therefore have religious merit by birth. Refusing to marry any other *kaom*, these latter resemble the Hindu Brahmins in their self-ascription of ritual purity.

Tangiri mythical history tells that the valley was originally inhabited by the *kaom* of Kameen, who were later joined by Yashkuns. A conflict broke out between the two *kaoms*, and the Yashkuns decided to cleanse the valley of Kameens. All Kameens were killed except a boy and a girl, who managed to flee northwards over the watershed to the princedom of Yasin where they were granted asylum (*feraazi*).

Shortly afterwards a skin disease broke out in the valley. Farmers were unable to gather in their harvests, and the community suffered a famine. The idea arose that the misery might be a punishment for some misdeed the community had committed, and a soothsayer (*danyal*) was asked to search for the cause. Working himself into a state of trance by dancing and inhaling smoke from intoxicating herbs, the *danyal* said: 'The only way you can escape punishment is to bring the Kameens back to the valley'. Villagers protested that it was impossible to do so, since the Kameens had been wiped out. The *danyal*, however, assured them that a boy and a girl had survived, and must be brought back. A search for the two was initiated, and at last they were found and brought back to Tangir, where their old *kaom* land was given back to them. For Tangiris today, the fact that Kameen land is still located close to the original settlements is evidence for the truth of this myth.

Later on a wave of new immigrants settled in Tangir. Due to their numerical strength and their superior weapons, they managed to acquire substantial areas of land. Now they live side by side with Yashkun and Kameen. These people are Shin, and their language, Shina, became the local language of Tangir.

There is linguistic evidence that the historical succession of settlements depicted in the myth is correct (Jettmar 1994). More important, however, is the fact that the three *kaoms* of Kameen, Yashkun, and Shin are categorized as *holosha* – meaning that they are the original or authentic inhabitants of Tangir. Those *kaoms* that have settled more recently are termed *uperah* – newcomers. These include Gujars, Kohistanis, Sayeds, Kashmiris, and others who have taken up residence in Tangir for various reasons. The dichotomization of *holosha* and *uperah kaoms* is said to have taken place six generations ago, probably at the turn of the last century. Settlers before that time have probably been assimilated into the existing groups irrespective of their original *kaom* status.

A hundred years ago, the *holosha* – *uperah* dichotomy was significant in terms of economic pursuits. Tangiris practice a transhumant system of agriculture, which utilizes niches in two different ecological zones: valley farming and high mountain pastoralism. Cereals, vegetables, and fruits are cultivated for subsistence in the valley. During the winter, cattle and goats are stable-fed, but during the summer season, the herds are taken to fertile pastures in the high mountains (*nirel*). Utilization of mountain pastures is thus integral to the farming system. But only *holosha* (authentic Tangiri) settlers are entitled to *nirel* rights. *Uperah kaoms* must either lease usufruct rights to mountain pastures from their *holosha* neighbors, or else manage on sparse valley-bottom pastures, which implies that they can only keep small stocks of animals. Generally, this means that *holosha kaoms* are wealthier than *uperah kaoms* in terms of subsistence.

Mountain pastures are not owned individually. The settlements of Tangir are divided into four territories called *raom*, and each *raom* is entitled to a specified part of the pastures. The *raom* pastures are managed as common property. Thus, pasture rights are defined according to a combination of ethnic (*kaom*) and territorial (*raom*) considerations. Only households belonging to *holosha kaoms* have pasture rights, and *holosha* households can graze their animals on their *raom* meadows only.

Recent events have enhanced the economic significance of the *uperah* – *holosha* categorization of *kaoms* tremendously. During the 1970s the Karakorum Highway was constructed along the Indus River, connecting Islamabad with Gilgit, and later with Xinjiang in China. Link roads were also constructed in the side valleys to the Indus, among them Tangir. By connecting Tangir to mainland Pakistan in this manner, the local mountain forests became highly valuable. The Tangir valley is surrounded by remnants of the original Western Himalayan forest cover, which is located at altitudes between 3000 – 4000 meters, just below the high pastures (*nirel*). Before the road was built, the forest had been only modestly used for building materials and for some hunting, but it had no value in the transhumant farming system equivalent to that of the mountain pastures. The link road made the forest accessible to timber contractors from the plains, who now feed the almost insatiable demand of the Pakistani furniture and construction industries.

Overnight, the high mountain forest became a gold mine to Tangir. The question of timber rights was easily solved by extending the institutionalized system of pasture rights (*nirel*) to include forest rights (*sith*) as well. It meant that only Kameen, Shin, and Yashkun were granted access to the new source of income. The business is managed in the manner that timber contractors from lowland Pakistan are allowed to cut timber themselves, occasionally using local labor, and to transport the logs to collection points along the Karakorum Highway. The contractors pay a certain revenue per log. The revenue is distributed among the right-holding families in the *raom* to which the particular forest belongs. And those right-holders all belong to the *holoshah kaoms* of Shin, Yashkun, and Kameen. A right-holding unit, that is, all the Kameens, Yashkuns, and Shins who live in the same *raom*, is known as a *dookar*.

The timber business is presently so significant that it is forcing a change in historical circumstances. The inhabitants of Gabaray *raom* decided recently to undertake land division (*taksim*) in the forest, thus converting the commons into individual property. The decision implied that timber rights became exchangeable. A wealthy and powerful Yashkun family has already taken advantage of the new arrangement. They managed to buy the rights of less fortunate Kameen neighbors, who are now deprived of timber revenues from the contractors. Interestingly, these particular Kameen families are no longer perceived to be *holoshah.* The notion of whether or not someone is an authentic Tangiri was traditionally derived from conceptions of how the valley settlements were originally established. The dichotomization of the population into *holosha* and *uperah kaoms* reflected the principle according to which pasture rights were allocated. Today, however, the definition of *holosha* status is undergoing a transformation, from something based on initial patterns of settlement into something based on timber rights. The more recent principle, timber rights, is itself becoming the prime definer.

In sum, the population of Tangir is differentiated according to three principles. First, Tangiris practise ideas about ethnicity (*kaom*). *Kaom* is primarily relevant in terms of marriage. All *kaoms* are mostly endogamous. When *kaom* intermarriages do take place, they tend to be arranged in a typical South Asian hypergamous manner, meaning that daughters are never married into *kaoms* of lower rank (see also Aase 1999). The logic is simple. *Kaom* identity is inherited through the male line. If a daughter marries a man of lower rank, her children will inherit the lower rank of their father. No families want to have grandchildren of lower rank than themselves. If, on the other hand, a woman marries a man from a higher *kaom*, her offspring will be ascribed the higher *kaom* status of the father, which is accepted by both families.

The second principle of differentiation is the distinction between 'authentic Tangiris' (*holoshah*) and 'newcomers' (*uperah*). This dichotomy bears resemblance to a class distinction, since it determines access to mountain pastures and timber rights. It also carries implications for the marriage pattern. The general Islamic (Shariat) inheritance rule, that daughters are entitled to half the share of sons, is also applied to the generational takeover of timber rights. A woman can claim a part of the timber revenues paid by contractors amounting to half of what a man's share would be. Such rights are inherited, in the manner that men inherit whole shares (*toli*) and women inherit half shares (*shik*). By implication, a *holosha* woman should not marry an *uperah* man. If she does, her rightful timber share will be transferred to the *uperah* family. All three *holosha kaoms* are vehemently opposed to the possibility of losing their timber monopoly through marriages with *uperah* men. In the local marriage pattern, this consideration overrules the principle of hypergamy. If a Shin girl marries a ritually high-ranking Sayed boy, the Sayed *kaom* will acquire timber rights. Such marriages are unheard of.

Thirdly, the population is territorially differentiated into four *raoms*. This distinction is also given meaning in relation to pasture and timber rights. The *holosha kaoms* living in a certain *raom* can claim exclusive rights to a geographically defined area of forests and pastures. Most importantly, the territorial division mitigates the danger of fatal conflicts along purely *kaom* lines. Since *kaoms* are mostly endogamous, Tangiris count their relatives within the same *kaom*. A blood feud between, say, a Shin and a Yashkun family might easily develop into a devastating ethnic war between two *kaoms* through mobilization of relatives on each side. The *raom* institution, however, introduces a set of territorial loyalties that helps prevent such developments. A Yashkun has *kaom* obligations towards Yashkun relatives who live in other *raoms*, but he also has common timber and pasture interests with Shin and Kameen neighbors in his own *raom* as against his outside *kaom* peers. Thus, his kinship loyalties are balanced by territorial interests. It is exactly this kind of 'conflicting loyalties' that Gluckman observed to establish 'peace in the feud' in his classical analyses of feuding societies in Africa forty years ago (Gluckman 1963).

Conceptually, Tangiris are well aware of these conflicting loyalties. The importance of balancing social forces is given meaning in the settlement myth cited above, in which a full *kaom* war between Yashkun and Kameen had so fatal results. The moral of the myth is that a fully-fledged ethnic *kaom* war has no victors, only losers.

The conflicting loyalties acquire further meaning when seen in a broader political context.

Tangir is part of the region traditionally called Yagistan, meaning 'the unruly country' or 'the ungovernable country'. The name refers to the independent valleys and settlements along the Indus river where it cuts through the Himalayan mountains. To the south and north, Yagistan was bordered by small princely states, each ruled by a mir or raja, and which retained their partial independence well after the partition of India in 1947. Yagistan, however, has been characterized by the lack of centralized political authority. In Tangir, the only intermezzo in the history of acephalous political organization happened in the early 20th century. In 1905, Pakhtoon Wali Khan, the son of an ousted mir of the princely state of Yasin in the North, was granted asylum in Tangir. Somehow, he managed to accumulate power and established himself as the ruler of Tangir. But institutionalized personal authority has never been held in high esteem by Tangiris, and ultimately he was killed in 1917.

Apart from the short intermezzo of centralized rule during the reign of Pakhtoon Wali, the only political institution of any significance prior to the establishment of Pakistani state administration in the 1960s was the jirga. The jirga is a council of influential elders that may be summoned for a number of purposes. It does not consist of a fixed group of people, but is composed according to the particular task in question. On the local *dookar* level, jirgas administer the common property of pastures and timber, and oversee vital tasks such as water channel maintenance. Issues involving two or more *dookar*s are negotiated by jirgas composed of members from all involved parties, and when there are border disputes between Tangir and the neighboring Darel valley concerning mountain pastures, a jirga involving both valleys is held.

5.2 Tournaments of power

The power of the jirga in resolving conflicts is, however, limited. It has little scope to impose sanctions on parties or persons who do not adhere to the solution suggested. Occasionally, the jirga is also unable to reach a unanimous verdict. If a verdict is not reached, or if the verdict is not accepted and adhered to by the families involved in a local conflict, the jirga is a lame duck. Since the sole function of the jirga is mediation, its role in a conflict is dependent on consent. Only when the parties involved agree that a jirga should be held can it fulfill its role as a mediator.

A peculiar trait of the feud is that families rarely agree to hold a jirga until some damage has been inflicted upon each side, as is demonstrated in case 2 below.

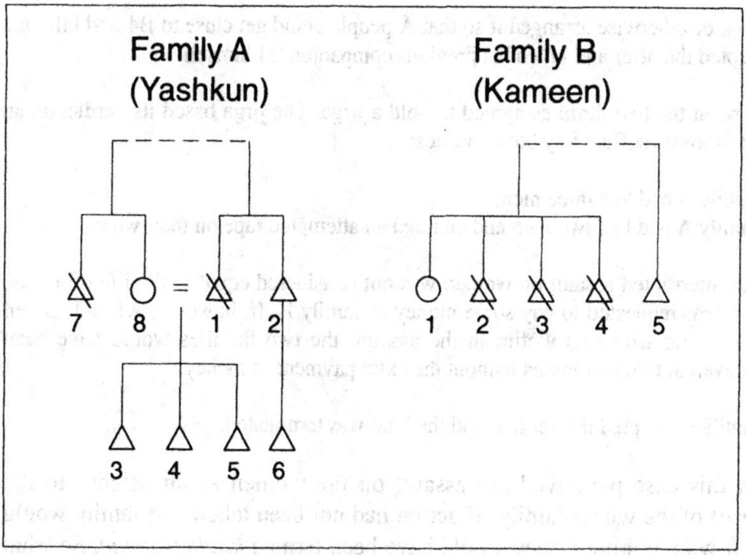

Figure 5.2 Case 2

Case 2
Two women of family A were working in the fields when no. 2 of family B and a companion assaulted them with the alleged intention of raping them. The women screamed, and other villagers managed to avert the crime. One of the women was A8, the wife of A1.

Soon after this incident A1 killed B2. Had there been the least suspicion that the women encouraged the assault, the menfolk of the A family would have killed them too. But since this was an obvious case of attempted rape, A1 did not kill his wife.

Family A was not willing to settle the *mar dushmani* even though they had gained an upper hand in the conflict. The reason for this may be that the A family were Yashkuns while family B belonged to the somewhat lower ranking Kameen *kaom*. In addition, the B family was considerably poorer and less powerful than A.

No. 4 of family B was an infant when B2 was killed. On becoming a young man he sought revenge for his brother and killed A1. A couple of years later A4 killed B3. The same day B4 retaliated by killing A7 with the help of a relative (R5) who did not belong to the B family.

By this time a police station had been set up in Tangir, and B4 and R5 were taken to jail in Gilgit. After some months they managed to pay their way out of prison,[1] but immediately after their release a dispute arose between them about who should bear the expenses. Family A heard about the disagreement and decided to exploit the situation. They promised R5 money and exemption from the *mar dushmani* if he

[1] There is a saying in Gilgit: "Why pay 100,000 rupees to a lawyer when you can get away with 10,000 to the judge?"

killed B4, or otherwise arranged it so that A people could get close to B4 and kill him. R5 accepted the offer and killed his previous companion B4 himself.

At this point the two families agreed to hold a jirga. The jirga based its verdict on an account of losses suffered by both families:

- Family B had lost three men.
- Family A had lost two men and endured an attempted rape on their women.

Since an interrupted assault on women was not considered equal to the life of a man, family A was requested to pay some money to family B. If, however, A1 had chosen to kill his wife who was victim in the assault, the two families would have been deemed even in terms of losses without the extra payment of money.

Both families accepted the verdict, and the feud was terminated.

Family A in this case perceived the assault on the women as an offense to the honor (*gheirat*) of the whole family. If action had not been taken, the family would have been left without honor; they would have been termed *bagheiratman*. So what is meant by *bagheiratman*? What is actually at stake here? A simple and frequently applied explanation runs like this: since honor is a family matter – a kind of corporate symbolic capital that is held jointly by all family members – violation of the honor of any one family member is also a violation of the honor of the whole family. In the case cited above, family A had to retaliate against family B in order to restore the honor of the women involved. By killing the offender or one of his family mates, the honor of the women is restored.

There is, however, something that does not quite match the reality of the case in such an interpretation. It is not the 'honor' of the involved women that is restored through a revenge killing. If the woman A8 had actually been raped, the family could only get rid of the shame by killing her. She would be the bearer of the shame, regardless of her own role in the matter. The only way to purge the shame that accrues in this way is to eliminate the person who embodies it. In many cases of rape the woman has been killed by her male relatives for this reason – even mentally retarded young girls. So what is it that has to be proven through a revenge killing? What does it mean to restore the family's honor?

When family A killed a member of the offending B family, they communicated to the latter and to all Tangir that they were capable of defending their interests, which in this case was the chastity of their women. The A people signaled that they were not to be fooled with; they were able to stand up and fight if necessary. This is the core meaning of honor in the sense of *gheirat*. By killing a member of the B family, the danger of being termed *bagheiratman* was transferred to the B family; thus it became their turn to prove their worth by killing a man from the other side. During the course of the feud, both families successfully demonstrated their power.

It is important to note that the jirga was not convened until killings had taken place on both sides. If the jirga had been set up earlier, it might have settled a *dushmani* (hostility) before it evolved into a *mar dushmani* (blood feud). But such an early appeal to the jirga would have missed the very point of a feud, which is to demonstrate power. Not until both parties had proved their worth was a settlement agreed.

The settlement of the case itself testifies to the assertion that honor is synonymous with power. The immediate aim of the settlement is to make the feuding parties even in terms of losses and compensation. But on another level, the verdict restores the power balance between them. Both have been able to defend their interests, and both can thereby withdraw from the feud with the assurance that their honor is intact. Even if women's chastity has been violated, the men emerge from the feud as honorable (*gheiratman*). *It is, accordingly, the men's ability to defend the interests of the family that is at stake in the feud.*

The assertion that honor is synonymous with self-defense, or power, is further confirmed by the fact that it is not only the violation of female chastity that can initiate a feud.

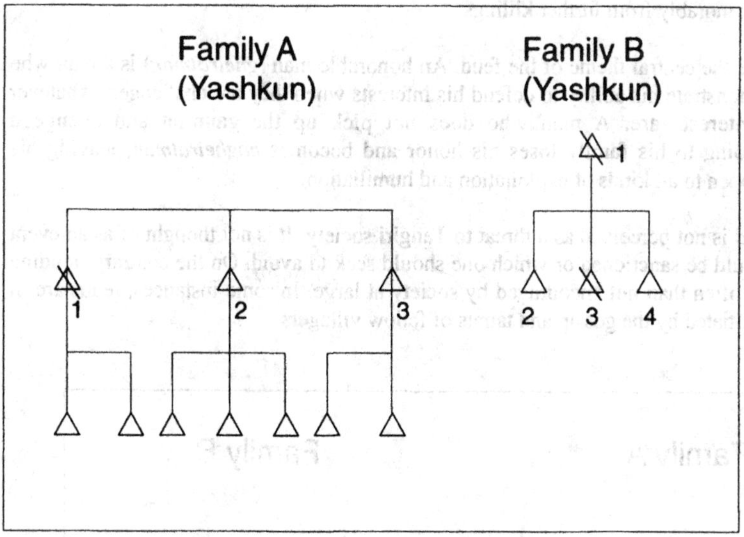

Figure 5.3 Case 3

Case 3
Families A and B both belong to the Yashkun *kaom*. One evening, while on his way home from prayers at the mosque, no. 1 of family B was killed by some unidentified person. Family B suspected various people of the homicide, among them no. 1 of family A, but all suspects claimed to be innocent.

The sons of B1 were infants when this happened. When they grew up, they resumed the search for their father's killer. One after the other, the suspected families came to them and swore their innocence. Some swore on the Holy Quran, and others declared to divorce their wives if they were lying. Both oaths are accepted as strongly binding. But family A claimed that it was not necessary for them to give the oath since they had not been involved in the matter whatsoever. Family B insisted repeatedly that family A take the oath, but A refused. At last B2 and B3 killed A1. Later on A2 killed B3.

After this the parties agreed to let a jirga try to mediate the conflict. The jirga asked family B to prove that the initial murder of B1 was committed by family A, which B could not. On request of the jirga, family A took oath that they had not been involved in the killing of B1. The jirga then decided that the killing of A1 was equal to that of B3. The killer of B1 is still not known and should be kept off the record. The two families were even in terms of losses caused by known killers, and the feud should be left at that. Both families accepted the verdict, and the *mar dushmani* came to an end.

The structure of events in this feud is quite similar to case 2 above, even if the immediate cause of the hostility is different. The jirga is summoned only after killings have taken place on both sides. The jirga's account of losses is accepted by both families, and a settlement is reached. The verdict of the jirga works as a public announcement of the equality of the two families in terms of power, and they can both refrain honorably from further killings.

Power is the central theme of the feud. An honorable man (*gheiratman*) is a man who can demonstrate his ability to defend his interests when they are challenged, whatever those interests are. A man who does not pick up the gauntlet and avenge a wrongdoing to his family loses his honor and becomes *bagheiratman*, leaving his family open to all kinds of exploitation and humiliation.

The feud is not perceived as a threat to Tangiri society. It is not thought of as an event that should be sanctioned or which one should seek to avoid. On the contrary, feuding is more often than not encouraged by society at large. In some instances, feuds are in effect initiated by the gossip and taunts of fellow villagers.

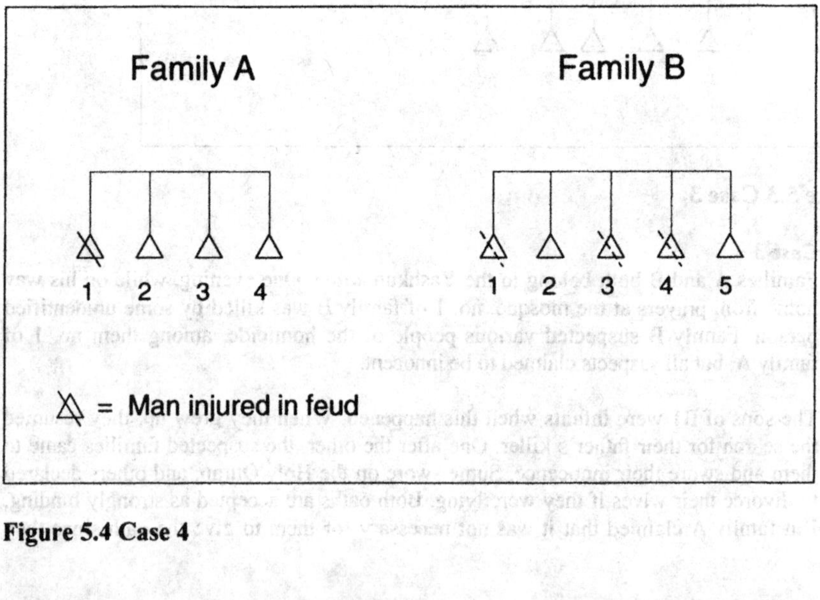

Figure 5.4 Case 4

Case 4

One night family A were woken by unfamiliar noises inside their home, which turned out to come from uninvited guests. Before the intruders managed to escape, one of them was identified as no. 3 of family B. The matter gave rise to mild enmity (*dushmani*) between the two families, but was left at that since no harm had been done. Soon, however, neighbors started to suggest that the aim of B3 and his companions' nocturnal visit to the A house was not theft. Their real intention was to get hold of the women of the A family. This possibility was insinuated by means of a metaphor: 'Hey brother, the other day I saw some young billy-goats trying to break into the shed of family A to copulate with their nanny-goats!' By repeated taunts of this kind, accompanied by sneers and laughter, the A family was challenged to prove and defend its honor.

Enraged by the village gossip and teasing, A1 went to the B house and attacked B3 with an axe. B3 was seriously injured in the neck. He survived treatment at a regional country hospital and returned to Tangir partly disabled. Later on, A1 again tried to kill B3, but this time B3 was armed and managed to kill A1 instead. A3 then attacked and injured B1, and A2 accompanied by A3 managed to inflict serious injury on B4.

At this point a jirga was held, and it managed to end the *mar dushmani* on the condition that the B family paid some compensation to A. In this way the losses of the two families were judged to be even and the account could be settled:

– Family A had suffered the loss of one man and a nightly visit to their house.
– Family B had suffered serious injury to three men and the cost of paying some money and cattle to family A.

What actually caused this feud was not the nocturnal visit to the A house in itself. If it were not for village gossip, the *dushmani* might have passed over peacefully. The incident was, however, an occasion to challenge the two families to prove their power. The opportunity was seized by co-villagers, whose repeated taunts could not be ignored by the A family without a loss of honor. They had to retaliate against family B in order to avoid becoming *bagheiratman*. After having done so, their position in society was restored. They had unwillingly been forced into a position where their honor was put in question, and they confirmed it by attacking the original offenders. In this way they demonstrated their honor – in the sense of their capacity for self-defense – not only to the B family, but also to the community as a whole.

5.3 What is honor all about?

Three aspects of honor can be elicited from the cases cited in this chapter.

Firstly, the actual events that trigger feuds are not all of a single type. The emergence of *mar dushmani* is frequently related to women's chastity, but other episodes may also generate blood feuds. Since no single action or event can ever be regarded as a necessary and sufficient condition for the feud, the core meaning of the blood feud must be sought at a deeper level. A revenge killing is more than a habitual response to the stimulus of a certain kind of event. In line with Black-Michaud (1975), I argue that the core meaning of the feud is found in the ability of a family to defend its interests. It is not the interests themselves that are really at stake, whether it is women's chastity or something else, but the ability and the courage to stand up and fight for those interests. The term *gheirat*, which is invariably translated as 'honor' by other authors (e.g. Keyser 1991, Ahmed 1996), is used in Tangiri to denote precisely this capacity for defense.

The validity of this interpretation of the feud is clearly seen in the cases of *mar dushmani* that have been settled. Even if men are killed and women assaulted, the offended family emerges from the feud with its *gheirat* restored. It is not the attempted rape of a wife or a sister as such that makes a man *bagheiratman* – a man without honor – but only his inability to avenge the offence. Thus, it is correct to conceive of honor as the ability to defend one's interests. This was also the conclusion of Black-Michaud's survey of the feud in the Mediterranean and in the Middle East (1975).

Secondly, the actual events that spark a feud, like an assault on a woman's chastity, are merely occasions when a man's power is put to the test. A man or family that experiences an event that can be seen to represent disgrace is actually invited by others to prove his worth. In case 4 above, neighbors' repeated insinuations of a sexual motive for the nocturnal visit ultimately forced the family who fell victim to the intruders to confirm its *gheirat* by attacking the house of the identified culprit. The metaphorical gossip about billy-goats and nanny-goats was far more threatening than it might at first seem to be. It implies something like, 'now we will see if you have the guts to defend your interests!' What is at stake in a situation like this is a man's *gheirat*, and not women's chastity.

A third aspect of Tangiri feuds is the frequent involvement of young men in their inception. In cases 1 and 3, decisions of revenge were left to the sons of the murdered man, to be taken by them when they reached adolescence. Shina language contains a special term for a young man in his teens, ***chakur***, which denotes someone who expected to be impulsive and unable to control his emotions. Indeed, the metaphor of the billy-goat used in the gossip of case 4 has wide connotations in Tangir. The Shina term for a billy-goat is *bal*, and this is also widely used to denote a young man. The coming of age is conveyed in terms of *bal* in the following proverb:

> When the young billy-kid *(bal)* is getting a beard, the mature billy-goat is losing his.

The beard is a symbol of manhood. As virility and power passes from father to son, so too does responsibility for the *gheirat* of the family. Young billy-goats are lively, uncontrollable, and continuously testing their strength against others. Applying the label *bal* to young men establishes a structuring metaphor between billy-goat and young man (A = B), by which knowledge about the one is transferred to the other (Lakoff & Johnson 1980). Thus, the metaphor makes it comprehensible to Tangiris that young men play an active part in the feud.

Even if the impulsive acts of young men and billy-goats are understandable to Tangiris, it is still a question why they are so eager to start and renew the feud, and why they are so preoccupied with honor. An answer demands that we look into another form of honor in Tangir, which is called *izzat*.

Izzat is appropriately translated as reputation, or merit. A person who is *izzatwala* is respected for some deed he has performed that has given him a good reputation. In contrast to *gheirat*, which a man either has or has not, *izzat* can be held in degrees. *Gheirat* is a dichotomous thing, while *izzat* is continuous. *Izzat* can be obtained through performance of valuable acts in various social fields. One of the most important fields for ascription of *izzat* is that of feuding. It can be accumulated by showing courage in combat, by negotiating a wise solution to a feud, and by acting generously towards a vanquished enemy, thus permitting him to keep his *gheirat*. *Izzat* accumulated in this way can be seen as a kind of symbolic capital, since it can be transformed into other kinds of capital. Most directly, *izzat* can be converted into political influence through appointment to jirgas.

The mediating jirga consists of influential men. Since the jirga does not enjoy any kind of delegated authority – neither secular nor religious – the effectiveness of mediation depends on the aggregate power gathered in the jirga. The verdict of a weak jirga would hardly be respected by anyone. Thus, only powerful men are asked to sit in jirgas. Power is measured according to the number of armed men a person can mobilize, usually brothers and sons. But power is also measured in terms of *izzat*, the symbolic capital a man has accumulated during his lifetime. A nobleman who is thus found worthy of sitting in *jirgas* is termed *justero*. *Justero* is a position that is much aspired to, since it is a clear index of a successful manly life.

The *justeros* of Tangir laid the foundation of their *izzat* during adolescence. The reputation they accumulated during their young years is exactly what made them *justero*s later in life. If a young man has ambitions in the direction of power and influence, which most Tangiris do have, he should prove his abilities in his youth. The feud is an appropriate opportunity to show bravery and a capacity for self-defense. Thus, a young man who participates successfully in the feud does not only save the *gheirat* of his family. By doing so he simultaneously enhances his personal *izzat*. Black-Michaud made similar observations in his survey, where he writes about, 'the reputation that older men acquire from the successful pursuit of honor in feuds in which they participated in their youth' (Black-Michaud 1975:180).

The feud is an ambivalent phenomenon to Tangiris. When it breaks out into an open tournament of power, fear is created and lives are lost. Those aspects are not, of course, appreciated, which was clearly expressed by the man who wanted to accompany me to Norway. But on the other hand, the feud is a golden opportunity for a young man to confirm his honor. Eagerness for revenge indicates that he has taken over responsibility for the *gheirat* of his family. Participation in the feud may thus be seen as an investment in symbolic capital (*izzat*) that can be embodied in the position of *justero* later in life.

Feud and honor have a strategic aspect as well as a cognitive aspect, as Coombe (1990) rightly observes. Strategically, the point of the honor game is to avoid a humiliating defeat. If an attack on the vital interests of a family is not avenged, the family loses its *gheirat* and admits being inferior to its opponents. Such admission can be fatal in an acephalous society where every family is the architect of its own fortune:

Case 5

Some time between the First and Second World War when Tangir was under the formal jurisdiction of Kashmir, a Sayed woman bought water rights to a spring in the hillside above the village of Shekho. According to the custom of the time, the purchase was made in gold. Later, when Tangir became part of Pakistan, the water rights were confirmed by the Pakistani administration.

The appropriation of the spring water by the Sayeds was not applauded by the remaining Shekho villagers. People complained that monopolization of water contradicted Shariat (Islamic law), which states that water is a public resource not to be privately owned.

An influential Yashkun family from the neighboring village of Rim owned some land below the spring. The Sayeds hoped to buy the land cheaply now that they controlled the water, but the Yashkuns did not want to sell, wealthy as they were. Around 1980, the Yashkuns started to construct a channel from the Tangir river in order to supply irrigation water to the land in question. This was resented by the Sayeds, whose spring would thereby lose its value.

In 1985 a young Sayed boy shot and killed a man from the Yashkun family while he was working on the channel. During the *mar dushmani* that subsequently developed, two Sayed men were killed by the Yashkuns in retaliation. The feud put an effective end to further channel construction.

In 1994, a public channel was constructed along the lines of the former Yashkun plan in connection with a Norwegian development project in the valley. The channel was primarily built for water supply to a hydropower station further down, but irrigation water was also granted to fields adjacent to the channel. Thus, the new channel rendered the contested spring water irrelevant. The Sayed family had no water rights to defend any more, and besides, they were by far the weaker part in the conflict. They therefore sent a message to the Yashkuns that they were willing to negotiate a compromise. A jirga was held in which the powerful *holosha* Yashkuns had an upper hand over the numerically weaker *uperah* Sayeds, and were able to dictate the conditions for peace. Even if the Sayeds held the disadvantage in terms of the balance of lives lost in the feud, having lost two men as compared to the Yashkuns' loss of one man, the Sayeds had to pay 500,000 rupees (approximately US$ 15,000) to the Yashkuns. In addition they had to give a daughter in marriage to the Yashkuns.

The marriage was a significant event in the ritual hierarchy of Tangiri *kaoms*. As noted above, inter-kaom marriages are usually practiced in a hypergamous manner, implying that women are given to marry men of higher *kaoms* only. Since Sayeds claim to be direct descendants of the Holy Prophet and thus the purest of all *kaoms*, they practise strict endogamy all over Pakistan. Bearing this in mind, the Sayed woman who was married to a Yashkun man signified the higher ritual rank of the Yashkuns. The compensation paid by the Sayeds in order to put an end to the feud thus consisted of material capital (money) as well as symbolic capital (acceptance of the higher rank of Yashkuns through marriage). The marriage is particularly significant, since it gives precedence to the *holosha - uperah* (authentic - immigrant) ranking in opposition to the traditional *kaom* hierarchy.

The settlement of this feud was not applauded by Tangiris in general. If the Yashkuns had not exploited their superior power to dictate an uneven peace, they might have been ascribed *izzat* (merit) for being generous. As things turned out, the Yaskuns were termed *magroor*, meaning haughty and arrogant, by fellow Tangiris. By accepting a humiliating defeat, the Sayeds for their part stood in danger of losing their honor and becoming *bagheiratman*. Again, we see that it is power and capacity for defense that is at stake. An uneven compromise like this one is not honorable to either of the parties, and the peace achieved is a fragile one. In all probability a young Sayed 'billy-goat' will eventually react to future taunts and allegations of cowardice by resuming the feud.

Until recently, killings were committed by means of daggers, axes, or old Enfield rifles left by the British colonists. Using any of these weapons, an avenger had to come quite close to his victim in order to be successful. The past few decades have, however, witnessed a technological modernization of the feud. Russian Kalashnikovs found there way into Tangir in the wake of the Soviet occupation of Afghanistan. During the Soviet presence, some Tangiris crossed the Hindu Kush mountains into Pansjir, where Afghan mujahedin offered captured Kalashnikov rifles for 30,000 rupees. In those days, the Kalashnikov was primarily the privilege of wealthy Tangiris, mostly *holosha* families who earned cash on the timber trade. During the 1990s, the famous arms manufacturers of Peshawar started to produce cheap imitations. A 'made in Pakistan' Kalashnikov could now be bought for 12,000 rupees. Curiously, the spread of Kalashnikovs in Tangir is partly due to the above-mentioned Norwegian power project. In 1993, the project disbursed 2.5 million rupees in land compensation for areas needed for the water channel, penstock, and power station site. Among the receivers were many poor *uperah* households who belonged to the village where the power station is located. On my subsequent visit to Tangir, there were more Kalashnikovs to be seen than ever.

The Kalashnikov has become the Mercedes, so to speak, of the valley. Proud owners of a Kalashikov gun 'style' it with plastic beads, colorful straps, and inscriptions from the Quran. It is a sign of wealth as well as of power. Modern weaponry may have a deterrent effect insofar as people think twice before provoking situations where it might be put into use. But when tournaments of power occasionally do break out, the results are dramatic.

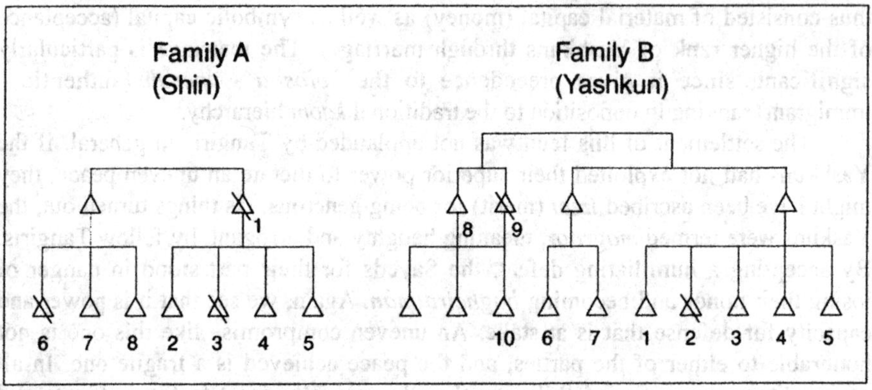

Figure 5.5 Case 6

> **Case 6**
> A young Yashkun man (B5) was wanted by the police for some illegal activity he had been involved in. One day police constable A2 arrested B5 in the house of his friend. The friend was a Shin and a relative of A2. Thus, a *dushmani* evolved between families A and B.
>
> One night some unidentified persons killed A3 and A6 on the road to their home. Neighbors had observed B4 on the road some time before the killings took place, which led the A family to accuse the B people of the killings. Family B for their part denied all involvement.
>
> Shortly afterwards family A launched a massive attack on the B homestead. The B people sought shelter in their stone tower, but B9, a relative of the B family who was not included in the accusation of the initial killings, was accidentally killed in the cross-fire.
>
> A few years later Family A repeated the attack and managed to kill B2.
>
> A1 was a well-known nobleman (*justero*) of Tangir, about 70 years of age. One afternoon when he was traveling down the main Tangir road in a jeep together with several other passengers, he was attacked by B10, a fifteen years old boy. The boy fired off a full magazine of his Kalashnikov at the jeep. A1, the target of the attack, died on the spot, as did three coincidental passengers.
>
> The original *mar dushmani* between the A and B families continues. Compromise was achieved through compensation for the families of two of the passengers killed accidentally in the shooting, and who happened to be Yashkuns like the killer. The third innocent victim was however Shin, and his family has entered into a *mar dushmani* with the B family. Thus, the initial arrest of B5 developed into two ongoing *mar dushmani* relations and two expensive compensations for family B.

In the hands of angry young men the Kalashnikov is a dangerous thing, not only to the intended target, but to the social surroundings as well. It might thus be expected that the introduction of effective modern weaponry would transform the feud from an accepted aspect of Tangiri society into a threat to the social order. But an event that happened outside Tangir indicates that this is unlikely.

5.4 The changing context of honor and revenge

In 1988, a violent conflict between Sunni Muslims and Shia Muslims broke out in the town of Gilgit. During a few days of intensive fighting, which included people from Tangir and other surrounding valleys, several hundred were killed before the army managed to impose a 24 hour curfew. Ever since, Gilgit and the northern areas of Pakistan in general have been plagued by annual sectarian fighting and a continuous state of tension and anxiety (Aase 1999). One day during my fieldwork, news reached Gilgit that four Sunni Muslims from Gilgit had been killed in the Shia stronghold of Shigar close to the Kashmiri border. The Gilgit bazaar closed immediately, and all inhabitants sought refuge in fear that a sectarian fight would break out. The next morning Gilgit citizens were however relieved to hear that the Shigar incident was a *mar dushmani* business. The bazaar reopened, and life returned to normal. A sectarian conflict was perceived as potentially devastating, as it had proved to be in 1988. But locating the Shigar killings in a *mar dushmani* context was no threat to society. This was just one more installment in the long list of power tournaments going on in Tangir and its neighborhood, only this time it had occurred outside Yagistan.

Effective modern weapons mean that the feud has become less 'sporting' than it may have been in the past (Jettmar 1960). Despite a heavy annual toll of human lives, the feud remains an integral part of Tangiri society. Moreover, the feud has so far survived the ongoing integration of Tangir into the Pakistani state. A Deputy Commissioner has been appointed to Tangir, whose mandate is to prevent crime and collect taxes. Land rights are regulated by the land register (*patwari*), and a District Council is democratically elected. In October1994, national political parties were allowed to campaign for local elections for the first time (Aase 1999). However, there are no signs that traditional honor is losing ground to modern dignity; the notion of *gheirat* is as strong as ever. Taking these processes of modernization into consideration, it is valid to wonder about the future of the feud. If, as argued here, the feud can only be understood in its social context, why does it not change in accordance with contextual changes? When spears and daggers are substituted by automatic rifles, and when the traditional political set-up is reinforced by modern stately institutions, why do Tangiris stick to old ideas of honor and practices of revenge?

Tangiris themselves maintain that some changes in the feud have, in fact, occurred: 'Earlier, we fought over land and water; nowadays, we mostly fight over women'. This 'emic' description of a recent change in the typical pattern of events indicates that changes are occurring in gender relations, which may explain the obstinate survival of the feud.

Tangiri men watch their women with a remarkable degree of jealousy. The Tangir valley can, for example, boast the dubious virtue of a hundred percent female illiteracy. Girls should not be allowed out of sight once they reach puberty, not even to attend school. A girls' school was set up by the government ten years ago, but the building is used as a secondary school for boys. Neighboring Darel is somewhat better off. There, a small girls' school has been established in the house of a local *mola* (priest). In 1995, the Director of Education in Gilgit came to Darel on a tour of inspection. He was duly shown the classroom, but when he asked to see the teacher, things turned difficult. The teacher was a young lady, and she was also the daughter-in-law of the *mola*. It would be a disgrace to let her talk to a strange man. But the Director insisted on seeing her. How could he otherwise know that there existed a teacher at all? If he could not meet the teacher, he would have to reconsider the monthly disbursement of wages. On this threat, a jirga was summoned to discuss the problem. It was decided that the Director should be allowed to talk to the teacher for seven minutes in the presence of four male family members. So the Director of Education got his meeting with the teacher, who was wrapped in clothes and shawls, her face kept to the wall throughout the interview.

Gender relations were probably more relaxed in the past, compared with the extreme seclusion of today. Old Tangiris remember that men and women used to have dance contests at weddings, and women are depicted as active romance partners in traditional folklore. Nowadays, neither men nor women dance, and the colorful lore has been substituted by Islamic rituals. Somehow, the increased importance ascribed to women's chastity is related to the particular kind of Islamization that is going on in Northern Pakistan and Afghanistan. The messages of mainstream Islam are spread throughout the region by an influential organization called Tablighi Jamaat – 'The Association of Preachers'. On frequent visits to Tangir the Tablighi exhort people to watch the chastity of their women, among other things. Since Tangiris are relatively recent converts to Islam, they regard the jealous guardianship of female chastity and Muslim piety as intimately interconnected virtues.

It may be argued, then, that the feud has changed in accordance with contextual changes. Since land and water rights are regulated by newly introduced formal institutions, and since crime is punished according to the official penal code of Pakistan, a *dushmani* (conflict) over natural resources can be resolved through official channels before it evolves into a *mar dushmani* (blood feud). On the other hand, no official institution exists to regulate gender relations. Ideas about proper behavior between men and women are left to individual families to decide. Avenging an assault on female chastity is not considered a crime, and it is thereby not included in any official jurisdiction. Indeed, local priests (*mola*) encourage vengeful behavior against violators of female chastity.

A possible explanation for the recent transferal of the feud from the context of land and water rights to the context of gender relations might therefore be found in the simultaneous processes of 1) the integration of property management into Pakistani administration, 2) the omission of gender from formal regulations of interpersonal relationships, and 3) the increased significance of female chastity in the name of Islam.

However, the statement that 'formerly we fought over land and water; now we fight over women', might be more hypothetical than real. Jettmar heard the same claim in 1958! (Jettmar 1960, 1994). At that time Tangir was a remote place, no more integrated into Pakistan than it had been into the State of Jammu and Kashmir a hundred years before. This observation renders the explanation offered above extremely dubious. The increased emphasis on women as objects in the feud can hardly be correlated with the administrative integration of Tangir into the Pakistani state. It seems that women played a similarly important role in the feud at a time when Tangir was still totally lacking in stately institutions and regulations. So how are we to understand the persistence of honor and vengeance? What alternative explanations are there?

As Black-Michaud has argued, the immediate 'reason' for feuding should be considered secondary to its core meaning. The cases in this chapter demonstrate that, although women's chastity is currently a dominant theme, feuds evolve for a variety of reasons. In one case vengeance is taken because a sister's chastity has been violated; in another instance a feud evolves because of the arrest of a son, or because of a conflict over spring water. The core meaning of the feud is, however, prominent in all the cases cited above. Irrespective of the immediate events that cause a feud to break out, the feud itself is an occasion to confirm two kinds of honor that are of the utmost importance to a Tangiri. Firstly, it is an occasion for a family to prove its ability defend itself (*gheirat*), and secondly, it is an occasion for a young man to accumulate merit (*izzat*) that adds to his personal renown. In a society where every individual family is the architect of its own fortune, these qualities are of immense social importance. Judges can be influenced, police officers can be bought, and land registrators can be threatened. Survival under such circumstances is preconditioned by a solid foundation of symbolic capital – of *gheirat* as well as of *izzat*. The particular occasion on which such capital is accumulated matters less. A tournament of power fought over the chastity of a woman is as good as any other cause.

References

Aase, T. (1999), 'The Theological Construction of conflict. Gilgit, Northern Pakistan', in Manger, L. (ed.), *Muslim Diversity. Local Islam in Global contexts*, Curzon Press, Richmond (UK)

Aase, T. (2000), *Clean Energy to Tangir. Review of a Norwegian Hydro-Electric Power Project in the Northern Areas of Pakistan*, Center for Social Research Paper 10, University of Bergen, Norway

Ahmed, A.S. (1996), *Pakistan Society. Islam, Ethnicity, and Leadership in South Asia*, Oxford, Oxford University Press

Black-Michaud, J. (1975), *Cohesive Force. Feud in the Mediterranean and the Middle East*, Oxford, Basil Blackwell

Coombe, R. (1990), 'Barren Ground. Re-conceiving Honor and Shame in the Field of Mediterranean Ethnography', in *Anthropologica XXXII*, pp.221-238

Gluckman, M. (1963), *Custom and Conflict in Africa*, Oxford, Basil Blackwell

Jettmar, K. (1994), 'Consequences of the Political Integration of Tangir and Darel into Pakistan', to be published in Allan, N.J.R. (ed.), *Himalayan Crucible: North Pakistan in Transition*, California, V.C. Davies

Keiser, L. (1991), *Friend by Day, Enemy by Night. Organised Vengeance in a Kohistani Society*, Fort Worth, Holt, Reinhart, and Winston

Lakoff, G. and Johnson, M. (1980), *Metaphors we live by*, Chicago, University of Chicago Press

Lakoff, G. (1990), *Women, Fire, and Dangerous Things. What Categories Reveal About the Mind*, Chicago, University of Chicago Press

Schomberg, R.C.F. (1935), *Between the Oxus and the Indus*, London, Martin Hopkins

Chapter 6

Honor, Feuding, and National Fragmentation in Kurdistan

Haci Akman

6.1 Introduction

The ideology of honor is widely accepted in Kurdish society, but for most Kurds, it rarely acts as a guide to action. Only in situations where the family or the tribe feel that their honor is threatened or when an insult calls for the restoration of honor, will the ideology be put into practice. This chapter illustrates how a coincidental event happens to evoke conceptions of honor in two neighboring tribes, and how these conceptions eventually lead to a tragic blood feud through an escalating series of ever more violent interactions. But since a text needs to be seen in context in order to be understood properly, it is necessary first to introduce the reader to the socio-political situation in which the actual feud occurs.

Since the Turks 'forced the gate' to Anatolia for the first time in 1071, the Kurdish nation has continuously faced the threat of annihilation. In that year, the aboriginal peoples of the region, Kurds and Byzantines, were defeated at Malazgirt. For the Kurds, the defeat initiated an era of social fragmentation and a vagrant way of life that has lasted to the present day. In 1639 Kurdistan was divided between the Ottoman Empire and Persia, who wished to have a buffer zone between them. Almost 300 years later, after the First World War, another fragmentation followed when the allied nations decided in agreement with Turkey to divide Kurdistan between the four states of Turkey, Iran, Iraq, and Syria. This fragmentation, in addition to oppression and external cultural influences, generated a political context that severely hampered the cultural development of the Kurdish people. Since Kurds were not allowed to establish cultural institutions nor publish books or journals, it was impossible for cultural leaders - artists and intellectuals - to create an atmosphere which allowed them to influence and guide their people (Uzun 1985:10).

6.2 The legend of Kurdish origins

Kurds have a strong sense of belonging to the land of their mythical origins and to their birthplace. In particular, they feel emotionally attached to the mountains, which are also central symbols in their present struggle for independence. There are various historical ways of comprehending the origin of the Kurdish people that are partly contradictory. The Kurds themselves prefer to present their genesis in the form of narratives. One of these is a legend that takes us 2600 years back in time to an age when Kurdistan was ruled by the mythical Dehag, which means 'the one who is loved by Satan'. During one of their occasional meetings, The Evil One touched Dehag's body, and as a result of this physical contact two snakes grew out of Dehag's breast. The snakes demanded the brains of young boys as food. By obeying the wishes of Satan and by nourishing him (i.e. the snakes) with the blood of the people, Dehag managed to increase his own power. He became stronger day by day while his people died at his feet.

Kawa the blacksmith had a son. When Kawa realized that the day was approaching when Dehag would demand the life of his son, he summoned the people to revolt against the tyrant. Kawa became the Messiah whom people had been waiting for. In a fierce rage, sword in hand, he managed to destroy Dehag. By this act, Kawa liberated his people from suffering and grief. After the victory he migrated with his people and settled in the high mountains. Kawa had avenged the wrongdoings and restored his own and his people's honor that had been defiled by Dehag. For the first time in their mythical past the Kurdish people experienced the spring in a condition of freedom, and since then springtime has been the symbol of a better future and a new life.

The legend of Dehag has become particularly significant for the Kurds since it tells of the Kurdish nation's capacity for unity and resistance. The fire of Kawa the blacksmith, which showed the way to the mountains, and which was later used to illuminate the cairns, is a frequently used symbol in the present freedom fight. Today a symbolic fire is lit on Newros (Kurdish New Year). The fire symbolizes freedom and renewal, but also mobilization and revolt. When young men and women set themselves on fire in order literally to illuminate the freedom fight, it implies a continuation of the mythical connotations of fire and struggle. Suicide by burning must also be seen in relation to the Kurdish perception of martyrs (*shehîd*). Martyrs achieve an elevated, almost holy position. Images of martyrs are produced in order to commemorate and honor their subjects during special festivals (Rugkasa 1996).

The historical suffering of the Kurdish nation has been the principle theme of artists and writers for centuries. The suffering is salient and beautifully expressed in a poem by Nali (1797-1855), which he wrote to his contemporary poet Salim during a period when he was living in Damascus. From his exile Nali wrote of his longing for his home country. He commemorates the rivers and plains and cities of Kurdistan and asks whether it will ever be possible for him to return:

To explain the pain of exile is to invoke the devastating fire of separation that flows from my eyes. Is the time come for me to return, or shall I stay here to my last day?

Salim responds by describing the ruin of Kurdistan and the cruelties of the occupiers. He turns to the wind in the hope that Nali can hear his cry:

> For the sake of God, give Nali the message that I beg him never to return to Silemani!

Today, the Kurdish people live scattered throughout the whole world and represent one of the most comprehensive diasporas of our time. But in spite of living in other countries, most Kurds regard Kurdistan as their proper homeland (*welat*), where they wish to return whenever the political situation will allow.

6.3 The tribe

Traditional Kurdish society is composed of tribes (*eshîr*) which are internally subdivided into several patrilineages. Tribal identity has been of greater historical significance to nomads than to settled Kurds, but still today tribal affinity means a lot to all Kurds. In traditional society the tribe was a social, political, and economic unit where loyalty among members was vital for survival. Members of a tribe were usually relatives (*kes u kar, xizm*), but there are also tribes organized according to other principles than kinship. David McDowell (1999) maintains that Kurdish tribal organization is based on the mixed principles of blood ties (*pîwend îy în xunî*) and loyalty (White 2000:18). This dual principle of organization seems to be a guarantee for the continuous reproduction of the tribe. The tribe inhabited a core spatial area which was perceived to be in its custody, although it was not marked by definite borders.

It has been argued that the Kurds never succeeded in organizing themselves above the tribal level. They have not developed alternative ways of organizing society, and neither have they tried to unite all Kurds under some kind of tribal superstructure. On the contrary, the world outside the tribe was ignored unless it had some direct impact upon the life of the tribe. The tribe was thought of as a miniature world in itself. Tribal rivalries have taken precedence over the common cause of the Kurdish nation, which has never had a fully developed idea of statehood. Many writers have argued that the fragmented tribal organization is the very reason why Kurds have never succeeded in making their own state. An early observer who called attention to this was Serefxan Bìtlis, who wrote the first Kurdish history in 1597. At that time Bitlis was in exile in Persia due to a conflict with the Ottoman regime. From his exile he reproached the Kurds for their continual tribal quarrels and encouraged them to unite and fight the common enemy (*dijmin*) instead.

The tribe was a central unit in the world of Kurdish life. It called for allegiance, and in return it offered welfare and security. Tribal communality (*hevbeshyîn eshîretî*) legitimated and defined persons as Kurds; without tribal affiliation a person was a non-Kurd, an outsider. The position of the tribe was strong and clearly defined until the First World War. Since 1920, tribal organization has undergone many changes, but even so, Kurds still perceive the tribe to be their prime reference of identity.

The historical survival of tribal structure must be seen in relation to the Kurdish struggle for land and a Kurdish identity. The outside world is perceived as a threat to survival, identity, and freedom, which are three basic features of national belonging. Due to the lack of civil rights offered by a state, Kurds have sought security and mutual support in kinship networks within the tribe. There are still different opinions about the historical function of the tribe and of the present importance of the tribe to individual Kurds. The tribe is probably ascribed different meanings by different persons in different contexts. Most Kurds, however, agree that tribes are usually organized on principles of kinship and territory.

Paul White (2000) is critical of the idea that Kurdish society has experienced a linear development from ancient times until today, with an unchanging tribal structure providing a stable core – the independent variable, so to speak. White refers to Dresch (1993:ff) who claims that Kurdish tribal structure has changed substantially during the last centuries, through a process of interaction with the outside world. The present tribes of Northern Kurdistan (Turkey) are radically different from their predecessors, reflecting general social changes within the region. The question arises, however, how far the tribe can change in order to adapt to a modern context. There seem to exist some contradictions between tribal society and the modern capitalist state that can hardly be reconciled. In the words of Paul Dresch, 'The language of tribalism is not that of the state, any more than it was in Islamic times' (in White 2000:18).

6.4 The family

The three basic levels of Kurdish social organization are 1) the family (*malbat*), 2) the clan (*êl*), and 3) the tribe (*eshîr*). Tribe refers to a kind of nation or state, even if it is based on the principle of blood relations between the members. The clan is a form of extended family. The family is the basic social unit. It is characterized by tight relations, strongly segregated roles, and systems of effective sanctions. A person is born into a family and a clan whose composition in terms of members is only changed by births and deaths. For most Kurds the kinship network acts as the prime social group through all phases of life. Thus, we can sense the importance of the family and the lineage in the formation of Kurdish identity. In times of difficulties, support and comfort can always be sought in the family. The social importance of the clan is correlated to geographical mobility, insofar as low mobility and close settlement in villages or small towns reinforces its position. In cities, Kurdish society is more fragmented into individual elementary families which only rarely interact with other clan members. Even so, most Kurds have a strong mental link to the clan irrespective of geographical distance and frequency of interaction. This mental link is a vital premise for action among Kurds, and it is important in the discussion of Kurdish identity.

The Kurds are not a homogenous group. The Kurdish people live in four countries and are accordingly exposed to different cultural and political influences. Still, most Kurds refer to their Kurdishness (*kurdbûn*) in various contexts. Whether such references are made openly or secretly depends on the actual political situation and on the ability and courage to challenge it.

6.5 Honor and duty

The Kurdish concept of honor (*hisyet*) can only be understood in relation to a tribal structure that is organized on the basis of blood ties between its members. In the introduction to this book, Aase presents a detailed discussion of the concept of honor and relates it directly to power. This chapter will not repeat a theoretical discussion of the concept. But it is vital to underline that Kurdish honor is intimately linked to the set of rules, values, and norms that exists within the tribe. Honor is linked to status and to the proper role behavior expected of men, women, spouses, children, oldest sons, and family heads, in what Berger (1974) sees as a typical pre-modern fashion. In addition, honor has a dimension that overrides individual statuses and somehow orchestrates the collective thinking and acting of the tribe (Akman 1988, 1994). Honor can only be understood in relation to the society in which is occurs, and particularly in relation to events and circumstances that can threaten the collective honor of the tribe.

Honor is closely related to notions of duty (*erk*). A Kurd has a duty to defend the honor of the tribe, women's chastity, and rights to property and land. If tribesmen adhere to the code of honor and defend their honor when it is threatened, tribal cohesion is reinforced. If norms are neglected, or if men fail to protect their own honor or that of the tribe, they will suffer loss of honor (*bê hisyet bûn*). In such cases, the tribe suffers a loss of credibility to outsiders. If an individual Kurd acts contrary to common ideology, he will be labeled 'without honor' (*bê averû*), and shame (*sherm*) will be ascribed to his entire tribe. Depending on the nature of the actual incident, such situations may have lethal outcomes.

Loss of honor can have various causes. If the event that leads to loss of honor is related to land or to women, consequences may be disastrous to individual men and women as well as to the tribe collectively. Reactions are directed against those who have caused the shame, in some instances also against innocent victims who have brought shame on the tribe by the very fact that they were molested. Women may lose honor by neglect of their husbands and children, by adultery, or by being raped. Reactions to such shame are verbal abuse and physical punishment. In extreme cases young women have been killed in order to restore the honor of the family or of the tribe (Keskin 1999). Sometimes, violations of honor have been used as a pretext to get rid of an unwanted wife. Morgan (2000) has documented that thousands of women have been killed in the name of honor in Southern Kurdistan. Irrespective of the causes, women are affected particularly hard by violations of honor. Even if a woman survives charges of loss of honor, she may be ostracized from the family and the clan and endure the heavy psychological pain that goes with such exclusion.

6.6 Kurdish narratives

A narrative differs from other forms of communication in having a clearly defined beginning and ending. It may contain various complicating elements that are given a final solution. An important aspect of the narrative is the fact that it often combines experiences and events from different spheres of life. Researchers who work on narrativity are fully aware that the relationship between narrative and experience is not static. The narrative is rarely a mere reflexion of people's concrete experiences, but must rather be seen as part of a process whereby experience is transformed into narratives which again exert influence upon future experiences, etc. (Drakos 2000:71). Below, I shall make use of the narrative in order to illuminate various aspects of the Kurdish code of honor as it emerges in a concrete feud between two tribes.

Oral tradition has a central place in Kurdish culture, due to its social function, as well as to the fact that many Kurds can hardly read themselves. Kurdish poetry has primarily been oral throughout the centuries. Poets found an audience at the courts of powerful tribal chiefs and in local coffee-houses in towns and villages. The ability to adapt the story and the form in which it is told to the expectations of the audience is a general trait of oral traditions (Tordarson 1985:6). Stories and poetry were given a popular form in the coffee-houses, while the courts expected a more refined twist.

In addition to more or less professional poetry, Kurds also have a folk tradition of relating real events and histories. Folk narratives are gradually given shape through the dialogue between storyteller and listeners, where all parties bring their interpretations into the stories. Themes are frequently taken from the lives of various tribes. Since Kurdistan is composed of tribal territories, a recurrent theme is honor and revenge related to tribal territoriality. There are numerous stories about peaceful neighborliness and friendship between tribes, but there are also stories about long-lasting feuds and blood revenge. Stories about feuds are highly moralistic, in the manner that families who act according to the code of honor are evaluated in positive terms, while families who show a relaxed attitude towards honor are frowned upon.

6.7 The conflict – a popular narrative theme

In the following pages, I shall write the history of two neighboring Kurdish tribes who inflict worries, grief, and damage on each other through what seems to be an endless feud. The actual event that triggers the feud happens when the herds of the one tribe pass through the territory of their neighbors, but the feud is not initiated until the neighbors interpret the incident. The story re-presents a real feud (*sherî*) between two wealthy tribes. For this reason, real dates and names of persons and places are avoided. The story is presented as a continuous series of events, even if there were long periods between the various attacks on one another.

The genesis of the conflict occurred some time in the 1890s. For years, the two tribes had been on friendly terms with each other. They exchanged goods and animals, used the same bazaars and coffee-houses in the nearby town, and shared the same water source – the wide and clean river that separated the two territories. Sharing of water sources is a traditional index of close friendship and trust in Kurdistan. Accordingly, it is difficult to understand how a longstanding friendship ended in a bitter feud and why no members of the tribes ever managed to settle it. It is still not settled after 110 years!

The tribes share a common origin, history, language, and culture. The people involved were all Kurds who had endured the same historical traumas. External powers have always tried to impose a divide-and-rule policy in order to control them, and mostly they have succeeded. It is therefore relevant to wonder why the Kurds have never learnt from history and united in resistance against intruders instead of fighting among themselves. Almost every Kurdish family knows the bitter experience and suffering of feuding, either directly through their own actions, or as an inheritance handed down to them over the generations. The disastrous events that generally characterize such feuds affect the entire tribe and leave deep wounds. They initiate a vicious historical circle from which it seems almost impossible to escape. The feud may have deep roots that spread effects far beyond the epicenter – even to diaspora communities in Europe and elsewhere.

Feuds can develop in many ways, even as a result of gossip. The initiating event may be a trifle. Retaliation may however be tougher than the initial wrong-doing, thus setting off a spiral of escalating violence. Some feuds are so far removed from their initial causes that tribesmen no longer recall them. But even if the cause is forgotten, the tribes continue their verbal and physical attacks on each other. Viewed from the outside such feuds can appear absurd, but those involved have to follow the logic of the honor code irrespective of their own valuations.

6.8 The feud

The territories (*cih*) of the two tribes, hereafter called A and B, are adjacent to each other. They are divided by the river which is bordered by fertile plains on either side. From time immemorial the two tribes have shared the river and the valley lands. In Kurdistan generally, territorial claims were negotiated by the tribes and agreement was either formalized in written documents or just based on oral consensus. The conflict between tribes A and B arose as a result of allegations of ignoring such agreements.

Both tribes had extensive flocks of sheep. Usually, it did not pose a problem to keep the flocks within the territorial limits of the owners. Still it happened one day that a few sheep of tribe A came over to the pastures of tribe B. When the sheep were discovered by the B people, the latter slaughtered them and carried them back to the land where they belonged. The B people perceived the incident as an improper trespass over the territorial border. From this violation of land rights suspicion arose as to the real intentions of tribe A. Did they have secret expansionist plans? Tribe B could not avoid suspecting tribe A of intending the dreaded message that the property of B was no longer inviolable.

Kurds are very conscious of the close relationship between property rights and honor. It was therefore an obvious response to perceive the sheep trespass as provocative. The suspected meta-message of tribe A was: 'we have the power to penetrate your borders'. Tribe B had two options: either they could contact A and try to elicit their real intentions, or they could retaliate by sending a similar message to A. Tribe B chose the latter option. Their chief perceived of the sheep incident as a hostile act and decided to burn the hay of tribe A in return. Such an act would have devastating effects on tribe A since a sufficient supply of hay is essential for animal survival through the winter, which in Kurdistan can be long and tough. Being left without hay, the tribe may be forced to sell animals when prices are low, which will in turn diminish their material wealth as well as their political influence. Fear of fires is widespread among Kurdish farmers, and great precautions are taken to protect hay against natural fires and hostile arsonists.

When a hostile act is followed by revenge, the tribes involved are caught in a spiral of acts and counter-acts from which it is very difficult to escape. Both parties live in constant fear of when and how revenge will strike next time; thus a psychological dimension is added to the physical damage.

Tribe B succeeded in burning the hay of tribe A. If the A people wished to avenge the arson, they would have to find a way of hitting B which was different from the damage they had incurred themselves. The degree of cruelty in the revenge must be correlated to the wrongdoing suffered by the avenger, or preferably slightly harsher. If revenge is not sought, the tribe who is willing to forget an offence stands the chance of being labeled 'afraid' and 'cowards'. In such cases the influence and social rank of the offender will increase. Tribe A therefore decided to show force by acting as fast as possible in the hope of putting an end to the provocations from B. Tribe A eventually demonstrated its power by killing all the kid goats of tribe B.

The spiral of tribal feuding is now firmly established. No effort is made to end it. On the contrary, much energy and creative thinking is invested in planning the next act of revenge. Tribe B does not hesitate long. The most influential men of the tribe meet for a brief deliberation and a decision is reached. The dogs of tribe A are the next target.

The people of tribe B slaughter one of their sheep and add poison to the meat. On a rainy night they succeed in enticing the enemy's dogs to the bait, and they all fall sick and die. The revenge takes tribe A by surprise and is effective. At this point in the feud tribe A cannot imagine how the people of B were able to penetrate their territory right up to the settlements. The message is plain: the enemy has demonstrated their ability to eliminate their innermost security system, namely, the warnings of their dogs. Dogs are vital on any Kurdish farm since they raise the alarm if predators or human intruders come too close to the homesteads. When a tribe loses its most able-bodied watchdogs this security is shattered, and it can hardly be substituted by human efforts. A Kurdish proverb says 'the enemy never sleeps'. A person who is involved in feuding should be on the alert day and night, for it is the art of feuding to strike when and where the other least expects it. If tribe A has the power to approach close enough to kill the dogs, they are also capable of killing human members of tribe B. After the killing of the dogs tribe B lived in constant anguish, suspecting all and everything that moved in their vicinity of evil intentions. But even if fear prevailed throughout the tribe, the next step in the feud was carefully planned.

During the early phase of the feud, actions and counter-actions were frequent. As the hostility (*dîsmuntî*) developed into a full tribal feud the time intervals between each reprisal become longer, but the nature of the acts became more serious. Sometimes ten years passed without any action, but both tribes knew that the next move would come sooner or later. The long intervals did not mean that people had forgotten and that peace had been restored. Feuding tribes continuously speculate on possible ways to hit the enemy. They are always on the alert, trying to be ahead of events.

Revenge calls for thorough planning no matter how long it takes until it is executed. The tribe knows very well that the enemy is also planning their next move. In order to succeed with their next revenge tribe A therefore had to think strategically. They surveyed the pattern of movement of tribe B, looked for vulnerable situations, considered the best way of attack, and identified possible constraints that might pose an obstacle to the action.

The river that divides the territory of the two tribes establishes a distance between them, but also a kind of proximity. The settlements of tribe B were located closer to he river than the A village. The proximity to the river afforded tribe B a peculiar defensive advantage. The river was inhabited by swans, which would scream if anybody came too close to them. Thanks to the swans, tribe B was warned when anyone tried to cross the river. Tribe B has an intimate knowledge of the behavior of the swans and their preferred part of the river. The tribal leaders have forbidden all hunting of the swans, and refer to ancient beliefs that to kill the swans would infuriate dangerous spirits who may lead the tribe into various kinds of catastrophes. Swans have been perceived as holy creatures for centuries, and they often occur in poetry, especially in love poems. The beauty and elegance of swans is a popular metaphor for female beauty, and their song is associated with the melodious voice of attractive women. The elevated mythical position of swans is expressed in the proverb 'the enemy may be false, but a swan never lies'. Thus, a warning by the swans is a certain index that someone has come too close to them.

The swans have become a serious obstacle to the revenge strategy of tribe A. They cannot reach enemy territory without the swans alerting the inhabitants. They decide to chase the swans away and debate various ways of doing so. First, they try to poison the river. Much time and money is used on this strategy, but the swans remain in their habitat. Nonetheless the people of tribe A are still convinced that they could gain easy access to enemy territory and thereby win advantage in the feud if only they could get rid of the swans. They just have to find a way to put an end to their treacherous song. They try to shoot in the air in a desperate effort to chase them away, but all they achieve by this is to alert tribe B who answers by shooting back. Tribe A feels compelled to give up hitting their enemy through the swans. After this follows a period of relative peace, both parties waiting for the level of alert to be relaxed.

There are certain rules pertaining to the feud that are taken seriously by both parties. The rules must be obeyed and the coded messages must be understood immediately. If not, tribal members may act impulsively and give the enemy just what they want. Feuding tribes use public space outside their own domain in a deliberate way, so as to avoid chance encounters with the enemy. Thus, the pattern of spatial mobility is delimited by the movements of the opposing party. The town with its coffee-houses and bazaars is a meeting place for the surrounding rural population. Cafés buzz with gossip and the exchange of news between friends from different villages who meet there, and on a lucky day the tribal leader himself (*serok eshîr*) may be consulted on a particular issue over a glass of coffee. Each tribe has its own regular café in town which is operated by a trusted person who also prepares the food. Sticking to one trusted café reduces the chances of food poisoning by the enemy. Killing by poisoning is a recurrent strategy of the feud, therefore it is vital to control the preparation of food and drink whenever a person has to eat outside his territory. Regular customers must also trust that the café host does not inform the enemy of their visits to the town and their habitual routines of movement there.

A long time lapses without any further events in the A versus B feud. Tribe A has a plan, but they keep silent and wait for the right moment to strike. One day a young male member of tribe A travels to town with a photo of a young girl from tribe B. He shows the photo to friends and relatives and tells that the girl has fallen in love with him and given him the photo herself. The strategy has the expected effect. Rumors about the illegitimate romance are soon spread to all villages. Since tribe A did not succeed in striking the property of B directly, they challenge the honor of B by broadcasting doubts about the chastity of B women.

The behavior of women is intimately related to tribal honor. When a photo of a tribal woman has fallen into the possession of the enemy, it implies a serious attack on their common stock of honor and can, if not avenged, have grave consequences for the social position of the tribe. A challenge to tribal honor like this one is especially threatening to the woman in question. Even if the intention was to strike the honor of the tribe and not primarily the young woman, she is the one to suffer most. In this case the woman was just a medium – a victim of a long-lasting feud. She has most probably never met the young man who carries her photo, she may not even know who he is. But still she must struggle to convince others that the photo was not handed over by her. The young girl portrayed on the photo was seriously affected by the rumors both within the tribe as well as outside it. The stream of rumors and gossip prevented her and other members of tribe B from visiting town in fear of humiliating laughter. The rumors were nourished by the fact that no one in tribe B could give a credible explanation of how the photo fell into the hands of tribe A. Suspicions were also raised among members within tribe B, which posed a serious threat to the integrity of the tribe.

In order to escape the impending danger of external disgrace and internal fragmentation, tribe B has to unite against tribe A. The first step is to identify the man who has the photo of the girl. Subsequently, they must map his habitual movements – the frequency of his visits to town, with whom he comes, where he goes, and which cafés he frequents. Once this survey has been carried out, the actual planning of the retaliation can begin. A united tribe B agrees that the man must die. In this way the feud enters a new and dangerous phase. The conflict has evolved from a manageable level where the mediation of a third party might have ended it, into a lethal feud that includes the call for blood revenge (*tola xûne*). The fact that tribe A possesses a photo of a B woman means that the reputation of the woman is ruined and she will remain unclean forever. Since it will not be possible to have her properly married, she will be a burden to her family as long as she lives. The young woman is socially dead. There is no way she can restore her reputation herself. The photo incident amounts to social murder and can only be properly avenged by killing a member of the other side.

The offended tribe mobilizes all its resources and contacts. By offering a generous commission to a secret informant, they come to know that a company of tribe A including the young culprit will pay a visit to town in a few days. The habitual movements of tribe A in town have already been mapped. The B people know that they tend to visit a certain coffee-house close to a vegetable market. In order to get close to the enemy, they let one of their menfolk act as a vegetable dealer outside the café. The plan is that he will shoot the culprit when he passes by. Only through blood revenge can tribe B restore the honor that is violated for as long as tribe A has possession of the photo.

Every day the bogus vegetable dealer takes up his position outside the café. The loaded gun is kept at the ready under his cart. If the assassin is lucky, he will also hit other members of the culprit's company. He is frightened, but also proud of having been chosen to execute the mission of honor.

After several days of waiting the targeted young man and several relatives are observed on their way to town. As they pass through the market, the fake vegetable dealer produces his gun and fires several shots. The main target of the operation dies immediately, and so does one of his mates. A third man is lightly injured. For the first time since the conflict started, retaliation has taken the form of manslaughter. The infamous incident of the photo has been thoroughly avenged. Whatever the consequences of the heinous act, tribe B has managed to demonstrate power against tribe A. If revenge had not been taken, tribe A would have maintained the upper hand in the conflict and thereby posed a constant threat to the social position and indeed the very existence of tribe B.

A century later, the two tribes are still feuding. They have continuously tried their best to disgrace each other over a period of 110 years. Innumerable attacks have been directed each way, ranging from minor irritants to grave violence and manslaughter. Many children have had to grow up without a father due to the ongoing feud. Generation after generation of men have been compelled to take part in the feud. Older generations have expected the younger ones to hate as passionately as they did, even if there existed no personal antagonisms any more.

6.9 Peace

From the 1970s onwards, several members of the two tribes migrated abroad to work or to get education. Two young men, one from each tribe, were enrolled at European universities at the same time without knowing about each other. At some point in the late 1990s, by which time they had both obtained postgraduate degrees, their paths crossed coincidentally. Both men were active in the same Kurdish party in their country of domicile, and they both dreamed of a liberated Kurdistan.

During the Gulf War in 1992, thousands of Kurds were forced to leave their homelands and fled to neighboring countries. In an effort to obtain international support for the refugees, the Kurdish party in question organized a conference in a

European city. Eager to support their unfortunate ethnic brothers and sisters, our two young men come to the conference. But during the presentation of the delegates they are utterly shocked. Neither of them was prepared for this kind of meeting. For the first time in more than a century, members of the two tribes sit at the same table. They have never before been so close to the hostile other. Situations like this are generally suspected to be possible traps, carefully planned by the other part. But nothing happens. Instead of avoiding each other, the two men are involuntarily attracted to each other. Apprehension and curiosity struggle for dominance, and a peculiar relation arises between them. They both acknowledge that for the first time in a century members of their tribes are brought together by a cause that is beyond their mutual hostility. The ancient tribal feud is preposterous when seen in relation to the suffering of the Kurdish refugees, which was on the agenda at the London meeting. The time had come to resist the age-old internal rivalry and feuding among Kurdish tribes and unite against external enemies.

In an effort at reconciliation, the young man from tribe A invites his party colleague from tribe B to stay with him for as long as the conference lasts. For a moment, the B man wonders about the real intention of such hospitality. A century of gruesome conflict leaves him frightened and skeptical. He hesitates, but accepts at last. The following night he stays awake expecting the worst. In the early hours he falls asleep, and wakes up a couple of hours later to the beloved smells of tea and Kurdish bread. He gets up and is met with the usual Kurdish hospitality and respect that he so appreciates from his home country. By means of the morning meal the host intends to end a long hostility (*dîsmuntî*) of which the two men have never really been a part; and without the presence of other tribe members the two men initiate their own cautious peace process. Hopefully, the peace will in due course embrace the entire tribes. But a similarly probable outcome is that the two young expatriates can never undertake an honorable return to Kurdistan since they may be thought of as renegades and traitors to tribal solidarity. Both men are aware of the fatal consequences their dawning friendship may have in their home area, but they are willing to take the risk in the hope of overcoming the never-ending and senseless feud, in order to unite forces against other and more serious threats.

6.10 Conclusion

On the one hand tribal structure has helped perpetuate Kurdish traditions, language, and identity; but on the other hand, it has proved an insurmountable obstacle to a wider national unity, and perhaps even to state formation. The interests of the individual tribe have always taken precedence over the common interests of the Kurdish people as such. Non-Kurdish political powers and organizations have exploited internal tribal rivalry to prevent the establishment of an independent Kurdish state.

Kurdish tribes do have the aspiration to establish broad alliances against external threats, but these efforts have more often than not been thwarted by internal fighting, in which honor and revenge have been the overriding issue. In this manner, it is possible to claim that there is a direct link between practices of honor and the present impasse as far as the Kurdish nation is concerned.

Tribal conflicts are more or less serious, depending on the issue at stake. Violent feuds generally develop out of smaller offences in terms of an escalating series of actions and counter-actions, until the level of attacks on property and humans is reached. Violations of women's chastity are a particularly effective way of devaluing an enemy's honor. Violations like abduction or rape are primarily committed in order to strike the enemy tribe; the abused woman is just an unfortunate victim in the power struggle that is primarily a men's game. Blood revenge becomes a valid response when the previous action amounts to homicide. It does not have to be an actual killing though. An attack on female chastity amounts to homicide since the offended woman remains unclean for the rest of her life and is thus perceived to be socially dead. In such cases the account of losses is settled even by a counter-killing. The account is brought out of balance again if the other tribe retaliates. In the final analysis the struggle over honor is an epiphenomenon of the demonstration of power, as discussed in the introduction to this book (Aase). The tribe who stands erect and is able to hit its enemies hard and mercilessly, is the one with power (*qawet*) and which is feared by other tribes. No one dares to fool around with the members of tribes that have honorable – that is, powerful – reputations.

In one significant respect, therefore, honor in the Kurdish context means to have the power to inflict a cruel revenge on any wrongdoer. Honor thus functions as a kind of protective shield, a deterrence that minimizes the chances of being involved in future feuds.

6.11 Epilogue

The future fate of the two men who met in Europe recently is obscure. Most probably, they will carefully suggest to their tribal co-members at home that mediation should be tried in order to achieve a peaceful solution to the century-old feud. Mediation between feuding tribes was institutionalized in Kurdistan a long time ago. The Kurdish word for mediation is *navbeynkari*. According to the Kurdish political scientist Abdollah Hejab mediation is applied in minor conflicts between neighbors as well as in comprehensive tribal rivalry. Tribal elders, mullahs, women, and, more recently, political parties, may act as mediators. The actual status of the chosen mediators depends on the conflict in question and the status of the parties involved. As a general rule the mediator must be of high social rank, he must enjoy a reputation of being honest and impartial, or he must be a particularly powerful person. Most mediation in minor family disputes is undertaken by elders; tribal leaders take care of prestigious conflicts that involve honor; and mullahs and religious leaders assist in matters where interpretation of the law (Shariat) is of paramount importance. The dividend to the mediator is increased symbolic capital, since a successful mediator is perceived to be of higher social rank than the contesting parties. Interestingly, women may mediate in conflicts that are too difficult for men to handle. During war-like conditions between tribes or clans, women sometimes go between and stop ongoing battles. A proverb says that 'when women go between fighting parties, even blood revenge may be forgiven'.

Mediation has a high rate of success. The reason why most mediated conflicts are settled may be found in the fact that few persons accept the role of mediator unless the involved parties reveal a sincere desire for reconciliation. Formal mediation is usually preceded by unofficial communication between the parties, mostly through a third person. As we have seen in the case above, initial talks of reconciliation were undertaken recently by members of the feuding tribes themselves in London. It is, however, questionable whether such direct contact could have been established in Kurdistan. Thus, it is to be hoped that the unfortunate diasporic situation of Kurdish tribes will at least have the positive effect of moderating the feud.

References

Akman, H. (1988), *Familien i endring. En etnologisk undersøkelse blant vietnamesiske flyktninger i Bergen.* Forlaget Folkekultur, Bergen

Akman, H. (1994), *Landflyktighet.* Forlaget Migrasjonslitteratur, Bergen

Borzaslan, M.E. (1990), *Serefname.* Stockholm

Dresch, P. (1993), *Tribes, government, and Yemen.* Oxford University Press, Oxford

Keskin, E. (2000), *Sexual violence: perpetrated by the state. A Documentation of Victimstories*, Istanbul

Kreyenbroek, P.G. (1990), 'Kurdish identity and the language question' in *Kurdistan in search of Ethnic Identity.* Papers on Ethnicity and Ethnic Identity (1), University of Utrecht, Department of Oriental studies, Utrecht 1990

McDowell, D. (1989), *The Kurds.* 2nd rev. edition. London: Minority Rights Group

Morgan, D. (2000), 'Honour killings in Iraqi-Kurdistan' in *Kurdistan Report No 30.* London

Rugkåsa, M. (1996), *Leve Kurdistan.* (Long live Hurdistan) M.Phil. Thesis, Institute and Museum for Anthropology, University of Oslo

Thordarson, F. (1985), 'Kurdisk litteratur – noen glimt' in *Kurdistan- nytt,* Oslo

Utas, B. (1985), 'Kurdiske dialekter' in *Kurdistan- nytt*, Oslo

Uzun, M. (1985), 'Kurdisk prosa' in *Kurdistan-nytt*, Oslo

White, P.J. (2000), *Primitive Rebels or Revolutionary Modernizers? The Kurdish National Movement in Turkey.* Zed Books, London and New York

Chapter 7

Kampung Revenge: Crime, State, and Neighbourhood Retaliation in Java

Eldar Bråten

Judging from newspaper reports, robbery is an extremely risky undertaking in Java, at least those infringements that are directed at local neighbourhoods. Few situations seem more likely to result in anger, murder and mutilation than the capture of a thief red-handed, or even of one merely suspected of theft. The only people ever likely to be as unfortunate, it seems, are the agents of traffic accidents, again especially when the accidents take place in or close to neighbourhoods. Newspaper reports and widely circulated oral narratives tell of perpetrators, typically discovered by perceptive neighbours, being run down by a handful of resolute chasers, and then killed and mutilated by a concerted neighbourhood mob. The ways in which the violence is carried out vary, but the destruction of the body appears to be an especially prominent feature of such narratives. The reading of signs of violence on the body is, as James Siegel has emphasised (1986, 1998), a major fascination in people's experience of crime. It is not so much the sociology of violence that is of concern, he argues, i.e. the identities of perpetrators and victims or the causes of action, as the very effects of violence, how violence marks the dead body.

One cannot deny that acts of murder and mutilation are crucial to such narratives and that the facts of mutilation often arouse interest. It does seem appropriate to read molested bodies as very tangible evidence of the force of violence. This article will however argue that stories about thieves and their destruction also make a series of other points. Reading such narratives for the finer details of their explication, as well as in terms of what they seem to take for granted, reveals preconditions, consequences and depths in the facts about murder and mutilation. I shall argue that we discover systems of meaning that illuminate the sociology of neighbourhood, the precariousness of community relations, and the encroachment of the state. My contention is that this wider context needs to be understood if we are to grasp the immense ferocity that confronts Javanese thieves caught in the act. We are dealing with a force of revenge that is fairly uncommon in other aspects of Javanese life, and the challenge is to bring out some of the deeper meaning that informs these horrendous acts. What are the 'in-feelings' of community and the structures of honour that can explain the viciousness of such revenge?

Let us approach this question through one particular narrative, an account of a robbery that took place in Batasan in 1985. Batasan is in many ways a rather typical wet-rice cultivating village in North Central Java. Although this was my fieldwork village at the time, I was not at the scene when the thieves attacked and were dealt with. A few weeks later, however, people could relate the following incident:[1]

> One early afternoon – in full day-light – three strangers on a motorbike parked in a neighbourhood close to the centre of Batasan, just outside the home of a prominent local landowner. Two of them rushed into the house, held the resident captive with a sickle around his neck, and ransacked his home while the third stood guard by the bike. The intrusion did not escape the notice of perceptive neighbours, however, and before the two robbers were finished inside, the third was already overpowered, and the bike had been taken away. Realising that their escape vehicle was gone, the other two took to their feet and initially managed to put some distance between themselves and their pursuers. One turned to the right at the nearest intersection thus heading out of the village, while the other chose the wrong direction, running right into the thick of village community. Tellingly, he suddenly found himself stranded in the very centre of Batasan, at the main intersection. Quite by chance, the village secretary, the *carik*, was also there, standing on the porch of his house just beside the main road. With a considerable crowd now rapidly approaching from behind, the thief desperately shouted for directions, but the *carik* declined to answer. Instead he promptly invited the man into his house for a cup of tea! The thief accepted this temporary safe haven, and a growing crowd outside respected the privacy of the *carik*'s house, but the ensuing standstill also allowed for a consolidation of positions. People now had sufficient time to go home to arm themselves, whereas the *carik* had reasons to pursue a different strategy: he wanted to call in the police. Ingeniously, he let his adolescent daughter out the back door. Apparently a young woman out to do shopping, she sneaked through a neighbouring village only to take a minibus to the nearest police station. Accompanied by two officers she later returned through the dense bushes in the *carik*'s back yard, and the circumstances changed.
>
> Agents of the state were now on the scene. Ideally, the thief would thus be taken into police custody, and ought to be removed from the local community altogether. But the crowd wanted it otherwise. Armed with knives and sickles and overcome by an immense fury, they effectively blocked all escape routes. The police officers were now trapped as much as the thief, and the only way out was through a confrontation with the local community. This is what ultimately happened, after a tense and prolonged standoff: taking the thief between them, the two officers tried to force their way through the front yard. But the strategy was futile. The thief was wrestled free from the police, the police officers were themselves knocked to the ground in the ensuing battle, and the theft was avenged in the prototypical manner: not only was the thief put to death, but his chest was cut wide open – and in the subsequent narrations of the event, this disfigurement was given major emphasis.

[1] This and two other Batasan incidents are described in Bråten, in press.

Before attempting an analysis, it is necessary to insist on methodological caution in dealing with such accounts. Although dramatic and no doubt memorable for eyewitnesses and participants, the time involved in events such as the discovery, pursuit, killing and disposal of thieves and other violators of local honour is very brief. Little of what happens in such circumstances enters the historical record as objective fact. With the passing of time, indeed from the very first recollection, the event is at the mercy of individual and collective memory and the transformative power thereof. From the somewhat sensational tone of the accounts related in Batasan, one senses that the case has already moved into the space of narrative rather than fact. The events as such are developed, embellished and modified in response to the need to make the story both significant and signifying. Once the immediate impressions of the chase, the sweat, blows, blood, murder and the police have faded, the need arises to make sense of what has happened. At the time of narration the Batasan story was not yet entirely free to develop its own meaning in this way, since people still feared how the police would react. Knocking down two police officers was hardly a trivial matter, and people chose to stand united against the possible response: each and everyone would come forward to claim responsibility for the murder. It didn't take long, however, for the fear of possible police investigations or retaliations to die out, and freed from the need to attend to the potential repercussions, the events could develop into a full-blown story. As far as honour and revenge are concerned, and the social units that cultivate their discourses, narratives serve to corroborate moralities: they confirm that, in the final analysis, the actions constituted the appropriate way to deal with the matter.

The methodological point to remember is that among all the stories to be gleaned from the newspapers, the gossip mill and from a handful of scientific observers, very few have actually been witnessed firsthand, even if all of them are narrated. It cannot be denied that neighbourhood retaliations are real enough; intruders, deliberate and innocent, get lynched in apparently substantial numbers. However, the power to ascribe meaning to these incidents rests mainly in the hands of the narrators, not with the historical facts. As analysts it is thus the spin given to stories that becomes our main occupation. Since firsthand observations of such cases are rare or non-existent, we have to deal mostly with narratives. The sensationalism of personal accounts of a chase and murder such as the one in Batasan is somewhat different but similar in spirit to the more factual, but no less sensational, accounts of neighbourhood revenge printed in the metropolitan press (Siegel 1998). They are but two products of the same transformative mechanism, which turns acts of violence into messages of 'violence', acts of honour and revenge into explorations of 'honour' and 'revenge'.

Although we might wish for a better vantage point for the (objective) study of violence, it is crucial to remember that honour and revenge move in a space of meaning. Again, the forces of honour and revenge do leave personal, social and material realities altered, but their operation is nevertheless founded on the specifics of 'honour' and 'revenge', i.e. on the meaning and import of the moralities that inform their working. Nothing of the drama in Batasan can be deduced, simply and squarely, from the structural positions of the village or its occupants. The acts and their narrations gain their import from the meanings they are accorded in and through their performance; even the savageness of murder and mutilation is embedded in 'webs of meaning' (Geertz 1973) that provide direction and interpretation. However, although heavily loaded with meaning, such accounts are not entirely free-floating and arbitrary. If they are 'fantasy', they certainly constitute a very informed type of fantasy, reflecting not so much the factual shape of events as their social embedding, the social space from which they acquire import. They speak of real concerns and the premises of real action. Whether sensationalist or moralising in tone, or styled according to some other narrative genre, it is not phantasms but real communities and moralities that are of concern.

Our methodological note of caution should therefore not deter us from taking narrations seriously. Although our understanding of honour and revenge in Java would no doubt benefit from more and better firsthand accounts, it would be erroneous to assume that stories of violent events, no matter how sensational, are worthless. They put us in touch with the very core of existential concerns and the social and cultural realities from which these concerns spring.

Another crucial question, however, concerns the extent to which such accounts are in fact integral to the social world from which they spring, the extent to which they not only comment on but also influence society, or to which they negotiate realities as much as reflect them. It is, I believe, in this respect that analysis of media reports differs from analysis of community narration. James Siegel has recently argued that the metropolitan press of Jakarta during the Suharto era helped nurture an entirely new criminal type (1998). Whereas violence and crime during Sukarno's rule were largely channelled within nationalistic trajectories, Siegel argues that Suharto's New Order failed to accomplish a similar transformation. The force that previously went into anti-colonial struggle and the building of a nation now ran wild between family and nation. Siegel claims that an entirely new type of criminal emerged within this space, a character of *kriminalitas* that intruded on local worlds in ways quite different from before. Whereas in the past theft and assault were committed by identifiable forces, thereby forming a recognisable pattern, the criminals of *kriminalitas* seemed to come from nowhere in particular. They seemed to burst onto the local scene without an origin, thus in a sense also escaping the identification and causality of 'ordinary' crime. In Siegel's view, this uncanny, non-recognisable character of *kriminalitas* is what the metropolitan media conveyed, thereby discursively creating a new type of criminal.

Siegel's argument relates directly to our field, since it delineates a set of social roles at the boundaries of state (or between family and nation in Siegel's phrasing), where patterns of violence – and I will argue, honour and revenge – become apparent. It is crucial to remember, however, that the expressions to be found in such media reports are not integral to real lives in the way that Batasan accounts are. Although newspapers also discursively shape notions of honour and revenge, these are not embedded in factual dramas at the same epistemological level. The accounts of a local incident given by the Batasan people are part of the local incident itself in a way that metropolitan discourse cannot be. In providing narrative models, press accounts certainly affect the formation of community and its defence in places like Batasan. It is important to recognise, however, that life in specific places takes shape in response to the way such models are articulated, and that there is no one-to-one correspondence between national or metropolitan discourse and the way local concerns unfold. Therefore, Batasan stories cannot be read *in terms of* a more overarching discourse; *pace* Siegel we do not turn to journalism to understand crime in Java. Rather, it is a most interesting empirical question, whether or not we see any correspondences between media narratives and local accounts of incidents. This critical point applies not only to inferences drawn from the discourse of *Pos Kota*, *Tempo* and other popular Jakarta media, but also to other attempts to understand situated life in terms of wider discursive fields. Also the notions of honour and revenge expressed through official state channels or in Islamic discourse need to be juxtaposed with local stories as they occur in living circumstances in order to trace possible correspondences, discrepancies or even resistance.

Local stories are thus situated and embedded in people's lives in ways that media accounts are not, and as such they may provide us with a somewhat different picture than the one that can be derived from the media. As situated events, both the factual action and the subsequent narrative sense-making reveal something of the way honour and revenge are constructed and actualised in real settings, and this is the methodological approach adopted here. What then does the Batasan story teach us about honour and revenge? What are the relevant groups in question in the Javanese landscape of the 1980s and how do they accomplish their defence? What are the collective social units that seem to be relevant, and what discursive figures of honour and revenge have they developed to maintain their unity?

It is difficult not to see the Batasan story in terms of boundary demarcation. Tracing the narrative shape of events, we see that the thieves and pursuers encounter socio-physical borders that affect the course of action, and we sense the diverse moralities held by the variously positioned actors. What both thieves and pursuers run up against (within the narrative structure) are fairly clear-cut notions of community and its limits: the thieves come up against the neighbourhood/village, the pursuers against the state. This triad of neighbourhood, state and crime, which reflects well-known patterns in both popular and scholarly discourse on violence in Indonesia (e.g. Siegel 1986, 1998, Nordholt 1983, Barker 1999), needs to be accounted for in order to understand the deeper aspects of honour and revenge in the Javanese case.

7.1 Whose honour?

In delineating the relevant collectivities of honour and revenge, we first need to take note of a comparative deficiency. Whereas the family is the core honour-defending unit in many societies, this is not a conspicuous feature of the Javanese situation. This is not to say that there are no breaches of honour between families, nor to deny that such violations sometimes lead to acts of revenge. But the Javanese family seems neither sufficiently corporate nor sufficiently self-centred to count in the formation of major honour collectives. Nothing of the scale or ferocity encountered in the above case seems to arise between families. This is no doubt a consequence of the Javanese principles of descent, and the typical patterns of family incorporation. The Javanese refer primarily to cognatic kinship, and trace rather shallow genealogies in terms of time-depth (H. Geertz 1961:15-30, Jay 1969, Hefner 1990:123). Moreover, families are very seldom incorporated above the level of the nuclear family (Jay 1969: 53, 174, H. Geertz 1961: 32, Hefner 1990: 166-67), and in many cases even the nuclear family dissolves into individual economic units (Brenner 1998).[2] Combined with inheritance practices that dissolve the estate between all the children in each generation, a lack of any significant tradition of marriage exchanges between families, and rather high divorce rates,[3] these patterns produce social units of rather limited importance. In most cases, neither the estate nor the incorporated unit develops beyond a minimal level (e.g. Dewey 1962, Castles 1967, Soedarmono 1987, Nakamura 1983, Abdullah 1994, Cederroth 1995, Brenner 1989, Tambunan 2000). There appear to be exceptions to this pattern in some business environments where there is a need to safeguard accumulated capital, and among nobles who are more concerned about genealogy. The general pattern is however that the family tends to be a rather small entity of limited influence in everyday social life. Both classical and more recent works on Javanese community emphasise the importance of other types of social relations, especially those based on territoriality (C. Geertz 1960:12, Jay 1969:188-238, Jellinek 1991:35, Koentjaraningrat 1985:146-47, Guinness 1986, N. Sullivan 1983:227, 258, J. Sullivan 1992). Over and above the typical nuclear family household we find a range of activities focused on the immediate neighbourhood and on the more encompassing structure of the village, and several of these forms of community are characteristic of both rural and urban settings.[4] There is a distinct emphasis on relations that arise due to physical proximity; both in rural villages and urban settings there are overt demands on individuals and households to engage in and manage neighbourhood relations. Residents of modern middle class suburbs and of the prototypical trade milieus of urban streets (*jalan*) seem less obliged to cultivate relations determined by physical proximity, but most Javanese in one way or another need to pay attention to neighbours. It is also common to cultivate neighbourhood relations in kinship idioms (Hefner 1985:79-81, Jay 1969:292, H. Geertz 1961:18).

Neighbourhood relations extend outward from any single household to delineate a series of fields of solidarity in the immediate surroundings. These fields are to some extent shaped by modern administrative boundaries and partly with

---

[2] According to the recent economic census of 1996 as much as 61.7 % of all business ventures in Java are single-person establishments (Badan Pusat Statistik 2000:85 and 87, Table C2).

[3] Divorce rates as high as 52% have been reported in certain areas (H. Geertz 1961: 69), but the incidence of divorce appears to be significantly lower in more staunchly Islamic contexts (H. Nakamura 1983:3, Alexander 1987: 20, Hefner 1990: 170).

[4] It is difficult to be entirely satisfied with this picture, however. Although neighbourhood does seem to take precedence over family in many respects, the current literature largely fails to account for some of the aspects of life that are in fact managed by the family. There is a notorious lack of newer firsthand, empirical studies concerned with upbringing, gendering and other formative processes of situated family life. To a large extent we still_rely on Hildred Geertz' eminent study from the mid-1950s (1961, but see Smith-Hefner 1988, 1989). A more focused reseach strategy might very well reveal a somewhat different picture. Despite rather fragmented and transient forms, we must assume that also families build and maintain forms of morality concerned with boundaries, infringements and retaliations.

reference to historical patterns of local allegiance. In the prototypical rural case, the village itself appears as the largest unit of such solidarity. Since this often consists of a clearly bounded area of settlement surrounded by rice fields, there is a physical aspect to the demarcation. Within the village, however, neighbourhood units are less clear-cut, and often overlap. There is an official administrative structure of wards (RK) and neighbourhoods (RT), which to some extent shape aspects of community dealings, but in other respects the RK and RT borders may be obscured by identifications in terms of *dusun, dukuh* or *kampung*, the 'natural' units of community as perceived by the inhabitants themselves (Guinness 1986:143).[5] One feature that has often been commented upon is that this sense of a 'natural' neighbourhood community extends well into urban structures as well, delineating rather well-defined local communities even in the larger towns of Java (Guinness 1986, 1989, J. Sullivan 1992, Jellinek 1991).

Whether in terms of administrative structure or traditional allegiances, local community is a rather dense and vivid field of activity. It is burdened with a series of demands on its own social, ritual and also to some extent infrastructural reproduction. With respect to physical maintenance and the upgrading of villages, the modern Indonesian state has partly emulated a system introduced by the Japanese occupation forces during World War II. According to this model, the state and local people are jointly responsible for the upkeep of local community infrastructure, such as roads and minor irrigation canals, the locals often providing the necessary labour force, the state supplying the required material input (Guinness 1989:58-59, Hefner 1990: 71-73). On the ideological level this mode of co-operation, *gotong royong*, has been elevated to an essential trait of local Javanese life and is much celebrated in state discourse as the 'spirit' of progress (Bowen 1986). In material terms it can be argued that local communities are drawn into and accorded responsibilities for state engineered 'development', *pembangungan*. The specific projects subsumed under these programmes are not necessarily locally conceived, and the *gotong royong* schemes are not always pursued with enthusiasm on the part of the local population, especially since the projects often serve the political interests of certain local groups above others (cf. Bråten 1988).

There are other fields of activity, however, where community solidarity is more apparent and to a larger extent driven by local agency. First of all it should be emphasised that neighbours generally spend a lot of time together. People encounter close neighbours when venturing out of their houses, and in most cases, such chance encounters demand a degree of polite chatting. The details of one's comings and goings are exchanged together with formal greetings. The minimal subject in such situations consists of where the person in question has just been and where he or she is heading, or what his or her concerns are. There is a certain expectation that people will pause, at least for a moment, to acknowledge others who are close to them, and although brief, these numerous separate encounters

---

[5] The terminology varies somewhat from place to place. In this article the term *kampung* is used for the 'solidarity unit' emerging in self identification. As will be clear from the discussion, this unit varies from situation to situation as the boundaries of local solidarity collectives are being negotiated.

ritually reinforce a kind of collectivity based on neighbourhood. More conspicuous, and certainly far more time-consuming, is the vivid socialising that takes place in the evenings – in the street, in courtyards and on verandas. In Batasan and many other localities, both rural and urban, the evening is a time for relaxation, recreation and pleasant gossiping (Siegel 1986:56, Hefner 1985:79-81), most often in the company of close neighbours.

Socialising in the sphere of the public neighbourhood appears to have two modes. The one is the very relaxed and amiable mood associated with gossip, sweet tea, snacks (*jajan*), light gambling, and badminton, table tennis and other courtyard sports. The other entails a more official commitment to community and often involves a wider range of neighbours. In everyday life, evening activities often shift between pleasant relaxation and a wide range of more formal activities. There are family rituals and celebrations to which close neighbours are the first to be invited, a variety of ritual and practical events connected to the activities of neighbourhood associations, as well as an occasional stagings of artistic performances, often financed from village coffers and organised in connection with national holidays. The most conspicuous feature of leisure time in many present-day Javanese localities is however the Islamic prayers at sunset and during the evening. People, mostly males, tend to gather in the local prayer houses (*langgar*) as time permits, but usually at least once during the evening, and, depending somewhat on the religious ardour of the locality in question, there might also be other religious events to attend. In Batasan for instance, which is seen as a rather staunch village, there are prayers, discussion groups, religious speeches, and Koran recitation training almost every night.

It is worth emphasising that although Islamic discourse does connect local communities to much larger, translocal fields of activity through its many social arenas, it also allows the formation of localised groups (Bråten 1988, 1999). This was evident in Batasan in the mid-1980s where several neighbourhoods lobbied to acquire their own *langgar*. The gatherings in these prayer houses no doubt activate and reinforce identities that exceed the local community, but at the same time they also provide a space for further neighbourhood formation. Although the religious content of these occasions is taken seriously, their very formality is often circumvented by the highly valued informality that characterises relaxation in the neighbourhood. In practice, at least in Batasan, the groups that gather to pray seldom pray together. Religious matters are very much regarded as an individual issue, and apart from the Friday prayer at the village mosques and occasional recitation sessions, people do not readily submit to collective religious activity. They also seem very reluctant to submit to religious authority, if that submission requires real alterations of personal practices or preferences (Bråten 1988, 1999). The result of this reluctance, or resistance, is that prayer houses and many other arenas and contexts of more recent origin tend to be of secondary importance to commitments closer to home.

It is remarkable to experience the ease with which such formal occasions are overcome. The shift from formal to informal, from ritual to mundane life, is often stunningly abrupt, the formal occasions themselves are often exceedingly brief, and little of the content of the occasion seems to carry over into subsequent communication. They seem in a sense to be occasions out of time, taking place in a distinct realm of experience. This is a behavioural pattern commented on in the anthropological literature on Java (Keeler 1987:154-55), and I have suggested that it may be read as a reluctance to commit oneself to official schemes with clear political implications (Bråten 1988, 1999).

In practical, everyday (evening) life, this concerted but not necessarily conscious or explicit effort to circumvent the power of official ritual creates in fact a sense of local community which takes precedence over other allegiances, whether to state politics or to the *ummat*, or at least its political projects. Javanese people form powerful social ties based on physical proximity and tend to prefer these to the formality of opportunities which external powers offer on the local scene. This adherence to relations of proximity is also evident in the fact that one's place of origin or residence is a primary source of identity, and this can be seen in the rich ideology of neighbourhood morality that forms around these relations. The quintessential term for this moral identity based on neighbourhood is *rukun*, a term that evokes conditions of both 'inexclusivity and cooperative harmony' (Hefner 1990:184, cf. Jay 1969:66, H. Geertz 1961:147-149, C. Geertz 1960:61, Guinness 1986, J. Sullivan 1992:106-108). On the one hand, *rukun* is evident in the inclusive amiability of everyday encounters, in the continual willingness to recognise the social other. On another level, *rukun* also points to the ideal harmony that is supposed to emerge from the wide variety of cooperative efforts that village life displays. In the ritual domain neighbours help out in various ways with household celebrations, and there are also institutions of cooperative work that deal with practical tasks, such as house building and road repairs.

At another level of investigation, however, we certainly find much ambivalence and reluctance also in relations between neighbours. Also neighbourhood rituals are to some extent circumvented or subverted through passivity or non-commitment, and the emphasis on local community should not deceive us into believing that neighbours act as an integrated collectivity. The distinct individualism that is said to mar the business ventures of Javanese families is certainly also a feature of neighbourhood relations (e.g. Brenner 1998, Cederroth 1995:208). Economically speaking, the nuclear family is the prime decision-making unit in most cases, consisting sometimes even of single individuals, and the economic integrity of this small-scale unit is well guarded. Everyday life does entail economic co-operation between neighbours, most often between female representatives of households and most often connected to the staging of family rituals. Although a strong ideology of community and fellow-being surrounds these transactions, there is no reason to assume that they entail the forfeiture of individual resources for the benefit of others. There is normally a carefully calculated reciprocity in such relations (N. Sullivan 1989: 84, 87, J. Sullivan 1992: 76-77, Hefner 1985:222), and the failure to reciprocate creates tensions. The same applies to loans between neighbours, whether they involve money or goods. In Batasan there *are* a few institutions in which individual resources are given over to the community for the benefit of all, but these seem rather insignificant in the total economy. It is for instance common for a given neighbourhood or village to collect money among the inhabitants in order to purchase a set of the plates and cutlery needed for large family celebrations. The justification for this collective effort is to provide the poorest villagers with the means to maintain their ritual life. Another institution that may entail a certain degree of capital accumulation at a collective level is the Javanese variety of ROSCA (Rotating Savings and Credit Associations), the *arisan*. The overall picture, despite the *rukun* ideology, is however that are few joint ventures between neighbours that create enduring collective corporations.

The ideology of *rukun*, often propounded by villagers themselves and certainly a main feature in state discourse on community ideals (cf. Bowen 1986, J. Sullivan 1992), also needs to be challenged on a deeper level. I argue that individuality does not easily give way to collective arrangements on the level of social organisation, and that neighbours only very reluctantly cooperate in shaping larger socio-economic units. It could also be argued that the economic uniformity implied by some versions of the *rukun* ideology gives a rather skewed view of economic structures in most localities. This can even spill over into social science discourse (cf. Geertz 1963), insofar as it is sometimes assumed that Javanese communities are in some profound sense both politically egalitarian and economically undifferentiated. The reality is quite different; Javanese villages are undeniably characterised by powerful structures of authority, often state engineered (Antlöv & Cederroth 1994, see Antlöv 1995:3-7 for a review), by internal class differences (e.g. Hart et al. 1989), and by distinctions of status and prestige (Keeler 1987:148-149, J. Sullivan 1992:72-75). My emphasis on neighbourhood relations should thus not be read as a simplistic or romantic idealisation of local community, although rhetoric on the Javanese side often suggests such views. Neighbours are certainly positioned differently in terms of economic assets and political power, and these differences entail diverse viewpoints and interests, and thus tensions between neighbours. Occasionally it also entails confrontations and conflict.

Nevertheless, the neighbourhood seemed, at least during Suharto's New Order era, the social unit most likely to evoke issues of honour and revenge.[6] The situation in which a collective unit was most likely to assert its identity through violence was that of neighbours acting in defence of community boundaries, as in the case presented above.[7] Despite the fact that most local communities, such as Batasan, are highly differentiated, politically divided, and lack commitment to overarching co-operative projects, it seems to be community honour that is revenged in such incidents. Indeed, Siegel seems to argue that neighbourhood as a principle is in fact founded on violence (1986:49), and that blows administered to thieves in some sense help establish the *kampung* community. This local concern for defence also takes a more mundane form in several practices that aim to deter thieves from attacking the community. The most celebrated form of defence is the institution of the *ronda*, a nightly patrol conducted by male household heads on a

[6] Presently both scholars and authorities are concerned that instances of neighbourhood retaliation seem to be increasing since the fall of Suharto.

[7] Another well-known case of collective violence is found in clashes between gangs from different junior and senior highschools (especially prevalent in Jakarta), and with the fall of Suharto and the re-emergence of political parties, threats of open violence between adherents of different political camps always lurk in the background of reform and democratisation.

rota basis (Barker 1999). In town the physical layout of the neighbourhood also helps discourage thieves, in that entrances to the community are narrow and often guarded by perceptive *ronda* watchmen. Apart from detecting and intercepting possible thieves, one of the most important tasks of these guards, it has been argued (Barker 1999, Siegel 1986), is in fact to keep the common neighbours awake, or at least keep them from sleeping too deeply. They maintain a degree of alertness among neighbours by producing noise throughout the night and throughout the territory defined by the neighbourhood *ronda*. Local security and defence, then, seem to be central ingredients in the formation of community identity.

Moreover, the spontaneity and ferocity of revenge, in narration and probably also in reality, indicate that the intrusion of thieves hits at a very basic concern. One gets the impression that a petty thief threatens to overturn the very conditions of existence, and that this threat appears so overwhelming and immediate that no conscious or reflexive deliberation ever has time to arise. Although the incident in Batasan included the temporary truce of a tea party, which we must assume gave people time for deliberation, reflexivity and consolidation, things often happen much faster. To judge from other reports, thieves are often killed on the run, and it is only in hindsight, it seems, that people come to their senses and attempt to give the event a structure of sense and meaning.

It is worth mentioning our methodological note of caution again: there are of course very few social scientists at the scene when such events take place, and it is often extremely difficult to ascertain the facts afterwards. It seems that the events are too important as meaning-making mediums to be reduced to mere facts. As analysts we are thus required to move in a space of narration, and with shadows of real events. Nevertheless, as I argue, these narratives are highly real and important in their own right, both because they deal with the meanings that drive the acts of honour and revenge, and because they contribute - as tellings and retellings - to the (re)constitution of neighbourhood relations. Unlike newspaper reports on similar events, the stories told by the Batasan people themselves are part and parcel of the meaning and sociality they shape between them.

7.2 Community narrated

So what does the 1985 incident in Batasan tell us about local community? What kind of community is constituted at the narrative point where petty thieves run up against the honour of a neighbourhood?

The diverse fates of the three individual perpetrators are illustrative of the way Batasan people, at least through narrative, choose to mark dimensions of community. The thief who lost his direction (in itself an indication of serious confusion, madness or outright stupidity in Javanese thinking) literally ran into his own death. Not only did he offend the local community, he ended up at its physical centre, utterly confused and surrounded. The treatment he received was both logical and appropriate, people claimed. He dared to stand up against the community, but 'not knowing where north is', he proved quite incapable of carrying through his intention. It was a different matter with the thief who turned right at the intersection. He was chased only to the village border, where people let him flee. 'That was OK', locals claimed; he had certainly learnt a lesson (*kapok*) and would not bother them anymore. He managed to escape, and in a sense the fact that he did so became its own justification: he had proven both that he knew 'where north is' and that he could handle the challenge he offered to the community. He transgressed, but managed to get away with it. The third thief, who was overpowered almost before the drama started, typifies a third ideal response to community solidarity: total surrender. As the story goes, after a brief moment of confusion he chose to submit to the approaching neighbours rather than take flight. Appropriately giving in to the overwhelming force of concerted community action, he apparently dismissed himself from schemes of honour and revenge altogether. The appropriate response to such submission was simply to turn him over to the police, to release him from the grip of the *kampung* community.

Through the narration then, a rather neat and logical account of the nature and value of local community is created - a story that people can at least tell each other about themselves, even if potential thieves refuse to learn from it. As such the story falls into a much broader category of expressions that people use to signify borders between themselves and others (Grønhaug 1975, cf. Barth 1969). On the one hand, the incident becomes a means to demarcate physical, political and social boundaries: the administrative village border beyond which one of the culprits managed to escape, the line of authority between villagers and police, and the line of social propriety that one of the thieves adhered to by surrendering flat on the ground. On the other hand, the narration also addresses the matter thereby enclosed, namely the human world bordered in by the infringement of thieves. Within this physical, political and human 'in'-space whatever existed of inequality, domination, injustice and diversity is suppressed in the narrative in the interest of a rather blank and anonymous, but extremely powerful 'community'. Apart from the crucial exception of the village secretary, who represents both community and the state, no local distinctions are activated in the course of events. Real local distinctions between rich and poor, powerful and weak, old and young, or between those who support Suharto and those who support Islamic groups and parties, are left out of the story; it is a homogenous community that emerges, 'us', against 'the rest'. This is no great surprise of course; the semiotics of boundary creation and maintenance often relies on the distillation of simplistic traits from complex realities.

However, if we study this story as a social event rather than a narrative structure, against the backdrop of local life itself, rather than in light of general and abstract hermeneutics, we again witness the stage being peopled with socially distinct actors. As far as the local community is concerned, it is clear that not everyone took part in the event. No matter how much people may sympathise with the killing, and I have no indication that anyone strongly resented what happened, it is obvious that people contributed quite unequally to its enactment. The story itself does not specify who took part in the chase, and since threat of retaliation from the police discouraged the mention of such information, we must assume that this kind of detail circulated as secret knowledge. At least it was the case that in private, certain people suggested they were somehow more implicated than others. In short, some did chase and kill, others did not. This distinction is implicit in the story and actively concealed in reality, but serves nevertheless to reshuffle neighbours according to parameters of community. In defending their community some applied the force of revenge, others were either too slow, too afraid, too ambivalent, or had other reasons not to be in the frontline. It is not difficult to see how such acts of revenge can play a part in the careers of certain local people, and it is also not too difficult to find cases, in Batasan and elsewhere, where individuals openly take pride in their violent assertiveness when collective moralities are threatened (cf. Bråten in press).

7.3 Gender

It is also obvious that the event serves to distinguish between local collectivities. Not all *categories* of local people took part either. Although we can assume that it may well have been women who discovered the crime, and that they might have provided important information along the route, and although the daughter of the *carik* served as an actual mediator in the events, still it is highly unlikely that women took part in the chase or the killing, even if it is not unthinkable that they were among the crowd outside the *carik*'s office. Judging from everyday experience it goes without saying that the chase and killing took place in the realm of male assertiveness; no sane woman would involve herself in such a pursuit. Although the narrative leaves the positive aspect of women's roles implicit, how they in fact contributed to the event, it is not entirely unreasonable to assume, again judging from daily community experience, that they played a part in moving the action forward. The logical thing to do when a husband or son ran off to join the chase would be to spread the word to other households.

Seen against the implicit understandings of everyday practices, then, the narrative draws on a gender contrast which is never stated, but no less inherent in the course of action. As a narrative it no doubt emphasises an almost instinctive male assertiveness and absolute resolve, but we should not assume that this implies a contrast with passive or subdued women. I believe Javanese everyday experience would rather warrant an interpretation that involves female complicity. In Javanese experience women indeed have powers of agency; they are no less communal actors than men (cf. N. Sullivan 1989, Brenner 1998, Keeler 1990, J. Sullivan 1992:121). They are certainly seen as different from men in their modes of engagement, but they should not be construed as agency-less. The male narrative is not played out against a female blank. The backdrop to male experience is rather the agency and power that women gain through controlling a flow of information back-stage to male events. Women are placed in wide-ranging local networks that are not necessarily gender exclusive, and to a certain degree they acquire knowledge and insights about local conditions that evade their husbands. It is certainly not the case that they live in seclusion, or that they have to make do only with male versions of reality. To some extent the men experience women's agency as both powerful and threatening. In its most harmonic function, it may serve to channel valuable information to the household unit, and in a more challenging form it may effectively undermine a male's authority in the local community through secrecy and betrayals.

There is no indication in the events discussed here that women in one way or another betrayed the community by withholding information, i.e. restraining the chase; I suggest it is implicitly assumed that female agency here functioned at its best, propelling the course of action in the service of the community. Since this female agency functioned properly, there is nothing for the story to comment upon, and the narrative stage is set for the male drama to unfold. At one point, however, the other side of the female coin does emerge. The daughter of the *carik*, relying on her unassuming appearance, sets off on an entirely female pursuit, namely to go shopping, and betrays them all. She sells out the entire community to the police. For reasons I will return to, this is not in fact seen as a real betrayal; understood in the context of state rather than local community, her sell-out is indeed rather appropriate. But even in the context of community, her actions play on moralities that are both understandable and appropriate. What the girl did - on her father's request, we must assume - was to initiate a conflict that threatened to turn the community on its head. Although the solution she (and her father) sought was adverse to the villagers' most immediate demands for revenge, her brave intervention was meant to solve the conflict by putting it in a broader perspective. She took on the role of an intermediary by assuming the full force of her female identity. This, I suggest, is fully in accord with another 'communal' experience, also very much celebrated both in Javanese philosophy and common sense: the ability to refrain from spontaneous emotional action in order to recognise events more soberly in their proper contexts. What makes this case especially interesting is the fact that, contrary to male ideology, it was a young woman who took on the role. Typically, state and male ideologies elevate Javanese *men* to the status of intermediaries and arbiters of community conflict. In the male view, women appear too emotional to be able to dampen conflict or restore sociality. It is implied that women often contribute to social strain through their lack of social sensitivity.

What is inverted in the narrative space of ferocity, murder and mutilation is therefore not so much female characteristics of passivity and ignorance, but rather a series of celebrated *male* characteristics. Javanese daily life abounds in idealistic discourses of male propriety, whether couched in Islamic concepts, derived from elevated tenets of *priyayi* tradition,[8] or implied by the behavioural campaigns of the development-oriented state. To an amazing degree, the average Javanese is concerned with the wider social and cosmic aspects of his behaviour and tends towards rather philosophical reflections on being (Bråten 1995). Ethnography has long been preoccupied with these orientations and has brought out the complex and pervasive theories on self, society and cosmos that emerge in Javanese thinking (e.g. Anderson 1972, C. Geertz 1960, Keeler 1987, Siegel 1986, Pemberton 1994, Sears 1996, Mulder 1978, Beatty 1999, Stange 1984, 1998). The various traditions of knowledge that can be delineated are quite diverse, but the major contenders for truth also seem to converge on a series of core values that are at the very forefront

[8] The tradition of Javanese 'high culture'.

of Javanese idealisations and self-understanding. The value of *rukun* has been mentioned already, pointing to the inclusiveness and mutuality of concerted community efforts. We also find an entire psychology of self-monitoring and self-management very much concerned with the restraint of emotional action. Crucial concepts such as *rasa* (best translated as 'acute sensitivity'), *sabar* (patient), *nrima* (accepting), and *iklas* (emotionally detached) were emphasised in early ethnography (C. Geertz 1960) and are still very much part of Javanese discourse (e.g. Keeler 1987, Bråten 1995, Stange 1984, 1998).[9] At the explicit level of community discourse, the ideal of *rukun* is often seen as closely related to, or even a direct effect of, the self-management accomplished through patience, acceptance and emotional detachment. *Rukun* in a sense manifests the submission of individual opinions, wills and emotions to collective effort through work on the self that requires *sabar*, *nrima* and *iklas*.

It must be emphasised that in everyday neighbourhood life, in Batasan and all over Java, these values are not wholly distorted mystifications of actual practices. There *is* a degree of harmony, or at least functionality, in Javanese community life that accords with the celebrated values of *rukun* (J. Sullivan 1992:71, 81). Women no doubt play a more important role in the creation of this functionality than male ideology might suggest, but it is important to remember that both males and females are generally very much concerned with the demands of community life. People do strive after viable social relations with neighbours and others. Personal engagement is one aspect of this effort, but there are also institutional means by which strain and conflict between self and other can be handled. Respected locals (religious leaders, village officials etc.) often intervene to restore working relationships between antagonists (J. Sullivan 1992:145), and if intervention is of no avail, the last resort is often the well-known Javanese pattern of mutual ignorance. Ignoring the other's presence through eerie glances and related forms of behaviour is naturally a rather strong symbolic statement in a local world where all social encounters demand polite mutual recognition. On the other hand this demonstrates my point: however strained, Javanese neighbours do struggle to maintain a degree of communal functionality (reified as *rukun*) in ordinary life. Where they occur, open challenges, quarrelling, confrontations or violence between neighbours are notable events, occasions where things did not work out the way they were intended. They are occasions where passion (*emosi*) broke through despite all good intentions.

Hence, when men run wild, furiously chasing through alleyways and front yards, beating and hacking a fellow human being to death and beyond, opening his chest and then topping it all with open assaults on the official representatives of the state, it is certainly not an event that accords with ordinary daily behaviour. It contrasts at almost every point with the cherished community values of male propriety: the gingerness of action, the postponement of judgement, the avoidance of conflict, and the beauty and strength of personal composure. Thus if Batasan males were telling themselves an important story, and it was indeed males who were eager to recount these events, it is a story about two modes of male being: a

[9] John Sullivan discusses several related concepts at the basis of *rukun* (1992:71-83).

mode within a community where masculinity is dictated by the idiom of *rukun*, and a mode vis-à-vis the community that justifies all-out revenge. It is less a story about women, I suggest. Nowhere in the account do we hear of males scurrying to defend the females of the community, and it is also hard to see issues of gender, chastity and sexuality playing into the story on a more subtle symbolic level. Gender contrasts, like all other distinctions of village life, serve as a backdrop, but the story as such is played out between and for men - between the furious male force of the community on the one hand and three stereotyped male thieves on the other.

7.4 Age

Looking back at the narrative we also sense another social division running through its events. Not only are women unlikely chasers and killers; not all males took part either. If we trace the narrative shape against the backdrop of ordinary community life, we sense that a whole range of men in Batasan distanced themselves from the action. It goes without saying that the village chief (*lurah*) did not take part in the chase; neither did the other state officials, nor the numerous religious leaders of the village. The heads of wards and neighbourhoods, we must assume, found themselves in awkward positions, being on the one hand embedded in the local space where the infringement took place, on the other hand responsible for the actions of their communities vis-a-vis the state authorities. The issue is the extent to which the state penetrates local communities like Batasan to shape diverse loyalties in the *sociology* of such a chase and murder. In the world of narrative, as we have seen, the boundary runs through the person of the *carik*.

This is not the only dividing line between males, however. It goes without saying that also many older males were unlikely perpetrators. In line with the ideal of a concerted community, there is no indication that the village seniors in any sense distanced themselves from the morality of revenge. However, there is good reason to believe that many of them watched the events from the sidelines, if they ever ventured to the scene. It is likely, from the point of view of everyday life, that the pursuers and killers were adults in their prime, or even more likely, youth. The narrative in fact begins with specific neighbours, adult men, who start taking action, but then male individuality dissolves into a mob that is never again individualised. Nevertheless, judging from other acts of revenge in Batasan (cf. Bråten in press), it is more than likely that adolescent males were in the forefront of the race. Youth energy is not wholly contained by boundaries of community, but is certainly an important operative force in events of retaliation where community is at issue. The capacity to act with agility, physical strength, and the eagerness to build local careers of respectability are factors that turn young males into likely perpetrators. It is also among male youth that the rather uncommon narrative genre of open boasting turns up. Javanese storytelling is generally quite vivid, with frequent physical demonstrations accompanying verbal accounts, although the personal deeds of the narrator are properly referred to in a rather subtle and indirect voice. It is only among those with real power that celebrations of personal achievements are appropriate (Berman 1998:65).

The open boasting of physical prowess among youths also stands in marked contrast to the prevalent patterns of male propriety. It appears inappropriate both in terms of *rukun* submission to collectivity, which erases individual traits, and in terms of the authority structure of the community, which suppresses subordinate signs of power. In a sense boasting stands out with the force of revenge itself, it is indicative of the form of male agency by which brutal killings can be accomplished. It is a sign of assertiveness manifested in daily life. Although violence generally tends to occur in events directed against community, here it threatens to invade the space of everyday life itself. It threatens to collapse the two modes of masculinity discussed into a truly terrifying male agency, doubly individualistic and subversive.

The subtext of the Batasan revenge is therefore extremely powerful: it unleashes violent energies that manage to defend and reinforce boundaries of community, but this successful reinforcement effectively demonstrates where these energies lie, thus threatening to strengthen the mechanisms in which they play a part still further. As a result, local agency threatens to realign as much as preserve established boundaries. Energies, and especially those of male youth, threaten to spill over into other projects and trajectories, giving rise to alternative forms of solidarity to those contained in neighbourhood relations. Turning inwards it may challenge established community orders, turning outwards it may subvert state structures through new forms of collective agency. In either case it also shifts the boundaries of local community.

One example of revenge turning in on the experience from which it derives, is seen in confrontations between local communities. Hostilities between villages do develop, sometimes also between distinct neighbourhoods of the same village, and there are examples of recurring violent clashes, raids, arson and occasional murders. We do not know enough about the sociology of such cases to understand the underlying structural features of antagonism, whether it is based in identifications of locality alone, or in other kinds of allegiances. In Batasan itself, two neighbourhoods were explicitly marked as 'problematic' by the local majority. The one was a group of people who were moved to the village due to a development project nearby, and who were alleged to have affiliations to the disbanded Indonesian Communist Party. The other was a neighbouring *kampung* just beyond the village border. I could not elicit any good reasons for the antagonism to this *kampung*, but in local memory several neighbourhoods in Batasan had been involved in rather severe clashes with the *kampung* a few years prior to my fieldwork. Whatever the sociological realities of the case, in the space of narrativity two features were especially prominent: the clashes took place between male youths, and they continued to be reported, several years later, in a rather boisterous and bragging manner.

Although much more restrained than cases of murder and mutilation, we again sense the force and celebration of male assertiveness and violence in the interest of community, the appropriateness of inverting accustomed norms of propriety when honour is at stake. In this sense, confrontations between local communities do not differ from the prototypical stories of thieves; both situations are characterised by concerted violence in the interest of the local community. The latter primarily explores the boundary of community as a collective unit, whereas the former seeks to demarcate the factual boundaries of – and between – actual communities: where does Batasan end and 'our neighbours' begin? In either case, it appears to be honour based on locality that occasions revenge.

An altogether *different* modality of honour and revenge is opened up in cases where male agency truly turns in on its own community, where the *insiders* become the violators. This I believe to be a real concern in many Javanese localities, where boundaries between the state and community are negotiated. Although male youth has long been construed as 'aggressively egalitarian' (Jay 1969:261, cf. Hefner 1990:210), a new phase in state-community relations was traceable in Batasan in the mid 1980s. At this point, the village was connected to nearby towns and cities by road and public transport, and there occurred a marked shift in occupational patterns from agriculture to 'modern' forms of work, the latter often situated in urban areas. The village was also 'modernised' in many other ways. The most vocal critics of this change were Muslim preachers who feared loosing their moral grip on local youth, but it was also evident in many older people's complaints about 'new ways'. Development (*pembangunan*) certainly also had its supporters on the local scene, but the discourse on youth manners had already assumed a somewhat worried tone: will the new generation manage to withstand the enormous pressure from the modern world? Towards the end of Suharto's regime, such concerns were voiced everywhere in Indonesia, and a central feature of this worry was nothing other than the agency of male youth; how to contain male energies at a time when established structures were being eroded through development, modernisation and westernisation. These moralities are no doubt also concerned with female propriety in fields of family and sexuality, but I would contend that this theme is not especially prominent in the narratives discussed here, neither explicitly nor as a subtext. What the chases and clashes of Batasan evoke is a ferocious male power, here successfully contained in a revenge intended to uphold community honour, but which is potentially subversive to the very structures of community itself through its enormous scope to create other outcomes. One fear is, as mentioned, that these energies may recoil on neighbours themselves.

It is possible to highlight this challenge by way of thieves. Obviously, also thieves reside somewhere; also thieves are someone's neighbours somewhere. In fact, Javanese communities seem to have a long tradition of accommodating criminals under certain preconditions. So long as they represent no nuisance to locals, they are to a certain degree accepted (Guinness 1986). Moreover, local thugs have played roles in organising local security (Barker 1999). Despite their dubious roles and often questionable personal character, they figure at the very boundary between community and outside threats. Whether the persons that take on such roles are also valued as defenders of local honour – i.e. to what extent their roles affect their local prestige – is not entirely clear, but we certainly find rather positive recollections of their role in some narratives. Traversing the boundary between community and its intruders, however, their roles were – and are – highly ambiguous (Siegel 1998:49). They are in a sense walking embodiments of male ferocity, the mode of masculinity that boisterous and bragging local youths only express in untypical situations. In fact they are the very persons that invade the boundaries of other communities, the very persons that other communities are eager to chase and kill. Their local containment is therefore of the utmost importance; it is necessary to prevent both their roles and their energies from being turned against their own communities. In one respect, namely as role models, they threaten to turn ordinary neighbours into emulators of criminality. In another respect, and perhaps more importantly, there is always the threat that their violent energies will be channelled into local conflicts.

It is important to remember, however, that local communities are not alone in their attempts to contain these energies. The space that thieves and thugs traverse is not only delineated by community and transgressors, but is also formed in the engagement between community and the state. This is the last aspect that needs to be accounted for in our attempt to bring out the meaning and import of local honour and revenge.

7.5 State

The state is apparent in the narrative structure in terms of two agencies - in the *carik*'s almost stoic engagement of the desperate thief, and in the assumed reconstitutive legal powers of the police. The narrative makes it clear that neither of these parties wanted to punish through assertive murder; both attempted to rescue the thief into the workings of the state machinery. The *carik* and his family no doubt emerge as the major mediating force between neighbourhood and state on the local scene itself; the police merely enter as a force from outside. As *local* mediators they are in a potentially precarious situation. The family does hold land and has local commitments of various sorts; they are definitely part of the *kampung* and village. On the other hand, they work and function, also in most neighbourhood affairs, as representatives of the state. They are referred to in daily life as Mr. and Ms. *Carik* (*pak carik* and *bu carik*), and they mostly engage their neighbours as bureaucrats, official arbiters and campaigners for state development projects. The *carik*s also frequently take part in ritual events in their capacity as village leaders *cum* state representatives.

It is in this sense appropriate that the *carik* became the very embodiment of the state when the thief happened to run into his front yard. Knowing the personal character and appearance of the *carik* in question, a rather stern and elevated figure, one can imagine him standing there in his front yard as a pillar of the state at the exact time when he was required. In the turmoil of chase and revenge, the story claims, he politely invited the culprit in for tea. Here we see how the narrative shifts back into the restrained, polite and highly valued mode of everyday male sophistication. As a grown-up, experienced and responsible male, the *carik* effectively ignores all the chaotic emotion building up around him, turning the drama into a tea party full of suspense. The narrative itself stretches out this momentary safe haven in order to allow a large and revengeful mob to gather outside, even providing time for people to go back to arm themselves. In reality, it would take one hour at least to go to the nearest town to fetch the police, so we must assume that people did have some time to prepare themselves.

The point to emphasise is that whatever went into people's interpretations, the *carik* and his daughter were not, as far as I could ascertain, confronted with what they did, either at the scene, or afterwards. The police were in fact knocked down, an immensely transgressive act, but at no point did people direct their anger at the *carik*. Rather, in the hindsight of narrative, his initiative was, if not celebrated, at least left to speak for itself: he stood there in his front yard as a pillar of the state; he politely conversed with his guest over a glass of tea; he ingenuously fulfilled his official duty by bringing the police into the arena. Together with the *lurah* and a handful of other officials, he embodies the local state, so to speak; the state *in* the *kampung*. Although Batasan people often feel ambivalent towards their agendas, at least these functionaries constitute a localised form of state; they are operative representatives of the state within the community. The police on the other hand are not of the *kampung*, but are outsiders to local propriety and honour, and this places them in another position.

The boundary between *kampung* and state, then, is locally embodied in the *carik* and people like him, and the narrative takes this fact fully into account: the *carik* and other boundary figures cannot but be mediators, it is suggested. They *are* the state. Despite the fact that the *carik* here stood up against a concerted and revengeful community and deceitfully brought the police into local jurisdiction, people seemed to understand, even value, his actions. At least this was the case after the fact, when the whole event had turned into a drama between *kampung* and state, the mob and the police, and when *kampung* honour and revenge ultimately won through. At least in the context of narrative hindsight, the *carik* emerged not only as an actual mediator between *kampung* and state, but also as a driving force in a signifying story. Had the police managed to take the thief with them, or had they managed to arrest his murderers, the case and the story might have taken on another shape and had other repercussions for the *carik*.

If we now turn to the social context of the narrative again, tracing the wider relationships between *kampung* and state as implied in the story, we find that the state re-emerges in a rather surprising way. We have seen that in explicit narrative terms, the line between *kampung* and state runs through the *carik*. It is here that the drama of local honour is challenged by the norms and powers of the state. In the overall narrative structure the opposite challenge to the *kampung* is that represented by the thieves. Whereas the state challenges local autonomy, as this is demonstrated through acts of honour and revenge, with the aim of upholding state order, it seems to be an altogether different force that encroaches on the *kampung* from the other side: that of disorder, violence and crime. Thieves are in the habit of bursting onto the local scene without forewarning, disturbing and disrupting everyday calm in their desire for property, or even human life. Narratively speaking they are a disturbing, disordering force, a kind of base intentionality that challenges every aspect of *rukun* ideology in its absolute pursuit of material goods.

The contrast between these two antagonists to community honour is however far from clear-cut in people's ordinary experience. I have already mentioned the ambivalence that arises from the fact that even thieves are someone's neighbours, and have their place in some community or other. And I have mentioned the security-maintaining capacity of local thugs: although they tend to be a disruptive force to other *kampung*, they contribute to the defence of their own. What is more, such characters are not only boundary figures in the sense that they mediate violence between one *kampung* and another, they are often also a rather powerful mediatory resource for the state. Although we do not know the specific backgrounds and connections of the thieves in the Batasan case, it is common knowledge that, during the New Order regime, the state recruited large numbers of thugs to their political projects (Pemberton 1994:316, Siegel 1998).[10] The specific tasks and roles given to these 'mediators' could be better understood, but it is apparent that a major objective of their operation was to threaten or intimidate people into voting for the regime's Golkar party and to support the state's various development projects and their local agents. Their role in the channelling of economic resources between state and local community is less well studied, but their political entanglements are both well known and significant.

Judging on the basis of everyday experience and common knowledge, rather than the apparent narrative structure, we do not necessarily see a hierarchy of state, *kampung* and crime, associated with the characteristics of order (of state), honour (of *kampung*), and chaos (of thieves), although we might find such construals in state ideology. What we see from the point of view of Batasan people is rather a *kampung* both surrounded and penetrated by the state. The *lurah*, the *carik* and several other officials are effective embodiments of the state's presence in the *kampung*; they both represent and execute state power in daily life, thereby constituting the local state in their fields of operation. On the one hand, the *kampung* is explicitly surrounded by the ordering powers of the state, the police. On the other hand, it is surrounded by the disordering forces of thugs implicitly in the service of state. Although there is no absolute correspondence between the two poles of the contrast, since not all petty thieves and thugs have been recruited by state, there are sufficient cases of overlapping identities to make the distinction somewhat hazy. On the one hand, the police themselves cannot be trusted to stay on the correct side of the identity line; there are enough incidents and rumours about police corruption and extortion to render most *kampung* people, if not suspicious, at least wary in encounters with police. The common wisdom is that the local community is best served by keeping the police at a distance. On the other hand, there are also enough incidents of thugs surveying or even policing local people to blur the distinction from the other side: some criminals appear to have state sanctioned powers.

These roles at the boundary of the state were clearly dramatised, and perhaps refashioned, less than two years prior to the incident in Batasan. In the latter half of 1983, Indonesia witnessed the so-called Petrus killings, or 'mysterious killings', the execution of large numbers of alleged thugs (Pemberton 1994:311-18, Antlöv 1995:67-68, Siegel 1998:103-16, Barker 1999). The killings took place on such a

---

[10] In this respect Suharto continued a practice from both the colonial state (Nordholt 1983) and the nationalist revolution (Cribb 1991).

scale and with such uniform methods of murder and disposal all over Java that it could properly be called a campaign. The government was at fist reluctant to admit its involvement, but later publicised it as a cleaning-up operation. During a few months, the state in fact disposed of thousands of its most violent collaborators, many of whom had helped secure a large Golkar victory in the national election only one year earlier. Typically, the killings took place in secret, but the corpses were displayed publicly. All over Java local people suddenly found mutilated and decapitated bodies placed uncomfortably close to their homes - on walkways, in sewers or in dustbins. This, observers argue, was experienced as a very uncommon intrusion of violence into everyday life. Formerly, state power and violence were usually a rather abstract and distant entity. For law-abiding citizens, at least, it was only in rare cases that the immense life-taking capabilities of the state were registered in terms of dead bodies. In 1983, however, the state seemed to accomplish exactly this shift by displaying its destructive powers within local communities. In a sense it thus symbolically obviated its own demarcation towards the *kampung*. It asserted itself within the physical boundaries of community by breaking down, literally, the intermediaries that had sustained a degree of separation. If the destructive potential of the state was formerly experienced in the very powers of the thugs, it could now, paradoxically, be read in their dead bodies. The state had powers, it was evident, to control in multiple ways and at several levels; it was not only able to control through violence, but also capable of controlling the agency of violence itself. Moreover, Siegel argues (1998), one sensed an altogether different shape of violence in Petrus, not the somewhat brute and mundane force of common recognisable criminals, but an entirely displaced and hidden, indeed mysterious, power that somehow managed to place corpses in people's dustbins without their noticing how they got there. No one ever saw the killers or the killings, it is claimed; people only registered the effects of a powerful state in operation.

Further studies are needed in order to determine whether Petrus in fact signalled a new approach to *kampung* and crime by the New Order regime, and whether it had any significant effects beyond the symbolic statements of the moment. It is important to emphasise, however, that Petrus did throw light on the relationship between state and crime in a very dramatic way and that people in Batasan and elsewhere were very much interested, even fascinated, by the overt killings and the new situation created by the state's offensive. In Batasan the general mood was one of relative gratitude and optimism. People highlighted aspects of security: the state had now shown itself strong enough to take issue with criminals. Now, people asserted, there would be no need to maintain the security arrangements of the *kampung* any longer; people could sleep safely at night. These responses indicate that people experienced thieves as a harassment that would henceforth be tackled by the state, although I would argue that this does not necessarily imply that people view the state and crime as entirely distinct. Rather, their enthusiasm followed from the view that the state now seemed strong enough to deter criminality itself; that the state was in fact sufficiently consolidated to leave *kampung* people alone. Disposing of its own thugs was a sign that criminal collaborators were no longer needed to secure the required Golkar victory, and the mode of killings carried a strong message for other criminals as well: crime itself was explicitly being targeted (Pemberton 1994:313). People did not believe, of course, that an enormous police force would start to take control locally in order to handle crime. The point the state made, for all who managed to *kapok*, was that crime has dire consequences, and this strong statement, it was hoped in Batasan, would render local security arrangements superfluous. They sensed a kind of new deal between the state and *kampung*, one in which the state no longer needed to burden local community with criminal attacks in order to sustain its powers. Both positively and negatively the state seemed to take on a new role: sufficient people appeared to be supportive of the regime to eliminate the need for intimidation, and at the same time the state also seemed willing to start tackling the crime that remained. It must have been something of a disappointment when, less than two years later, the three thieves entered the village, proving that *kampung* security was as vulnerable as ever.

Through thugs, and then invertedly through Petrus, the state made itself felt in people's lives as a forceful power, and this experience needs to be remembered when trying to account for the honour and revenge of *kampung*. People felt both invaded and surrounded by the state at the time when the thieves entered the stage. The state was experienced overtly in terms of such figures as the *carik* and the police, but it was also traceable in thieves. Moreover, there was also no clear distinction between the modes of violence of state and *kampung*; by means of assertive thugs, as well as of the mysterious Petrus killings, the state showed itself as capable of destructive action as *kampung* people themselves. Rather than state-*kampung*-crime coupled to order-honour-violence, we sense both a *kampung* and a state alternating between order and propriety on the one hand, and destructive violence on the other. The state also proved itself capable of shifting between the everyday sophistication of regulation and composure (ideally the police), and the extraordinary events or incidents of brutal and telling violence (like Petrus). Like the *kampung* the state was also capable of telling a story through violence, and it did so in order to assert its own influence in people's lives, in local arenas and elsewhere.

7.6 Conclusion

Thus the Batasan narrative talks through its silences about several contexts of concern to local people. We hear of a very subdued and restrained masculine modus shifting abruptly into an outrageous, but in that context proper, life-taking and mutilating force, and what resounds through all the violent acts and boisterous retellings is first and foremost the horrendous agency of the prototypical perpetrator, the male youth. Capable and willing to kill and dismember, this agency both dramatises and realises the boundary at which the *kampung* community comes to life: united against thieves. It also highlights another point of unity: community solidarity against police; on the one hand criminals, on the other the state. At another level, however, and read in the context of the story of Petrus, I believe the narrative also talks about a much deeper ambivalence. What we sense is a state power that approaches from both sides, and through both order and violence. The distinction between thief and police is not altogether clear in people's experience; at least it is blurred in the behavioural mode of honour and revenge. At least in the mode of violent *kampung* assertion, it is not felt appropriate to turn the honour-defaming thief over to the police, to surrender to the state an agency that is not only *kampung* transgressive, but also, I would suggest, possibly encouraged or sanctioned by the state.

Within this mode, the state is regarded both as transgressing honour, in its failure, despite Petrus, to contain crime, and as subverting honour, through its insistence on legal powers. It invades the *kampung* only to obstruct it from realising a local response. It entails infringements on people's feelings of local community while at the same time impeding their means of defence. Giving the thieves up is in a sense to give up the very justification of community – the concerted action that, through killings and tellings, guarantees a space for local agency.

This encroachment of the state, I have argued, works on a type of community that is very vulnerable in sociological terms. The social entity of a *kampung* is not an unproblematic given; the structure of everyday life itself does not guarantee a concerted local community. Most property is private, economic pursuit is to a large extent individualistically oriented, and even nuclear families seldom manage to co-ordinate capital and labour above a very low level due to fragmentation within the household. The general picture is rather one of a carefully calculated and defended individual independence, both in economic, social and religious affairs; the basic social unit of the Javanese *kampung* appears in many ways to be the adult individual person. In rural settings there are economic dependencies that crystallise around the utilisation of agricultural land which create more enduring relationships, but these tend to create factional allegiances, thus also threatening the celebrated *kampung* unity. The same is the case in fields of politics. Although the New Order regime rather effectively constrained open political activity at local levels, distinctions of opinion and interest were to some extent channelled through social and religious organisations instead. Finally, it has been shown that individuals and families in urban settings also create allegiances ('cells', J. Sullivan 1992:45-55) that greatly restrict wider relations of solidarity. In short, it is difficult to maintain a picture of Javanese *kampung* as homogenous, uniform entities.

On the other hand, as I have argued, the corollary to such individualism and factionalism is a very strong emphasis on *rukun* over and above divisions, on the need to cultivate friendly relations with neighbours in daily *kampung* affairs. Smoothness in social relations is highly valued, especially where there is a danger of tensions and conflicts that might threaten the functioning of neighbourhood. The low degree of economic incorporation and political homogeneity is therefore balanced by a degree of *social* integration: in terms of recreation and ritual, diversity and antagonism are often smoothed over in favour of a *rukun* appearance. It is widely acknowledged that this social harmony does not come of itself, but can only be achieved by means of significant efforts. It is indeed experienced as a demanding task to maintain one's own independence and integrity in a world so intensely social as the Javanese. It takes continual self-monitoring and emotional control to create the operational mood that allows the pursuit of personal agendas. The functionality of the *kampung* therefore depends on a carefully crafted sociality, a constant effort to shape viable relationships on the basis of proximity. The community of the *kampung* is not a solid given, but a rather precarious entity constantly being built from efforts at solidarity.

On the one hand, the demeaning intrusion of thieves allows the *kampung* to realise yet another of its community constituting potentials. Apart from recreational amiability and a ritual evenness of temperament, the *kampung* is concerted in and through defence. As the Batasan story indicates, thieves provide the *kampung* community with an opportunity to define itself by exploring its own boundaries: the lines within which honour and revenge play a role, and the lines beyond which crime and/or the state operate. On the other hand, I argue, the intrusion of thieves also illuminates the very precariousness of community, the likelihood of neighbourhood solidarity *failing* to materialise in *kampung* defence. When three thieves enter the stage to rob one of the richer villagers, there is always the possibility that their base desire for material goods or their outright disregard for local authority will evoke a similar response among the neighbours themselves. There is always a possibility that the *kampung* will dissolve along the lines of different factions and individual desires. There is always a possibility that the victim will be abandoned at the point when neighbourhood solidarity is most required. This threat, I argue, goes a long way to explaining the ferocity with which thieves are met. It is the total subversion of everyday propriety and sociality evinced in attacking thieves that releases outrageous responses. This is a violation that cannot be equated with the sophisticated practices of everyday social encounters. It is an attack that belongs to a very different register of action and needs to be handled accordingly. It calls forth the modus of revenge by which the force of male youth is mobilised in the reconstitution of *kampung* community through chase and murder. These horrendous acts not only manage to dispose of thieves, they also create a local space in which neighbourhoods seek to reassert their agency vis-à-vis crime and the encroaching state.

References

Abdullah, I. (1994), *The Muslim businessmen of Jatinom: religious reform and economic modernization in a Central Javanese town.* Ph.D. Thesis, Universiteit van Amsterdam

Alexander, J. (1987), *Trade, traders, and trading in rural Java.* Singapore: Oxford University Press

Anderson, B. R. (1972), The idea of power in Javanese culture; in: C. Holt (ed.): *Culture and politics in Indonesia.* Ithaca: Cornell University Press. pp. 1-69

Antlöv, H. (1995), *Exemplary centre, administrative periphery: Rural leadership and the New Order in Java.* Nordic Institute of Asian Studies Monograph Series, no. 68. Curzon Press

Antlöv, H. and Cederroth, S. (eds.) (1994), *Leadership on Java: Gentle hints, authoritarian rule.* Curzon Press

Barker, J. (1999), Surveillance and territoriality in Bandung; in: Vicente L. Rafael (ed.): *Figures of criminality in Indonesia, the Philippines, and colonial Vietnam*. Ithaca, New York: Southeast Asia Program, Cornell University. pp. 95-127

Barth, F. (ed.) (1969), *Ethnic groups and boundaries: The social organization of cultural difference*. Oslo: Universitetsforlaget

Beatty, A. (1999), *Varieties of Javanese religion: An anthropological account*. Cambridge University Press

Berman, L. (1998), *Speaking through the silence: Narratives, social conventions, and power in Java*. Oxford Studies in Anthropological Linguistics. New York, Oxford: Oxford University Press

Bowen, J. R. (1986), On the political construction of tradition: *Gotong-royong* in Indonesia; in: The Journal of Asian Studies, vol. 45:545-61

Brenner, S. A. (1998), *The domestication of desire: Women, wealth, and modernity in Java*. Princeton, New Jersey: Princeton University Press

Bråten, E. (in press), Against community, beyond humanity: Grasping 'violence' in Java; in: Frans Hüsken and Huub de Jonge (eds.): *Violence in Indonesia*

Bråten, E. (1999), To colour, not oppose: Spreading Islam in rural Java; in: Leif O. Manger (ed.): *Muslim diversity: Local Islam in global contexts*. Nordic Institute of Asian Studies, NIAS Studies in Asian Topics, no. 26. pp. 150-172

Bråten, E. (1995), *Riddles of inverted being: A case of self and fellowship formation in Yogyakarta, Java*. Dr. Polit. Dissertation. University of Bergen

Bråten, E. (1988), *Respect for power? Islamization and impression management in a Javanese village*. Cand. polit. Thesis, University of Bergen

Castles, L. (1967), *Religion, politics and economic behaviour in Java: The Kudus cigarette industry*. Yale University, Southeast Asian Studies. Cultural report series no. 151

Cederroth, S. (1995), *Survival and profit in rural Java: The case of an East Javanese village*. Nordic Institute of Asian Studies Monograph Series, no. 63. Curzon Press

Cribb, R. (1991), *Gangsters and revolutionaries: The Jakarta poeple's militia and the Indonesian revolution 1945-1949*. Asian Studies Association of Australia in association with Allen and Unwin

Dewey, A. G. (1962), *Peasant marketing in Java*. New York: The Free Press of Glencoe.

Geertz, C. (1973), *The interpretation of cultures. Selected essays*. New York : Basic Books

Geertz, C. (1963), *Agricultural involution: The processes of ecological change in Indonesia*. Berkeley and Los Angeles: University of California Press

Geertz, C. (1960), *The religion of Java*. Chicago and London: The University of Chicago Press

Geertz, H. (1961), *The Javanese family: A study of kinship and socialization*. Prospect Heights, Illinois: Waveland Press, Inc

Grønhaug, R. (1975), Transaction and signification: An analytical distinction in the study of social interaction. Unpublished paper. Department of Social Anthropology, University of Bergen

Guinness, P. (1986), *Harmony and hierarchy in a Javanese kampung*. Singapore, Oxford, New York: Oxford University Press

Guinness, P. (1989), 'Social harmony' as ideology and practice in a Javanese city; in: Paul Alexander (ed.): *Creating Indonesian Cultures*. Oceania Publications. University of Sydney. pp. 55-74

Hart, G. et al. (1989), *Agrarian transformations: Local processes and the state in Southeast Asia*. Berkeley, Los Angeles, Oxford: University of California Press

Hefner, R. W. (2000), *Civil Islam: Muslims and democratization in Indonesia*. Princeton and Oxford: Princeton University Press

Hefner, R. W. (1990), *The political economy of mountain Java: An interpretive history*. Berkeley, Los Angeles, Oxford: University of California Press

Hefner, R. W. (1985), *Hindu Javanese: Tengger tradition and islam*. Princeton, New Jersey: Princeton University Press

Jay, R. (1969), *Javanese villagers: Social relations in rural Modjokuto*. Cambridge, Mass.: MIT Press

Jellinek, L. (1991), *The wheel of fortune: The history of a poor community in Jakarta*. Honolulu: University of Hawaii Press

Keeler, W. (1990), Speaking of gender in Java; in: J.M. Atkinson & S. Errington (eds.): *Power and difference: Gender in Southeast Asia*. Stanford: Stanford University Press. pp. 127-152

Keeler, W. (1987), *Javanese shadow plays, Javanese selves*. Princeton, New Jersey: Princeton University Press

Koentjaraningrat (1985), *Javanese culture*. Singapore, Oxford, New York: Oxford University Press

Mulder, N. (1978), *Mysticism and everyday life in contemporary Java*. Institute of Southeast Asian Studies, Singapore: Singapore University Press

Nakamura, H. (1983), *Divorce in Java: A study of dissolution of marriage among Javanese Muslims*. Gadjah Mada University Press

Nakamura, M. (1983), *The crescent arises over the banyan tree: A study of the Muhammadiyah movement in a Central Javanese town*. Yogyakarta: University of Gadjah Mada Press.

Nordholt, H. S. (1983), De jago in de schaduw: Misdaad en 'orde' in de koloniale staat op Java; in: De Gids 146, 8/9, pp. 664-675

Pemberton, J. (1994), *On the subject of 'Java'*. Ithaca and London: Cornell University Press.

Sears, L. J. (1996), *Shadows of empire: Colonial discourse and Javanese tales*. Durham and London: Duke University Press

Siegel, J. T. (1998), *A new criminal type in Jakarta: Counter-revolution today*. Durham and London: Duke University Press

Siegel, J. T. (1986), *Solo in the New Order: Language and hierarchy in an Indonesian city*. Princeton, New Jersey: Princeton University Press

Smith-Hefner, N. (1989), The linguistic socialization of Javanese children in two communities; in: Anthropological Linguistics, vol. 30, no.2, pp. 166-198

Smith-Hefner, N. (1988), Women and politeness: The Javanese example; in: Language in Society, vol.17, pp.535-554

Soedarmono (1987), *Munculnya kelompok pengusaha batik di Laweyan pada awal abad XX*. Dissertation. Gadjah Mada University

Stange, P. (1998), *Politik perhatian: Rasa dalam kebudayaan Jawa*. Yogyakarta: Lembaga Kajian Islam dan Sosial (LKIS)

Stange, P. (1984), The logic of rasa in Java; in: Indonesia, no. 38, pp.113-134

Sullivan, J. (1992), *Local government and community in Java: An urban case-study*. Singapore, Oxford, New York: Oxford University Press

Sullivan, N. (1989), The hidden economy and kampung women; in: Paul Alexander (ed.): *Creating Indonesian Cultures*. Oceania Publications. University of Sydney. pp. 75-90

Tambunan, T. (2000), *Development of small-scale industries during the New Order government in Indonesia*. Aldershot/Brookfield USA/Singapore/Sydney: Ashgate

Chapter 8

Hatred, Revenge and Sorcery

Reflections on the personalization of violence in contemporary societies[1]

Bruce Kapferer

Sociological (including anthropological) approaches to violence are marked by ambivalence. Violence is seen as emergent in the absence of the social or else its product, often the two positions are simultaneous in analysis. Thus in a Durkheimian analysis violence takes different shapes as a function of the kind of normative and social integration involved. This was most famously developed in Durkheim's own path-breaking study, *Suicide*. Here the violent taking of one's own life, self murder, is, for example, a function of over socialization (altruism) or else of radical isolation within the social (egoism, anomie). Other perspectives, but not necessarily unrelated, conceive violence as both a force of and against social and political control and regulation. Thus the state is a violent order, appropriating violence to itself. Resistance to the state, especially from within a statist conception of the social, is conceived to be intrinsically violent. It denies the state's appropriation of violence and its ordering claims. Such claims are often viewed as the repressive, overordering, oversocializing functions of state apparatuses that are thoroughly violent, excluding and marginalizing, in these aspects and provocative of the violence of resistance. Approaches as diverse as those of Durkheim, Weber, Marx, Freud and Foucault approach violence as intimately connected with sociality or social and political dynamics. Violence is a force emergent in relation to the social, produced through the social or anti-social dynamics. It is not something beneath or outside social and political and social forces, something intrinsic to human beings as essentializing socio-biologists often argue. Broadly, violence can be conceived of as the paradox of the social and strongly functionalist approaches have, for instance, described rituals as the institutional means for ridding the social of its destructive violence (e.g. Gluckman 1954, Girard 1972). But as so much research has demonstrated ritualized violence (an example is sacrifice, see Kapferer 1997, Bloch 1996) far from expunging violence engages violence to social formation, violence is intimate with social generation.

[1] This paper is a revised version of a presentation delivered to the Sawyer Seminar, University of Chicago, February 11, 2000.

It is violence as a destructive phenomenon that I am specifically concerned with here, but as a violence which is emergent in socially and culturally generative processes, a violence moreover that draws and expands its violence from particular cultural and social dynamics in which it is already integrally part. The anthropology of feuding and revenge and of honor and shame has specifically stressed such aspects, though the stress has been upon the functional force of their associated violence in maintaining the status quo. Much of the emphasis has been upon violence as a social sanction or violence that somehow immediately sets up counter processes of a socially reformative nature against the very distructive force of violence. This was Gluckman's (1956) interpretation of Evans-Pritchard's seminal analysis of feuding among the Nuer (see Harrison 1993 for a different interpretation with regard to New Guinea). I will take a somewhat different position but one which nevertheless is strongly indicated in studies of feuding and the anthropology of revenge. It seems to me that social processes built around notions of the feud and honour and shame are of an intensely personal kind. They focus on the character of persons and the infusion of their social relations with deeply personal consequences. The social or rather relatedness is the agency and the channel for the flow of injury and hurt. This is powerfully shown in notions surrounding hatred. I take hate and love out of a conventional psychological domain and place them firmly in the problematics of relatedness and the emotional energies that flow in the dynamics of relatedness.

The discussion opens with a consideration of hatred as an intense emotional expression of negative sociality. This argument is expanded through the exploration of a Sinhalese myth central in diverse sorcery practices which joins the passions of hate and love. In so doing the act of revenge, so much the motivation of sorcery, is moralized. The sorcery myth I discuss is also active in contemporary remythologizing rhetorics of the state and Sinhala nationalism, rhetorics which have given some fuel to violence in Sri Lanka. It is to this violence, largely ethnic, to which I turn and which appears to be formed through a discourse of revenge which, of course, the passions of sorcery have much to say. What follows is not merely applicable to Sri Lanka as I hope what I have to say should make clear.

My argument is simple and straightforward. Hatred is distinguished by its intensely personal nature. The conventional pairing of love and hate establishes the character of hatred's intimacy that is also integral to the potential cruelties of its violence. But I extend. Hatred not only arises in deeply personal relations, and gathers its furies accordingly, but it *makes* relations and situations powerfully personal. Hatred transforms relations and even contexts into highly charged personal ones. Hatred denies all abstraction and distance. It transmutes the inanimate into the animate. An object or thing, a category, an identity, institutions, organizations are, as it were, filled with a personality and are imbued with a living, embodied, personal force in relation to the agent of hate. Hatred is, in the view I develop here, an anthropomorphizing potency in the extreme. And here is its potentially dreadful and frightening paradox. As it makes intensely human and personal that which is drawn into the realm of hate, hatred is directed to the shattering of that which it creates or invents. This is the madness of hatred that must deny or extinguish that – the being and the relation to the being – that is the very fire and fury of its emergence.

There is a close connection between hatred and sorcery. Before I continue I should make it perfectly clear that 'sorcery' (colloquially in Sinhala it is referred to as *vina*, action, or *kodivina* or *huniyam*) is not to be grasped in common western terms as merely a magical practice usually of a thoroughly irrational nature. Such perspectives gloss far too quickly and inaccurately sorcery in Sri Lanka as a thoroughgoing pragmatic practice embedding notions that might be better understood as part of a 'realistic' practical sociology of everyday life.[2] Among Sinhalese Buddhists the fear of sorcery is related to its foundation in hate, and the deeply personal nature sorcery establishes with its victims. A sixteenth century Sinhalese poem/song which relates the anguish of Queen Kuveni expresses the intimacy of hatred in sorcery most powerfully. In Sinahala traditions Kuveni is the sorceress supreme and a figure whose story parallels that of the Greek sorceress, Medea, daughter of Hecate. As mythological traditions tell (that are also set out in the great textual traditions),[3] Kuveni is the daughter of the original inhabitants of Sri Lanka. But she betrays her people. Kuveni falls in love with a foreign prince, Vijaya, who is stranded along with his men on Sri Lanka's shores.[4] The prince vows to marry Kuveni if she would use her magic to help him slay her people. This she does, but once Vijaya achieves his conquest, he rejects Kuveni, banishes the sorceress and their two children to the jungle fastness, and marries another queen whom Vijaya brings from South India. In her anguish Kuveni curses Vijaya. This is Kuveni's cry as the poem records.

---

[2] This point has been argued extensively in Kapferer 1997, 2001. I stress it here because some scholars seem to have taken my arguments as perjorative statements that implies that Sinhalese are irrational sorcerers prone to beliefs and practices of the European kind described by those who have extolled the 'victory' of Western rational science and the dismissal of superstition (e.g. Thomas, Gellner). In the contemporary situation in Sri Lanka there is a great commitment to scientific rationalism which has a powerful class-based import. The bourgeoisie, for example, distance themselves from many in the peasantry and urban working classes on the basis that they are 'forward looking' rationalists separated from the irrational cultural traditions that once characterized practice and survives among the lesser educated. Such attitudes are a legacy of Colonial Rule and a culture of modernization (see Obeyesekere, Gombrich and Obeyesekere for more extensive discussion) and very far from my perspective on sorcery which has sought to separate its analysis from in fact a colonialist understanding of the phenomenon, an understanding which paradoxically continues in some post colonial approaches (e.g. Senanayake). My own approach to sorcery practice is concerned with exposing the sociology which is engaged to its routine practice, a sociology that, furthermore, can inform practices – very modern and contemporary practices – well-beyond Sri Lanka and might not be grasped *as sorcery*.

[3] I refer to those of the Mahavamsa, Culavamsa, Rajavaliya etc. all of which have been important in contemporary remythologizations of Sinhala nationalist identity. See Kapferer 1988(1998), 1997; Kemper 1990, Tambiah, Seneviratne.

[4] Important texts in the popular and ritual traditions concerning the myth of Kuveni are presented by Obeyesekere 1984.

The golden moon brilliant above the eastern hills
Has become a burning ball of molten iron
The scented flowers that made our lover's bower
Are now a bed of thorns
The cuckoo's once passionate call
Drives as a shaft of iron into my ear
The darts of love are now the arrows of war

My Lord, you have cut the bond of my devotion
Your affection lies elsewhere
You have banished me and our children...

Kuveni thus poured out her tearful grief
And took herself and her children into the jungle
While her lover, the Prince Vijaya, married and was consecrated king.

Agonized by Vijaya's terrible hurt
The sorceress seething with hate
Took the form of a leopard
Her tongue of sharp diamond, more than two leagues in length
Pierced seven protective gateways
And struck for Vijaya's heart........

The story of Kuveni and Vijaya is a central foundational myth of kingship and state in Sri Lanka, both of ancient Sri Lanka and, now, reinvented and revitalized as a key myth in contemporary nationalist history. The events of betrayal, hatred and revenge is conceived, in a vein similar to Herodotus's Greek history, as the primordial engine of history itself. The beginning of Sinhala history is founded in slaughter and revenge and their endless cycle and enmity is the continuing force in history. Sinhalese at all social levels will comment that the suffering occasioned by the current ethnic civil war and other related turmoil manifests the power of Kuveni's curse which like much sorcery and revenge recorded worldwide relentlessly pursues its victims down the generations. The events surrounding Kuveni's curse and its enduring effect expresses karmic principles and other ideas central to Buddhist thought, for example, suffering as the result of action and as a consequence of the inescapable fault that is at the root of all mundane existence.

There is much sympathy with Kuveni in present-day Sri Lanka. Many see her revengeful action as appropriate to the wrong committed by Vijaya and in their own crises will identify with her in their own actions and feelings for revenge. In village sorcery rites and in an expanding number of sorcery shrines in Sri Lanka, Kuveni's hateful potencies are invoked. Kuveni is for many an image of legitimate and moral fury returning anguish and hurt to its source, the quintessence of the reciprocity of violence, of a Nietzschean ressentiment. There is an ambiguity about her . While she is seen as a thoroughgoing evil force there is, nonetheless, a sense that her destructive action has been provoked and is the return of that which has been initiated by another. She has been made evil by another. In other words, Kuveni's overcoming anguish and self-consuming anger which becomes her destructive force is ultimately the responsibility of the person who is seen to have caused the distress in the first place. Such an orientation to the personal perpetration of violence as legitimate revenge is often used to absolve individual acts of violence, in Sri Lanka and, perhaps, everywhere.[5] Furthermore, it can contribute to the expansion of violent acts through precisely this kind of moralization, as has been widely commented upon.

But my general point is other than this. What the Kuveni story and associated practices of sorcery highlight is the potency and particular destructive potency of hate as well as its source. The engine of hatred emerges from out of the construction (as much imagined as actual) of an intensely intimate and personal relation between the agent of hate and its subject. They are created as consubstantial; the hated is virtually embodied in the hater and the energy of hatred is directed to the breaking of such an impossible union. In sorcery, whether in Sri Lanka or elsewhere this drives towards an extermination of the other as it also risks the self-extermination of the agent of hate – a possibility that mythologies of sorcery recognize worldwide. The consubstantiality and personalization of hatred, which hatred shares with sorcery, is associated with the visceral cruelty of the violence of both sorcery and hatred and, as well, with the emotions of disgust and revulsion that so often seem to go along with them.

This is well-exemplified every day at often crowded sorcery shrines in Sri Lanka. There individuals curse those who have in some way obstructed their lives or caused hurt. The cursing is accompanied with actions that describe the hurt and the pain that is to be meted out, glass and chillies are pounded in a mortar; an egg, drawn with the intended victim's name often with the blood of that who wishes the harm, is smashed; an effigy of the victim burnt or else a symbol of the victim's hitherto well-being (one, for example, that represents a happy and productive marriage) is destroyed. The magical words that accompany these actions give expression to a host of imagined cruelties that are to be visited on the subject of hate. The bodies of victims are to be utterly broken, their faces are to be horribly burnt and disfigured, their entire worlds of existence to be obliterated. Rancid oil, fecal matter, and other decaying substances are engaged to the destructive work. These are the forms of destruction and of pollution that are associated with sorcery work and, indeed, those who come to curse at the shrines regard such work and their own action as disgusting. This disgust is often how they feel in themselves as victims of another's hate – the reason they say that has brought them to curse. In other words, they are filled with the other's hatred, with another's disgusting hateful life-taking decay. It is their self-repulsion that cursers conceive as originating from a source outside themselves which becomes integral to their destructive energy. This energy is fired in the curser's radical break with that

[5] I might add that the concern to moralize and legitimate violence in the Sri Lanka context might have something to do with the current ideological stress on the importance of Buddhist virtue. Such a stress is to be expected in a context where the fact of everyday existence framed by the on-going ethnic war and general civilian disturbance demonstrates a constant threat to Buddhist ideal virtues of, for instance, non-violence (*ahimsa*).

I might add that in Sri Lanka victims of sorcery are often conceived as being in some way responsible for their ensorcellment. The Kuveni story recognizes this but underlines that her behaviour is nonetheless justified.

which is regarded as consuming and determining from within. The radical break becomes the force whereby such innerdestructive potencies are flung back to their source. (see Kapferer 1997, 1998 for extensive developments of these points.)

What I have described for sorcery in Sri Lanka has much resonance with accounts of sorcery practice in many parts of the world. The cultural specificities of particular practices may be different but, I contend, they often bear a similar dynamics whether this be in Europe, Africa, Asia and so on (Comaroff and Comparoff 2000, Geschiere 1999, Kapferer 2001). Such sorcery dynamics extend an understanding of the nature of violence that takes the personalized shape that is hatred. The violence is extreme and demands the destruction of bodies. This is so even when the subject hated is an abstraction, a category, an institution, an organization. Such abstractions in the personalizing energy of hate become embodied in particular living human beings who are the specific instances of the abstraction anthropomorphized by hate.

Thus with ethnic violence. The ethnic other, certainly in the constructions of so much nationalism, is often nothing more than an abstraction but through a discourse of hate is reified into living persons who are now conceived as contaminatingly and repulsively consubstantial. What the hater comes to see through the imagination of nationalism as the destructive force within the hater's body is, in its expulsion and rejection, now played out on the bodies of the victims of hate. In the dynamic of the return, bodies are burnt and defaced, and torn limb from limb. Bosnia, Sri Lanka, Rwanda are only recent examples. Christopher Taylor (1999) in a book detailing the Rwandan genocide of 1994 and the tragic experiences of his Tutsi and Hutu relatives and friends, describes the cruelties of the killings. The expressions of hatred involved metaphors of the body concerning the obstruction of fluids, the blockage of inner passages, the inhibition of movement; metaphors associated with the destructive effects of sorcery. Those who were killed or maimed had enacted on their bodies what they were conceived as causing: their tendons were cut to stop them from walking, they were impaled.

In much contemporary violence the state, an abstraction if ever there is one, is conceived of as a subject of hate. Accordingly, it is anthropomorphized. It becomes a person and the persons who inhabit the concentrated spaces of the state, or act as its officers, become synonymous with the state; the individual parts of the state stand in for the whole. The person is the state. Thus individuals, living manifestation of what is an abstraction, attract the extreme, often body-fragmenting, violence that can build in the formation of the hatred that is the possibility of intense personal relations. Such hatred yields a further destructive dimension, for example, to violent acts of revenge which gives added force to its annihilating possibility. This additional force is impelled by the revulsion, self-purification and moralization that flows in hatred. The perpetrator of the Oklahoma bombing, we are told by his sister, acted in revenge for the Waco killings but she also insists that her brother hated the state with a passion. His passionate hatred, I suggest, like the sorcerer, needed bodies for the revenge. Features of this phenomenon seem to be continued with reference to the almost unimaginable outrage in the destruction of the New York World Trade Center. The attack, of course, is seen as an act of 'evil' motivated in hate and of a powerfully personalized nature (see ZNet, Guardian). Sri Lanka has in the last thirty years experienced two major anti-state revolts within the Sinhalese population which, quite apart from the Tamil-Sinhala ethnic war, has probably claimed in excess of a hundred thousand civilian lives. The rhetoric of both anti-state and state propaganda was one which took the form of an intensely personal dialectic of hate. A feature of the anti-state terror was to select out individual functionaries of the state and kill them and often members of their families. The violence enacted upon their bodies was generally of a highly personal kind, akin to the revulsion at the person who is the subject of sorcery. I add that some of the violence was a moral violence – if this is conceivable – the manner of the killing in its sorcery of hate being its own legitimation. The bodies of victims were disfigured in a way which communicated publicly their moral offense. [6]

I have argued that hate discovers its particular violence through the nature of its personalization. It is an intensely anthropomorphizing and social anti-social antihuman phenomenon. It works within social relations and, I have stressed, even proceeds to create them where there was no social relation. The rhetorics of hate are extraordinarily dangerous and destructive because of their personalization, a process whereby contexts which may have been minimally social are made intensely and negatively so. Much has been written about the distortions of many nationalisms, for example, and their imaginations of community and society. These and their constructions of history are seen as implicated in the disasters that may follow. Those who are excluded from the community are then scapegoated and demonized and essentially dehumanized, it is frequently argued precisely because of the fact that they are defined as not part of the community that does the scapegoating and demonizing. My point does not necessarily oppose this position. However, it suggests an additional possibility which an exploration of hate and its peculiar dynamics indicates. This is that in the circumstances giving rise to hate or created through a rhetoric of hate the victims of violence, often these days of ethnic violence, are also conceived as being deeply inside society – not outside it – and as thoroughly human beings (not as demons or as some non-human monstrosity) who stand in a powerful and destructive relation to society and community and to each and every individual member with whom they are conceived as having a personal relation. Thus, as in sorcery, the terrible violence of hate and the particular attacks on the bodies of the hated that hate conjures.

[6] I should note that the structure of my analysis – the personalization of violence expressed in notions of hatred and revenge – is systematic with the globalization of violence attendant on state reformations and structures of deterritorialization. In such contexts networks of ties and of personal relatedness (a kinship of the global) becomes stressed, a kind of 'rhizomization' along the lines discussed by Deleuze and Guattari (1987) occurs, in which the dynamics I have examined through sorcery becomes increasingly relevant shaping both a contemporary violence and reactions to it.

Chapter 9

The Attraction of Power: Honor and Politics in a Japanese Village

Leif Selstad

9.1 Introduction

Words 'do' things, according to the philosopher J. L. Austin (1962:12). The word 'honor' might evoke thoughts of a historical debate over morals, in which people take it upon themselves to defend their own social interests in some absolute sense against those of all others. Our thoughts turn to feuds, vengeance, and feudal conditions. In order to see the relevance of honor in the modern world it is necessary to move beyond what words 'do' connotatively, to how concepts make sense in the wider workings of everyday social life. This entails looking at how honor is contested, defended and negotiated in the social relations in which people are constantly involved. My claim is that social concepts such as honor should not be viewed too narrowly, but must be related to the wider complexity and multiplexity of ongoing social life. To substantiate this claim materials from Japan will be presented that may supplement and problematize the prominence of Mediterranean and Middle Eastern materials on this topic (Gilmore 1987:3). By linking honor to the contests and negotiations of local politics in Japan its relevance in modern social life will become apparent. Questions of honor, face and reputation range from considerations of morality to conflicts over power and interests – in short much of what goes on in social life – all of which come together in games of interest between actors in different contexts. In this example honor may be viewed as a template through which local power and standing is negotiated.

The prevalence of considerations of honor and shame in Japanese society has been noted by several scholars (Asano-Tamanoi 1987:104; Befu 1971:169; Benedict 1946:157). Although the historical background of rank and honor is emphasized, their present-day relevance is usually apparent as well.[1] A general way of referring to honor and shame in Japan is in terms of keeping face and losing face. The theme of face and social standing might suggest that honor in Japan has a different focus than it has in the literature of the Middle East – a focus on protection and conformity instead of on assertive defense. Keeping one's face may

[1] While Asano-Tamanoi uses slightly outdated and literary terms like 'na' - family name or reputation - and 'meiyo' - honor, she clearly links the question of honor and shame to current considerations of marriage, rank and gender (1987:113).

sound more personally protective than the extroverted defense of family honor found in the Levant. Even so considerations of face in Japan have much to do with the support of groups to which individuals belong as members. In one analysis the strong emphasis on family reputation and continuity in Catalonia is compared to a comparable situation in Japan (Asano-Tamanoi op.cit.:107). The house ('ie' in Japanese) becomes a central arena for people's standing, insofar as it is an arena for social relations, gossip, and the social demand for heirs to perpetuate the house. Yet house or household is not the only social arena in which considerations of honor and standing apply. In fact, house has been used as a prototype for the ideological solidarity found in other institutions in Japan ranging from companies to the state, and with the village community as one of the strong exemplars (Nakane 1970:11; Nakane 1967).

Personal considerations of face and rank are constantly being invoked in a variety of situations in Japan, at home, at work and in public. The literature portrays a culture where privacy and individuality are subordinate to demands of group conformity (Doi 1973:173). In the same vein Japan has been called a group-oriented society (Kalland 1986:112). This leads to an argument about differences between Japanese and Mediterranean notions of honor. One version of this argument is that whereas social values such as honor are internalized and individualized in Catalonia, they are contingent to situations of group involvement in Japan (Asano-Tamanoi op.cit.:116). The argument would be that while a person in Catalonia may act individually in response to a code of honor including chastity and integrity, the response in Japan would be contingent on situational criteria such as a person's rank and standing within the group. This recalls the distinction between 'sin' culture and 'shame' culture, where people are motivated respectively by personal considerations of conscience and guilt and by group-oriented expectations of exposure and sanctions (Benedict 1946:157; Doi op.cit.:48). There is a danger of essentialized simplification here – individual guilt and group sanctions may be mutually informed phenomena – which calls for a wider exemplification of how people master their social reputation. I could then be shown that keeping one's face in Japan certainly involves group standing, but also contains many nuances of strategy, performance and negotiations.

The importance of honor and shame and their many facets in social life is reflected in their continuing relevance in modern life in Japan. Japanese modernity differs markedly from that of the West, and has been labeled non-modern by some scholars, due to its rootedness in a feudal past and the continued emphasis on duty and collectivity (Iwatake 1993:103). In the same vein Japanese modernity has been labeled postmodern, since it lacks the universalized and depersonalized attributes of western modernity (Clammer 1999:13). To all intents and purposes Japan is a modern society, at least as far as its economic and technological developments are concerned. One challenge posed by Japanese modernity is to go beyond essentialized differences and to realize that there are several modernities in today's world, not only the western version, with its focus on ideas of individualism and universalism, which is itself a simplified construction. To study the complexity of different large-scale modernities is a challenging but rewarding task that may provide a better understanding of the multiplexity of social life in the global anthropology of today.

Although social theory in Japan commonly invokes relationships between individuals and groups of various sorts, such relationships are not at all straightforward and simple (Befu 1971:165). There is a huge and polysemous vocabulary for relations of various kinds, such as for duty and obligation (cf. Benedict 1946). The same goes for honor and shame. Many words apply, some outdated and others quotidian, but their application will depend on the situation and what interpretation is made of it. The word of primary interest in this case is 'tatemae' or 'front', the social front or mask of individuals and groups that is usually represented as standing in contrast to 'honne', a person's 'real' or underlying self. The social 'front', the face or mask through which relations are negotiated, can in turn be linked with concepts of duty and dependence, such as the word 'on' or debt of gratitude and obligation (Doi 1973:34).

The example I will present concerns a Japanese local politician and his road to power. I did fieldwork in a village-like community in Tokyo called Tsukuda (Selstad 1998:1). The place was famous because it was a former fishing village that had been preserved against all odds. The village consisted of a densely packed jumble of houses occupied by people who in general had been born locally, worked in the fish industry and spent much of their time keeping up local traditions such as ritual celebrations and festivals. In this manner the village was clearly distinct from the surrounding metropolis of Tokyo. One aspect of the traditional appearance of the community is a stable leadership, to which only two families contributed with local leaders in historical times up until the 1980s, and where leaders held power for life. However, the latest leader, Fujima, does not come from either of the two leading families, although he is closely linked to them through ties of work and obligation. His road to power is associated with paternalism, a form of particularistic relations that are widespread in Japanese society (Bennett and Ishino 1963:38). Cultivated as a patron and client relation, such relations can be found in many arenas, ranging from family and village to fish market, urban ward and metropolitan politics. Even at the level of state politics in Japan relations of patronage and clientship are at work (Bestor 1989:100).

This entails that in Japan considerations of honor and rank can be found at virtually every level of social integration, from personal acquaintance to household, local community, and all the way up to state politics and national concerns. The task is to indicate why questions of honor can gain prominence in a modern and technologically advanced society like Japan. My claim is that honor, in the form of keeping and losing face, is part and parcel of contests of power, which in turn play a part in wider exchanges and negotiations of ongoing social life. Contests of honor, keeping and losing face, can be described as discursive events that are not as far removed from the realities of modern life as they seem at first glance.

9.2 The two faces of local power

In parts of his work Foucault describes social discourse as imbedded in a field of social 'inertia' or sluggishness (1972:227). I venture to borrow this concept in distinguishing between two aspects of local politics that I will term ingrained inertia and dynamic negotiation. The first aspect concerns the duty bound character of local leadership. Where relations involve the preservation of face and the duties within a group, it may seem as though a permanent leader holds a very firm power position that may be described in terms of social inertia. Externally the emphasis will be on keeping a solid front, showing unity, and the leader may use this unity to dismiss criticism and manipulate support in the name of the common good. This raises the question of how the struggle for local power and honor can be said to involve an aspect of negotiation - a question that will be addressed as the example progresses.

The unique position of the local leader, Fujima, may be illustrated by the following anecdote. On New Year's Eve in 1987 the office of the local association, a hut used mainly by men, hosted a so-called 'wake night' where people could bring greetings and presents of money. On this occasion, the secretary of the local association referred to Fujima both as a potentate and as an 'attraction', a local sight worth seeing and which people had to come to visit. Not only local residents, but also representatives of the police, fire fighters, the mafia and city politicians stopped by to show their bonds of gratitude and to renew relations of obligation and patronage. Fujima could on this occasion be spoken of as an 'attraction of power' in the village.

Fujima was a colorful person who came to power partly as a protégé of the former leader, partly through his busy-body character and not least through paternalistic political contacts. It could be claimed that Fujima became a leader against all odds. His family was not even native to the village, but had moved there when Fujima was three years old. As a youth Fujima was restless, but involved himself in the local festival with great vigor, and obtained a job as a broker at the fish market alongside the former local leader.[2] In this fashion Fujima managed through various means to get the former leader to appoint him informally as his successor, and this became a decisive step on his road to power.

When it comes to local elections in Japan they are interesting in several ways. Partly this reflects the circumstance that local political arenas, the local associations, became linked with militarism and were dispelled from the formal political system after the war (Bestor 1989:75). Nevertheless the local association continued as the smallest political unit in the Japanese political system, and was gradually rehabilitated. In the present case what may be emphasized is that even in major cities in Japan, local associations incorporate a mixture of traditional forms of succession and democratic ideas of elections and voting. In Tsukuda the practice

---

[2] Fujima got involved in the festival before the war, when there was talk of curtailing the celebration for public security reasons. In 1941 he incited the young men to ram the godcart, a piece of festival paraphernalia, through the wall of the official shrine supervisor. From then on Fujima was hooked on festival life, taking part and defending it against external encroachments.

is such that the leader is elected every second year. Each household has one vote, and the elected leader himself appoints all his subordinate officers. In Japanese prose this reads: 'The leader conducts the election according to his clients' request to become assistant leader and to obtain other offices' (Sawara 1972:291; my translation). It becomes apparent that local elections primarily serve as a confirmation of who is to become leader. The leader has already been appointed, and only a part of the electorate takes part in voting to confirm the leadership. The leader then brings his own faction as a bloc into the local association, by appointing his clients to different offices. Since leaders are elected for life, only a small part of the electorate takes part in the local elections every two years.

At the time when Fujima was elected leader around 1982, there was another local man who felt that he had performed many services for the village. Among other things he had helped protect the village against urban development by 'borrowing the power' of politicians, that is, by having politicians stop the plans for local razing in return for promised votes and backing at elections. Through most of the period from 1960 to 1988 Tsukuda was under threat of razing for purposes of urban development, such as high-rise construction. This threat still remains today. Most local potentates were opposed to urban development, however, and equally important is the second candidate's belief that he had been appointed by a former leader to become the new leader in the village. At the election in 1982 this second candidate was sidestepped. His candidacy was not taken seriously, and Fujima was elected practically unanimously. At the local elections two years later the opposing candidate once more tried to challenge Fujima, but again lost overwhelmingly.

On both occasions reference was made to the fact that Fujima had been appointed as a leader because he had a client relationship to a powerful city politician who protected the village. The former leader, who appointed Fujima, explicitly stated that the village had a debt of gratitude to this politician. The word in Japanese is 'on', which may be translated as a debt of gratitude or duty-bound obligation incurred as a result of assistance or services rendered. This debt cannot be repaid 'ten thousand times', but creates a lasting bond of duty that is demonstrated through a unified front or face, 'tatemae' (Benedict 1946:81). The villagers had a duty to vote for this politician and for his client Fujima in future elections. This obligation was shown by almost en bloc local votes for Fujima and the city politician's leading Liberal Democratic Party in many elections (Selstad 1998:84). In this way Fujima remained a life-long local leader and representative, with several elected and honorary offices in city politics and commerce.

The candidate who ran against Fujima lost face. His defeat was interpreted as a personal shame (haji), not so much for losing but rather for failing to assess his support before the elections. As a consequence of this humiliation he withdrew from public life and remained indoors, a bitter and crushed man, who henceforth had little contact with other villagers. Even so it would be wrong to assume that the loser forfeited all power. He continued to have influence through his former supporters who now formed a sleeping faction in the village, opposed to Fujima but not active in elections. The opposing candidate continued to defend local traditions, deploring the threats of urban development. He could express his opinions in private and in writing, and in this way continued his fateful defense of village life (Ishii 1980). Whether he would ever get even with Fujima would depend on the latter in turn losing face, but old age would probably prevent the opposing candidate from running for leader in the future.

Fujima was therefore effectively left as an unopposed local leader, and could demonstrate his position by taking liberties without losing face. His first wife left him because of his 'fervent involvement' in the village festivals. He was in a position to keep himself with both a wife and a mistress, and owned two houses in the village that he moved between as he liked. In public he was a master at gathering support. His style was both boisterously authoritarian and heedfully appraisive at the same time. Still it seems pertinent to ask how Fujima could retain his power throughout his life. In the village there were several factions, partly linked to the arrangement of local festivals, and the leaders of these factions were Fujima's rivals, and in some cases his enemies. In order to grasp the texture of Fujima's leadership it is necessary to look at the many negotiations, conflicts and mediations that went on behind the scenes in some of the informal arenas in the village.

9.3 Stable leadership and social negotiations

Rather than regard stable or life-long leadership as a traditional attribute of a village-like setting, it may be viewed as bringing together different interests in mutual, practical activities (Bestor 1989:255). Political leaders in Japan can often be spoken of as figureheads, who bring together a wide array of interests under the guise of unity. Local leadership in Tsukuda might be described as a double-bind situation in which the leader has to both satisfy his patrons in the city government, and bring together the villagers in unified action under his auspices (Bateson 1972:201). In order to grasp how this feat of leadership is possible, a look at what takes place in different social arenas in the village is called for.

Leadership in Tsukuda was not connected only to the local association as a political arena, but also to different associations based on occupation, notably the fish industry, and not least to associations organized around the execution of religious celebrations and festivals. The most prominent local celebration is called the Great Festival. It is performed every three years in honor of the local patron deity, the sea god Sumiyoshi (Selstad 1998:139). The Great Festival requires months of preparation and lasts for four days. Aside from feasts and gatherings, three days of the Great Festival center on events in which sacred paraphernalia are carried through the streets by local men. The main paraphernalia are called 'lion heads', wooden heads weighing fifty kilograms, and the 'godcart', a small shrine carried on wooden beams and weighing half a ton. The men are divided up according to a proper age-grade system, with cyclical initiations of new members and strict gerontocracy, a rule by old men. The association that organizes the Great Festival is based on the system of men's age-grades, in addition to a division into three local residential areas or sections. The festival association has a central leader accompanied by three assistant leaders, one for each local section. All the leaders belong to the age grade of old men.

The leadership of the festival association manages prominent local traditions, and thereby the stage is set for competition with leaders in the local association. In order to avoid conflict, the rule has been that the local leader also serves as leader of the festival association, but the correlation is not absolute. Fujima may be said to have anticipated events, in becoming leader of the festival association several years before he became leader of the local association, thanks to his vigorous participation in the Great Festival. As noted the festival association includes other leaders attached to local sections, and these in turn recruit factional supporters who can challenge the local leader over time. The rule is that one of the section leaders in time will advance to become leader of the festival association, and thereby also a candidate to lead the local association and local political life.

The apparently dominant position of Fujima as a political 'attraction' is a feature of a situation marked by negotiations in multiple associations. On the one hand he had to maintain his client relations to leaders in urban politics, often involving a give and take with local interests. On the other hand he had to make an effort to gather local actors in a mutual ritual performance under his leadership. During the 1980s Fujima tried to solve this dilemma by creating a written 'program' for the Great Festival that could publicize or 'sell' the village to urban authorities, tourists and the media. He had several glossy posters made of different sacred paraphernalia, and marketed the festival as a series of 'events' for the media and city dwellers. In this work Fujima allied himself with the religious figurehead of the festival, the shrine priest, and with the festival secretary. The section leaders in the festival reacted to Fujima's intervention. One view was that the Great Festival was a ritual event that constituted a single whole, and that it could not be produced in a piecemeal or fragmented form. At least one section leader ventured to bring up this objection by carrying on negotiations with Fujima through the secretary as an intermediary. There was a complaint that the leader 'would not listen'. For a while fairly intense negotiations went on behind the scenes – in the street and in other informal settings – although outwardly there was no sign of any conflict going on in the village.

When the Great Festival was performed in 1987, the participants simply elected to ignore the fancy plans and the 'program' Fujima had made. Instead, the festival took place according to received practice, based on the practical schedule of preparatory work and ritual performances. On one occasion Fujima wanted to signal the raising of the festival banners at a certain hour, but the participants started raising the banners long before he was ready. Fujima virtually became an observer at the Great Festival, who gave interviews on TV and snapped some photographs in order to record what took place. His passive role might in part be attributed to his socially elevated position as leader, but there were several comments about his distance from festival participants. One question would be how much Fujima could be ignored and how many defeats he could take before he started losing power, face and 'attraction'. This further reflects on the issue of how honor and face can be related to any actual wielding of power on Fujima's part over the villagers.

9.4 Honor, performances, and gender relations

So far it is Fujima's special position as a potentate in the village that has been emphasized. Although there were complaints about his leadership and negotiations over how to perform events, his position as a leader remained unchallenged. What has to be brought into the description is first of all the many interests, expressions and considerations involved in local social and ritual life, and not least those that relate to gender. While gender ethics may not seem as central to honor in Japan as in the Mediterranean, it would be a mistake to overlook the gender implications of honor and power (Asano-Tamanoi 1987:115). The second consideration is the way in which Fujima could actually serve his own ends in a context that put emphasis on unity of face, consensus and stable political leadership.

At a concluding meeting of the Great Festival in 1987, Fujima held a short speech in which he summarily deposed his strongest competitors among the leaders in the festival association, including the section leader who had voiced complaints about the program. This event almost passed me by unnoticed, because he spoke very rapidly, nobody voiced a word of opposition, and he used a standard formula about retirement 'due to personal circumstances'. And Fujima had another card up his sleeve. A female TV journalist had persuaded Fujima to make concessions on the question of whether women should be allowed to enter the Great Festival. In 1993 he introduced a decision that there would be a round of carrying the sacred paraphernalia 'by women only' during the Great Festival. At the time I interpreted this as an indication that the local residents were trying to incorporate women in the festival due to external pressure, and that they tried to do this according to traditional rules of exclusion and inclusion. In the festival there is a symbolism of gradual inclusion, in which different groups, determined by age-grade and section, first carry paraphernalia around separately, later to be brought together in a joint procession where also women take part (Selstad 1998:305). Many things must have taken place behind the scenes, thus rendering my first interpretation too simple. My surprise was considerable when I returned to the village in 1999 and discovered that women again had been excluded from carrying any of the sacred paraphernalia. The woman who told me this added that the participation of women was 'just something that Fujima made up'. By this time Fujima had become senile; all he said on meeting someone was 'who are you'. So the festival members had quite simply decided to overlook what the leader had decided and reverted to the former practice of men carrying the paraphernalia.

One implication of this situation is that Fujima may seem to have lost face in the end, albeit only after he was so weakened that he could no longer defend himself. Honor may easily be conceived of as a static attribute of a person, something a person either has or has not. In my opinion the examples indicate that honor can be described as a game, what might be called a 'tournament', where factors have a tendency to even out in the end (Aase, this volume). The village residents readily acknowledged that they had a lot for which they had to thank Fujima as a leader. In the 1980s he managed more or less single-handedly to prevent the village from being razed, by visiting his political patrons in the city government and imploring them to abandon plans for urban renewal in Tsukuda

(Selstad 1998:345). The grievances against Fujima, local disagreements and conflicts over his role, were almost equally strong, however, and for this reason Fujima constantly had to maneuver his position to keep in power. Many of these complaints concerned festival life, which in turn touched on deeper issues about local life and integration. At times it seemed like Fujima treated the Great Festival as his own venture, such as when he offered to sell kimonos used as festival uniforms to American tourists, uniforms that were supposed to be worn only by festival members. While local concerns relating to ritual rules of purity, exclusion and inclusion may seem restricted in scope and relevance, they interrelate with wider concerns in the sense that festival life may be seen as a commentary on everyday social life in the village, in a complex interplay between traditional involvement and modern change. Hence Fujima's interventions in the festival were not taken lightly by the residents.

Here another implication of ritual change comes to the fore. The move to exclude women once again from festival participation can be interpreted as an expression of traditionalism. In my opinion it would be too simple to claim that the villagers had reverted to an archaic or reactionary use of local cultural codes. The main considerations would seem to involve negotiations over performances that could make sense in the setting of local life. As noted, the ideas of honor and shame are associated with gender relations in Japan as they are elsewhere (Tamano-Asanoi op.cit.:116). During the village festival itself some local men did not hesitate to point to ritual pollution as a reason for women's exclusion. A group of female tourists from the metropolis seemed shocked when told by a local man that women are not allowed to touch the sacred paraphernalia because women are 'dirty' or shameful. Other participants would dissociate themselves from such crude statements. In order to show how composite the game of honor and shame can become in relation to gender, I return to the expression of 'tatemae', a person's public front or face. Everything that takes place overtly during the festivals, and ideally in all social life, is spoken of as 'tatemae' or 'front', whereby a person's 'honne' or real self is not to be shown directly. During the Great Festival young men have to fight in order to be allowed to carry the paraphernalia, jostling for carrying positions. There was pushing and shoving, even beating and kicking to find room, and at times people lost their temper and attacked each other physically. At such moments the older men quickly stepped in and subdued the combatants, at the same time emphasizing that what happened was 'tatemae', front, not real emotions.

Such interpretations of social front provide scope for a considerable amount of ritual play involving symbols and representations. In one celebration local women make fun of men by dressing up as pimps, bums or hen-pecked men during a dance in the street. In the Great Festival there is the opposite symbolism when women take part in the procession dressed as 'maiko', a kind of prostitute. At night during the festival, as people sit in the streets and alleys drinking under the lights of lanterns and open windows, exchanges between women and men become much more personal, ranging from quarrels and small talk to crying and drunken declarations of love.[3] During the festival period it is permissible to go beyond the restrictive codes of everyday life - as long as these can be reinterpreted in terms of ritual play as a 'front'. Among other things women can address sexual allegations and jokes to the men taking part in the festival. Concepts of ritual purity and exclusiveness may furthermore be tied up with threats of ridicule, ostracism and loss of face. One rule states that the festival uniform can only be worn by men taking part in the festival, and lending the uniform to non-participants, in particular to women, is forbidden under penalty of ostracism and expulsion from the festival. When in the 1970s a young woman was seen wearing her brother's festival uniform, the young men physically attacked the brother and beleaguered his family's house, demanding that he be expelled from the festival. The seriousness of the incident was demonstrated when the father of the young man, a prominent old man, offered to resign from the festival. The case was smoothed over as a matter of ignorance - the young man had not yet learned the rules - but it can also be interpreted as a loss of face through breach of rules. For years the other young men prevented the offender from taking part in the festival or going near the sacred paraphernalia, even after the old men had pardoned him.

In spite of modern change, considerations of face and rank continue to have considerable bearing on ritual and social life in Tsukuda. My claim would be that ritual relations of purity and pollution, honor and shame, constitute part of a ritual and social play that represents a commentary on everyday negotiations of gender relations and residential conditions. One reason why honor is not personalized more often in terms of gender would be that rank is depersonalized as an integral part of relations, such as in the minute ranking of age-grades. Gender is ritualized in terms of pollution and distance, allowing conflicts and negotiations to be reinterpreted as play and license. One observation in my material was that women were as forceful as men in expressing support for the perpetuation of festival life. One statement made by women was that if a husband refused to take part in the Great Festival this would constitute grounds for divorce on her part (Selstad 1998:175). Women may be represented as subordinate and underestimated, especially in the Great Festival with its emphasis on old men's rule and ritual exclusiveness. At the same time women were insistent in their expression of interest in and support of festival life. One claim was that women refused to cook during the festival because they got tired from all the preparations – a kind of silent protest against men's dominance. The men interpreted this differently, claiming that they needed specially purchased ritual foods during the festival.

While honor is not personalized in terms of gender, it is still women who administer face and shame through gossip and other forms of gender negotiations (Asano-Tamanoi 1987:116). Women did not hesitate to use the ritual room for license and play against male leaders. When Fujima ran around trying to 'administer' the Great Festival according to his plan, he was not only ignored but subjected to some teasing and jeering. On one occasion, as he hastened past a group of housewives sitting on a bench with a camera in his hand, one of the

[3] Windows have to remain open at all times during the Great Festival, a practice conducive to the social atmosphere called festival life.

women called out in mock deference, 'oh, mister village chief' – an outdated and ironic-sounding term. He pretended not to hear her as he hurried on. Fujima in his turn could ignore much of this ridicule because of his permanent position as leader. When he took command he knew that he would not be overtly opposed, even when working to depose his closest rivals for the local leadership. Behind the stable 'inertia' of public honor, then, room is created for conflicts, mediation and negotiations that may be linked with group relations, but which also allow individuals to express their interests, whether in subordination or as a dominant 'attraction'.

9.5 Reflections on the re-negotiation of power

When presenting a political dynamic which on the surface appears static, characterized by life-long leadership and displays of honor, it becomes a pressing task to demonstrate the considerable complexity and multivocality of the interests that underly this surface stability. Tsukuda is clearly distinct from the surrounding metropolis and from modern Japanese society in a number of ways; it stands out not least on account of its village-like setting. In fact this distinctiveness is what raises a first question in visitors' minds: how can a village survive in a giant city? In my research I have shown that this question is too simple, and may lead to reified and essentialist preconceptions of local life (Selstad 1998:302). Many factors, historical, economic and political, have helped preserve Tsukuda as a unique but living place.

A pertinent question at this point concerns the extent to which Tsukuda can be considered representative when compared with the far more complex and change related conditions of Japan as a late modern society. When researchers claim that Japanese modernity represents a transition from and an intermixing of 'premodern' and 'postmodern' societies, they seem to imply a unidirectional, if not always smooth, transition from tradition to modernity (Clammer 1995; Iwatake 1993). When local residents in Tsukuda insist that they are both traditional and modern, they may be interpreted as supporting such a view, but they are also commenting on the multiplexity and compositeness of modern social life. This became clear during my latest visit to the village in 1999, when the Great Festival was being performed as vigorously as ever, although at the same time residents felt a stronger pressure than before toward urban development and loss of local control. One woman expressed it rather desperately by exclaiming that many people 'have no money' to take part in festival life. Perhaps the current economic and social crisis that Japan is going through is an expression of the new values and relations that are taking over. The new prime minister has aired the idea of instituting a welfare state in this formerly group-based and family-anchored society. In spite of this there is every reason to believe that considerations of face, duty and dependence will continue to play a role in Japanese social life (cf. Doi 1973:163).

In many ways, events in Tsukuda reflect this trend toward increased heterogeneity alongside persistent forms of social relations. Local residents continue to emphasize bonds of honor and obligation, as evidenced by Fujima continuing to be the leader of the festival association even after becoming senile. Today he is more of a figurehead than anything, while the practical implementation of the Great Festival is managed by the echelon of section leaders. In the midst of intense developments and social change the villagers have tried to revitalize the festival by reverting to former practices. The godcart is once more taken out to sea on a boat that circumnavigates the island, a practice abandoned in the 1960s due to the construction of flood barriers. Special ramps and gates had to be constructed to make it possible to take the godcart by boat. As noted, women were excluded from carrying the sacred paraphernalia after being permitted to do so in 1993. Viewing events in isolation may easily lead to misinterpretations of traditionalism or ritual exclusion. Moreover, in 1998 I learned that for the first time in history a woman had been elected as leader of the village. It is noteworthy that she came from a prominent local family, not one of the two leading families, but still a kin group with strong interests in local traditions and festivals. Perhaps women are better situated than men to preserve the village as a residential area bound by ties of honor and duty. A more prosaic explanation would be that she serves for her husband, since most women members of the local association are widows who serve in the name of their husbands.

The point to be emphasized is that any simplified view of honor and power is bound to run up against the multifaceted considerations and negotiations that constitute the fabric of social life. When asking what words 'do', honor and duty easily lead our thoughts to feudal conditions of submission and chivalry. In stead it would be worthwhile to view contests of honor in the context of constant negotiations and re-negotiations of power and standing in social life. In order to avoid essentializing conceptions such as sin culture and shame culture, it becomes mandatory to describe culture discursively in terms of the many facets of its manifestation, whether in everyday detail or in overall claims of direction (cf. Benedict 1946:156). I would like to paraphrase Foucault on this point, by saying that social life has to be captured in the totality of its emergence (Foucault 1972:35).

Perhaps anthropology has matured to a point where it recognizes how composite and opaque images of persons and social relations can be. At least representations such as habitus, 'thick' interpretation and discourse point to such a human complexity (Boudieu 1977; Geertz 1973). The tendency remains to think too simply about what it means for individuals to get involved in social life. The continuing relevance of honor and duty in modern life can be just such a topic, where the danger of oversimplifying person images is imminent. Honor should not be conceived of too narrowly nor too widely. When interpreted as personal 'dignity' or integrity, honor concerns all people. When viewed as a 'tournament of power', honor becomes a question of how people manage their interests in relations that are inscribed by rules, heavily coded and loaded with symbols. The political career of a Japanese leader exemplifies the way in which honor, or losing and keeping face, is closely connected to the manipulation of power. It is tempting to claim that honor corrupts as much as power corrupts, without drawing an equation between honor and power. In any case the question of honor and reputation will to a large extent depend on an exposition of the contexts where interests are played out. When viewed as a static concept, as a privileged position that can be defended within a group, honor can easily be interpreted as a breach with modern relations marked by situatedness and individuality. When honor is viewed as a face, front or veil through which power is exercised and negotiated, then it becomes apparent that this is an area where individuals may subsume their self-interests under the umbrella of group interests. Thus honor and power become phenomena of acute relevance to the shifting allegiances of negotiated relations in today's modern world.

References

Aase, T.H. (this volume), 'Introduction.' In: Tor H. Aase (ed.): *Tournaments of Power.*

Asano-Tamanoi, M. (1987), 'Shame, family, and state in Catalonia and Japan'. In: D. D. Gilmore (ed.): *Honor and Shame and the Unity of the Mediterranean.* Washington, American Anthropological Association

Austin, J. L. (1962), *Doing Things With Words.* London, Oxford University Press

Bateson, G. (1972), *Steps to an Ecology of Mind.* New York, Ballantine Books

Befu, H. (1971), *Japan: An Anthropological Introduction.* New York, Chandler

Benedict, R. (1946), *The Chrysanthemum and the Sword.* Boston, Houghton Mifflin

Bennett, J. W. and Isao I. (eds.) (1963), *Paternalism in the Japanese Economy.* Minneapolis, University of Minnesota Press

Bestor, T. C. (1989), *Neighborhood Tokyo.* Tokyo, Kodansha

Bourdieu, P. (1977), *Outline of a Theory of Practice.* Cambridge, Cambridge University Press

Clammer, J. (1995), *Difference and Modernity: Social Theory and Contemporary Japanese Society.* London, Kegan Paul International

Doi, T. (1973), *The Anatomy of Dependence.* Tokyo, Kodansha

Foucault, M. (1972), *The Archaeology of Knowledge.* New York, Tavistock

Geertz, C. (1973), *The Interpretation of Cultures.* New York, Basic Books

Gilmore, D. D. (ed.) (1987), *Honor and Shame and the Unity of the Mediterranean.* Washington, American Anthropological Association

Ishii, K. (1980), *Jinzai eika.* (Life's elegy; in Japanese.) Tokyo, privately printed

Iwatake, M. (1993), 'Tokyo' in the postmodern world order'. In: J. Kivisto et al. (eds.): *Modulations in Tradition.* Tampere, University of Tampere

Kalland, A. (1986), 'Japansk gruppisme.' (Japanese groupism; in Norwegian.) In: *Japan bak fasaden.* Oslo, Cappelen

Nakane, C. (1967), *Kinship and Economic Organization in Rural Japan.* London, Athlone Press

Nakane, C. (1970), *Japanese Society.* Harmondsworth, Penguin Books

Sawara, R. (1972), *Tsukudajima no kondyaku.* (The past and present of Tsukudajima; in Japanese. Tokyo, Yukibana-sha

Selstad, L. (1998), *An Island of Tradition: Ritual Life and Local Traditionalism in a Tokyo Bay Community.* Bergen, PhD Dissertation, University of Bergen

Tokyo-to kyoiku iinkai (1984), *Chuo-ku Tsukudajima-chiku bunka-zai chosa hokoku.* (Investigative report of cultural assets in Tsukudajima; in Japanese.) Tokyo, Tokyo-to

Chapter 10

A House that Lacks a Man, Lacks Respect

Marit Melhuus

10.1 Introduction

In 1967 Peter Rivière wrote an article entitled 'The Honour of Sánchez'. The article was prompted by two significant works in anthropology in print at the time: the volume edited by Peristiany, *Honour and Shame: The Values of Mediterranean Society* (1965), and Oscar Lewis's book *The Children of Sánchez* (1961, Spanish edition 1965). More specifically, Rivière responded to a call from Pitt-Rivers that '[a] comparison of the values and symbolism of honour in Spain and in the New World is badly needed' (quoted in Rivière 1967), while at the same time wishing to 'see how far the type of ethnography produced by Oscar Lewis is amenable to sociological analysis' (1967: 569).[1] Thus he sets himself the task of analysing *The Children of Sánchez* in terms of honour and shame.

This exercise is fruitful. Rivière finds that such notions can in fact be gleaned from the ethnography presented by Lewis, and that honour and shame are of relevance in the context of a poor, tenement neighbourhood in Mexico City. Hence, the analysis is also a step towards a more systematic comparison of these value systems.

Arguing for a distinction between 'communal or family interest' and 'individual or self interest' (to parallel the distinctions made by Pitt-Rivers between 'honour = virtue' and 'honour = precedence'), Rivière proceeds to show how notions of honour and shame are intrinsically gendered, i.e. linked into local values of *machismo* as well as feminine values of virginity and chastity. He finds that Mexican ideals echo those reported from Spain, with one main difference: in the Spanish setting there is a correspondence between ideals and practice, whereas Rivière finds this connection far more tenuous in the Mexican case (1967:575). Therefore, he turns his attention to grasping the significance of this discrepancy.

It is, perhaps, not surprising to discover that notions of honour and may prevail in Mexican *mestizo* communities, considering the overwhelming influence of Spanish culture as well as the Catholic Church in the formation of the modern

[1] Oscar Lewis's family studies/life-histories were variously received and controversial at the time. For further discussion, see Melhuus 1997a; Rigdon 1988; see also Lewis 1959, 1961.

Mexican state. Historians have documented the prevalence of a morality tied to the notions of honour and shame and their significance for the colonial social order (see e.g. Johnson and Lipsett-Rivera 1998; Seed 1988a). Although such notions may still occur and carry meaning in contemporary society, they will most certainly differ radically from their historical antecedents, not only with respect to meanings but also with respect to the implications in cases of moral breach. Hence, any understanding of these notions must take into consideration the specific contexts in which they operate. In this article I am concerned with the workings of contemporary forms of a morality grounded in honour and shame. Therefore I will not focus or debate the transformations of meanings of honour and shame through time (but see Seed 1988b for an illustration of such transformations in the colonial period). With a special emphasis on women and their efforts to be respected as morally good, I will, however, indicate particular social processes, which may serve to undermine a local morality tied to honour and shame. These will, to anticipate the conclusion, be related to Pitt-Rivers observation: 'once the sexual division of labour breaks down, women become men and where this occurs there can be neither honour nor shame' (1974:70). Finally, there is one salient feature which is worth noting for its recurrence in the literature: discussions of honour (and shame) invariably invoke the themes of sexuality, and thereby marriage and procreation, and more specifically the legitimacy of children. My case is no exception.[2]

Despite the cue given by Rivière, anthropologists working in Mexico – or even Latin America more generally – did not rise to the challenge at the time. Other issues presented themselves as more pressing (in particular those of modernisation and change, with the concomitant focus on theories of peasantries, underdevelopment, and subsequently dependency, and the substantial critiques following in their wake). In fact, the notions of honour and shame as relevant concepts for grasping aspects of social reality resurfaced with a renewed focus on gender and gender relations, personhood and identity (see e.g. Archetti 1991; Stølen 1996; Melhuus 1997).[3] More specifically, the interests in masculinity and homosexuality prompted a re-examination of the significance of these terms (e.g. Lancaster 1988; Prieur 1998; also Melhuus 1998).

10.2 Honour and shame, once again

Given the criticism that has been raised with regard to the use and status of the notions of honour and shame in anthropology, some mention should perhaps be made of the major objections. Moreover, since these concepts are not just

[2] This thematic slant is also prevalent from studies carried out in the Mediterranean region. See e.g. Gilmore 1987; Delaney 1987.

[3] One exception is a study by Martinez -Alier (1974) from Cuba, which explicitly focuses on honour and shame in a historical perspective; other studies from the Caribbean (e.g. Clarke 1979, Eidheim 1981, Wilson 1973) have focussed on gender relations and the gendered notions of reputation/respectability.

analytical categories but are also empirically grounded, being at one and the same time part of local discourses as well as anthropological discourse, they leave ample room for misunderstanding. To this we can add arguments of modernity, which contrast honour (and chastity) with dignity (e.g. Berger et al. 1997: 78ff), associating the former with pre-modern societies and viewing the latter as a thoroughly modern feature. Arguments to the contrary nevertheless merit our attention.[4]

Within anthropology, the concepts of honour and shame have generally been employed to characterise the value system of the Mediterranean region, so much so that they can be considered gate-keeping concepts.[5] They are usually associated with rural communities, typically characterised by face-to-face, multiplex social relations. Not only has the relevance of these concepts – as universals for the region – been contested, several authors have also stressed the androcentric and ethnocentric bias that has permeated the use of the terms (e.g. Piña-Cabral 1989; Gilmore 1987; Goddard 1987; Lever 1986). Research on the honour/shame syndrome has also been criticised for re-enforcing a rural-urban stereotype (Brandes 1987).

In much of the ethnographic literature, notions of honour are coupled with those of shame. They are often viewed as mutually constitutive of meaning, in the sense that they are seen as implicitly or explicitly referring to the same social phenomena.[6] However, this intrinsic linking of the concepts has been problematised and questions have been raised as to whether honour and shame are semantically equal terms (e.g. Wikan 1984). The conceptual pair were considered neither necessary nor sufficient to describe the reality from which they were extracted. Hence the forceful plea to elicit indigenous meanings and usages of the terms, with an emphasis on situational and local expressions and context. Moreover, empirical evidence suggests a variation with respect to which of the two concepts predominates in any local context (e.g. honour for Greece, shame in Spain). Thus, for example Brandes (1987) and Wikan (1984) find that in Andalusia and Oman, the concept of shame is much more prevalent than the concept of honour. Brandes even goes as far as to say that 'it is reasonable to draw upon this

---

[4] For a discussion on the concept of shame and its relevance for contemporary society see Wyller (2001), an edited, interdisciplinary collection of essays.

[5] Most anthropological discussions on honour and shame depart from Peristiany's now classic essay collection *Honour and Shame. The Values of Mediterranean Society* originally published in 1966. See in particular Pitt-Rivers (1974 [1966]) and Bourdieu (1974[1966]). See also Schneider (1971), Herzfeld (1980), Gilmore (1982) and Gilmore (1987), also an edited collection, where Asano-Tamanoi discusses the concepts with respect to Japan.

[6] See for example Pitt-River's (1974) discussion of the different meanings of honour as virtue and honour as precedence (1974: 35 ff) and his discussion of honour as synonymous with shame (1974: 41 ff) and as constituents of virtue. He says: "while ... certain virtues are common to both sexes ... they are not all so ... This is particularly evident in the differentiation of the sexes. The honour of a man and of a woman ... imply quite different modes of conduct ... A woman is dishonoured, loses her *vergüenza* with the tainting of her sexual purity, but a man does not." (42) And he goes on to make the following observation: "Yet the concepts of honour and shame also extend to the point where they are no longer synonymous ... when they are not equivalent, [they] are linked exclusively to one sex or the other and are opposed to one another" (1974: 42-43).

concept [i.e. shame] to explain Spanish values and social relations; emically and etically it makes sense as an organizing principle' (Brandes 1987:123).

The relationship between the concepts of honour and shame, then, is problematic on several counts. Partly this is due to the multiple meanings of both concepts. Their meanings vary not only with respect to place (regionally) but also according to situation and gender. In addition, the positioning of the individual researcher will invariably influence the images projected. Feminist theory and a more general incorporation of gendered perspectives have contributed to different and more nuanced understandings of honour and shame. The fact that the meanings of these concepts have been investigated in Latin American (Melhuus 1990, 1997b, 1998; Lancaster 1988; Prieur 1998; Stølen 1996) and urban (Goddard 1987,1996) contexts has yielded new ethnography and thereby also expanded the comparative field. This book, with its comparative focus on contemporary forms of honour is a further step in that direction.

10.3 A particular moral order

As mentioned, much of the empirical as well as theoretical observations suggest that the nexus for a morality based on honour and shame are the notions held of sexuality. Gilmore claims that where honour and shame prevail as primordial values 'these values are deeply tied up with sexuality and power, with masculinity and gender relations' (Gilmore 1987:16), suggesting that 'since the honor/shame syndrome regulates both inter- and intrasex relations, it may be regarded as a total social fact' (ibid. 5). Brandes echoes this view, claiming that 'these core sexual values become metaphors in terms of which other realms of life might be conceived' (Brandes 1987:132; see also Melhuus and Stølen 1996 for a similar argument with respect to gender more generally). Thus, it seems that any understanding of meanings of honour and shame has to take into account gender relations and their social significance for the construction of masculinity and femininity. It is in these constructions, gleaned from everyday practice and discourse, that idioms of power are embedded and ideas of (and behind) moral restitution (be it through vengeance or otherwise) can be traced.

Insofar as the concepts of honour and shame have been linked to so-called traditional societies (implying rural, premodern), it is surely because the concepts articulate a particularistic moral code and because it has been assumed that such particularistic moral codes only prevail in small, tightly knit communities permeated by multiplex relations. The main characteristic of such a morality is that it is grounded in difference. It is a morality which anchors and orders social relations and social organisation on the basis of differentiation and hierarchy – such as gender, class, and race.[7] This is in sharp contrast to a universalistic moral

[7] For example in the case of colonial Mexico (and elsewhere in Latin America, as well as Spain) difference was established and people classified according to blood and degrees of blood mixture. See Lippsett- Rivera 1998, Martinez-Alier 1974, Baroja 1974; for Southern USA see Wyatt-Brown 1982. What many of these studies show is the significance of "pure blood" with regard to reputation and

order, grounded in universal values of human worth, dignity, and equality, irrespective of gender, race, age, religion etc. Crucial to such a moral order is the idea of individual autonomy (and rights), and anonymity is an important dimension of social organisation. In theory, these two moral orders are incompatible, operating with qualitatively different notions of personhood. Thus, in theory, there is no room for honour and shame in modern societies. They are classified as pre-modern phenomena. In reality, however, we encounter a very different picture.

Much anthropological research has demonstrated that ideas of honour and shame do belong to our times. The classic studies of honour and shame were in fact carried out in local communities within modern nation states: Algeria, Greece, Italy, Spain, Turkey. Thus, empirically one could assume the presence of co-existing yet contradictory moralities. However, little attention has been paid to the implications of such contradictory moral constellations for the people living them or those studying them.[8] One important line of investigation, therefore, would be to locate and explore a possible interface between co-existing moralities as they are expressed in social relations and social practice. Examining the nature of moral dilemmas might be one place to start. Moreover, to what extent notions of honour (or shame) are on the wane or being reinforced depends on a series of factors, and can only be documented empirically. I would suspect that a hypothesis which posits that notions of honour are being fragmented and gradually becoming obsolete would immediately be met by a counter proposition: particularistic codes are becoming more entrenched as a response to modernity's constant transformations. In social reality, these processes occur simultaneously and the challenge is to understand how.

One of the observations that Rivière makes in his analysis of *The Children of Sánchez* is the discrepancy between ideals and practice, in particular with respect to female chastity and men's willingness to defend their honour (and that of their families): women are not virgins when they marry and men do not readily turn to violence as forms of vengeance. This observation concurs with my own findings based on research in San Felipe, a *mestizo* village in the State of Mexico.[9] The fact that values are expressed but not necessarily adhered to is, I think, common to most human experience. Thus, my approximation to morality implies a perspective that shifts from a predominant concentration on moral rules constituting a mechanism for sanction, to the more complex focus on significant ideas and values as a set of cultural presuppositions that inform and create social relations, and not just sanction and maintain them. Moreover, as the meaning of moral values also hinges on imagination and emotions, morality will always be open to interpretation; it will necessarily be less than certain (e.g. Evens 1982; also Edel and Edel 1959). A perception of morality as multivocal does not imply that central values are not

honour. For an analysis of hierarchy in terms of modern and premodern see Dumont 1980.

[8] One exception is Pitt-Rivers (1974) who in fact poses the question, but does not pursue the implications in ethnographic detail.

[9] Fieldwork was carried out for over a year in the period 1983-84; with a follow-up in 1989. At the time of my fieldwork, the population of San Felipe was about 6000. As in previous texts that I have written from this area, all names of people and places have been changed.

shared or recognized. It does, however, imply that their meanings may be contested.

10.4 San Felipe – a quiet place

So let me now turn to the village of San Felipe, nestling in the *sierras* at an altitude of over 2700 metres, not far from the major urban centres of Toluca and Mexico City. San Felipe is a district capital, where the church and the 'presidencia' or town hall – each representing power, authority, and tradition – face each other across the town's plaza. At the centre of the plaza, surrounded by trees, is a small bandstand used for festive occasions. There are many days of *fiesta* throughout the year. Christmas *posadas*, Easter processions, the day of the village saint, Mothers Day, the Day of the Dead, as well as the day of the Virgin of Guadalupe are all celebrated. The narrow streets leading off the plaza are cobbled, and give way to pavement only beyond the immediate centre, from where they connect San Felipe to nearby towns and major highways. Pathways criss-cross the surrounding countryside, between fields of maize, which is the main crop.

San Felipe is primarily an agricultural community, drawn into state policies through credit schemes, local and ambulant health services, schools, and of course the political apparatus. Agriculture has always been the mainstay of the district, and the agrarian structure is based on the *ejido.*[10] Maize is the staple crop and together with the keeping of domestic animals and the exploitation of the 'maguey',[11] those represent the traditional adaptation. The majority of the people still rely on farming for their subsistence, and many own their own small plots as well as having access to the *ejido*. However, agriculture does not provide sufficient financial income and additional sources have to be sought. Emigration has been common, causing great concern to local authorities, especially as it is the young who tend to leave. Characteristic of this local trend is that children or young single persons migrate, not household heads (neither husbands nor wives), although many (men and women) were migrants before marriage. As I have argued elsewhere, this particular migratory pattern should be understood in terms of a local morality where notions of honour and shame are central (see Melhuus 1992).

San Felipe is a Spanish speaking community, and the majority of the people are Catholic. At the time of my initial fieldwork, the village had a primary and secondary school. When I returned several years later a technical school had been constructed as well as a public library, as part of a plan to keep youth in the area. The older villagers valued education, aspiring to better futures for their children, and hopefully better security through them in their old age. For the younger ones, education was seen as the best way of achieving some social mobility.

[10] The *ejidos* were a result of the major land reforms in Mexico, granting peasants usufruct rights to the land. The original land grant for San Felipe was given in 1936.

[11] The "maguey" is an agave plant used for the production of "pulque", a fermented beverage based on the "agua miel" or "honey water" extracted by scraping the hollow of the plant.

Although a local seat of power, this village was no bustling centre. In fact people complained about the difficult times (it was a period of major recession in the Mexican economy) and the lack of local job opportunities. The inhabitants of the village centre, 'el centro', described their village as backward ('atrasado'), not very civilized ('no muy civilisado') and closed ('cerrado'). They were comparing themselves not only to the urban centres but also to the nearby predominantly Otomí villages, who, they said, had been able to 'superarse', i.e. get ahead in the world, being successful in their commercial ventures and open to initiatives. Some of the villagers associated this with the fact that many of the Otomís had converted (to Protestantism) and this made them more united ('más unidos'); moreover they had stopped drinking, and become more responsible. Or so I was told. The people of 'el centro' represented a different segment of the population than the surrounding area. Here live the professionals, doctors and teachers, shopkeepers and artisans, the 'pulqueros',[12] the baker, butchers etc.

According to the villagers, San Felipe had been notorious for being a violent and dangerous place. Vivid tales of 'tiroteos' (gunfights) and arbitrary killings flourished. It was said that those driving transport vehicles would refuse to enter the village after sunset and women would never venture to the centre after dusk. But this was 'antes' – 'before'. At the time of my fieldwork, the refrain 'somos un pueblo muy tranquilo' or 'somos muy pacificos' (characterising the village/people as tranquil, or peaceful) was reiterated constantly. Moreover, people would stress, as a positive trait, that the village was like a family, everyone knew each other, 'la vida es transparente' ([village] life is transparent).

When discussing issues of violence with Don Fidel, he said: 'Violence usually arises from situations where honour has been tainted. These situations are nearly always related to the family and have to do with either women or land ... In order to defend the honour of the family, they [the men] would seek vengeance, to rid themselves of the mark.' And he continued: 'But this was before. Today, it seems that parents are softer, as if the honour of the family is losing something. No one has the right to take anyone's life.'

It is always hard to grasp local ideas of 'before'. These will, obviously, depend on the age, position, and hence frame of reference of the speaker. If anything, such expressions sum up a mood or feeling of changing times. Don Fidel is an elderly, well-educated man. When talking about these issues, he used expressions such as 'mancillar el honor' (literally 'to taint honour'), and that a man 'se siente mancillado' ('feels tainted, humiliated') and this would provoke acts of vengeance. Such expressions were not common, and the community was not riddled by violence, although gossip was extremely vicious. Don Fidel's reflections about the demise of honour echo perhaps some overall trends, which are not always easy to pinpoint precisely, but which may have to do with gradual shifts in

[12] The production of pulque was one of the few local commercial activities. However, with changing tastes, other alcoholic beverages are now preferred and pulque has lost its commercial value.

notions of moral worth (and thereby means of moral restitution). These shifts may become more apparent by turning to the prevailing gender ideology.[13]

However, the fact that honour is not explicitly invoked does not mean that incidents of violence were not framed in those terms. In addition to tales of 'antes', there were recent cases of murder and rape, as well as domestic violence, involving people I knew. What is striking is the local interpretive frame through which these events were filtered. All of them locate women as a focal object in the struggle between men (see Melhuus 1998), and defence of honour (through vengeance) is perceived as the reference – and means – whereby the chain of events unravels. These local interpretations point to a particular construction of male virtue (which can be glossed as honour, covering local terms such as respect, being responsible, generous, being in command, independent, virility – in sum: being a *macho*), which implies a specific construction of female virtue (understood as a woman who has shame, is chaste, modest). However, the fact that people tend to understand violence in these terms, attributing to it a certain meaning, does not necessarily imply acceptance of the violence or the reasons for it. Nor does it necessarily concur with the intentions of the offender or the interpretations of the victims. Such matters were part of the local gossip.

The following example is interesting precisely because it does not (initially) seem to have anything to do with sexuality or women or land. Ignacio, a young, active man was murdered. The motives for the murder were unclear but did not have to do with either his wife or the wife of the assailant, but appeared to be a case involving corruption. Ignacio was, among other things, in charge of a group receiving fertilizer through a local government scheme. Ignacio's widow, Carlota, was left with four children to support. She had married very young, had had no education and felt ill-equipped to cope with the situation. She said she knew nothing of how Ignacio had run his affairs. He had been better off than many in the village, cultivating several hectares of land, while at the same time raising cattle and running a taxi. When I asked his brother (who was also the closest neighbour) what would become of Carlota, how she would manage, he answered: 'We will help her in what ways we can, if she behaves.' I countered: 'Behaves, in what sense?' 'That she does not remarry. She has to look after her children. If she is a good mother, we will give her a hand.' Ignacio's brother felt obliged to help his sister-in-law only insofar as she remained chaste (i.e. refused potential partners) and thus maintained her husband's honour. However, this is cast in terms of being a good mother. A good mother would not remarry since it is assumed (and this is generally confirmed in the village, by both men and women) that one man will never care for the children of another man. Hence, in remarrying, Carlota would forsake her children. This would be a selfish act and in local terms she would be considered an egoist and a poor mother. This would not be condoned.

[13] These shifts in moral worth will in turn have to do with notions of personhood, which implies *ipso facto* notions of gender. For a discussion of *machismo*, men and power see Melhuus (2001a). See also Gutman 1996 with respect to changing notions of masculinity; and Levine (1986, 1993) with respect to womanhood; also Villareal 1994.

Soon after Ignacio's murderer had been apprehended and put in jail, rumours began to circulate in the village concerning the assailant's wife, Dolores. It was said with some scorn that Dolores was claiming she had been Ignacio's lover, implying that her intention was to change the nature of the crime (from one of corruption to one of passion). By admitting publicly that she had been mistress of the deceased, she was obviously shaming her husband. However, she was at the same time giving her husband legitimate grounds for having killed Ignacio: he was only defending his honour. In a sense she was offering her virtue for that of her husband (in the hope that he would be let off on a minimum charge) and thus helping to restore family honour. However, the rumours did not say anything about the husband's reactions to Dolores' provocative acts.

Leaving aside the more obvious point – that violence is typically masculine (something which is amply confirmed through other incidents) – this little tale also points to the significance – and ambiguity – of female virtue. Two women are left without their husbands: Carlota, a widow, and Dolores, the wife of a murderer. Both have to find ways to fend for themselves in a situation where alternatives are few. Moreover, it is not just a question of economic survival – moral survival is equally precarious. They do not want to be classified as women who have no shame ('que no tienen vergüenza'). The implication of Ignacio's death for Carlota is to remain a widow and depend on her brother-in-law (who thereby also gains access to her land). This entails being a good mother (which is ultimately what being a good woman is all about) which in turn means loyalty to her (dead) husband which is tantamount to chastity. Dolores, however, has opted for a different path. She openly flaunts her dubious virtue – i.e. her shame. Her claims to lack virtue (saying she was the mistress of the deceased) are an attempt to restore her husband's honour, thereby transforming a 'bad' act to a 'good' one. She wants her husband back at any cost.

Taken together, the example of these two women illustrates the discrete categorisation of women that permeates the local community, where the virtuous woman (the one who has shame) is contrasted to the immoral woman, i.e. one without shame. However, Dolores' actions also serve to highlight the ambiguity with which all women are potentially imbued: if bad acts can become good acts, the opposite is also possible.

In most discussions of honour (and violence) the focus is on men and the violent acts they perpetrate. Violence is a male form of moral retribution. It is intrinsically tied to masculinity and power and is seen as one way of restoring honour – and thereby maintaining respect and manhood. Elsewhere I have suggested that this form of moral reasoning rests on a perception of masculinity as continuous – you are more or less a man, and hence you can achieve more masculinity by acting more 'like a man'. Obviously, the converse also holds true: masculinity can be challenged and even 'lost' in a contest between men (see Melhuus 1997b, 1998). This is in contrast to the discrete categorisation of women, where women are classified as either decent or not. In this Mexican context, violence among men serves to underscore the stereotypical image of the *macho*. Needless to say, there is much more to being a good and respected man than being violent. Situations of murder are the exception, not the rule (and can be used as exemplars indicative of moral values if not representative of them). In fact, most of the time, men are *not* violent and they uphold their reputations as good fathers, husbands, sons or brothers by other means. However, intrinsic to their claims to manhood are their relationships to women, be it mothers, wives, daughters or sisters. Thus, this little tale of violence (as it was retold) is instructive as it also points to ways that women can be implicated in acts of violence which on the surface do not appear to have anything to do with them.

10.5 The keepers and the kept

In what follows, I have chosen to focus on women, leaving aside the issue of men and violence as a form of moral retribution. Perhaps it is precisely because women do not usually revert to such outright dramatic acts that their moral footwork has been overlooked. The very grounding of significant values is often harder to discern, as they are embedded in daily chores. Sharing with housework that peculiar quality of only becoming visible the moment it is not done, this moral work is like a hidden script, the clues to which are revealed through gossip. However, that does not make a woman's efforts to maintain her moral worth any less strenuous and the stakes may be just as high.

I will illustrate this moral footwork by way of Ana, a woman who is struggling to be accepted by the community of which she is a part. This is a story about everyday life and continuous moves for moral survival in a community that is wary of change. The tale is in many ways ordinary: a woman is abandoned by her husband, tries to do something about it and meets local resistance. The person, however, is extraordinary. Ana is exceptional because she sees what she is doing and is able to reflect upon the moral limits of her own community. In order to render Ana's precarious situation comprehensible, however, I need to highlight some general aspects of this local morality.

Like any moral code, one based on honour and shame is grounded in significant distinctions. In this local context, these distinctions are represented through gender and obtain not just between men and women (i.e. cross-sex relations) but also between men and between women (same-sex relations). A central trait of this moral order is that rules of conduct apply unequally to men and women: what is appropriate for men is not appropriate for women and vice versa.[14] In other words, it is a code that discriminates according to gender. Central to this

[14] This is most obvious with respect to sexual conduct.. Men are expected to be sexually promiscuous and have many women; this enhances a man's masculinity, as does the number of children he has, a sign of his virility. Women, however, are expected to "have shame", protect their virginity and remain chaste after marriage. The concept of shame "vergüenza" (and "sin vergüenza", shameless) have many connotations; depending on context, it can be used to comment on shameful acts, relating to the particular behaviour of men or women or children, or it can also be used more significantly to allude to a woman's lack of propriety.

gender differentiation is a specific division of labour, which is reflected both spatially and occupationally and which ties notions of work to ideas of sexuality.

Briefly stated: a man is expected to work and through his work maintain his family. That is the role of the husband/father. Concomitantly, women (mothers/wives) are not expected to work (outside the house) but to attend to their families. Women do not inherit land, as they are supposed to marry and are therefore not in need of land of their own.[15] A man who lives off a women (his wife or mother) is called *un mantenido* (literally a maintained one, i.e. one who lets himself be kept), and locally this has very unmanly connotations. As I was told time and again: 'A man who lets his wife work is not a man'. It is not only assumed that a kept man is 'un flojo', i.e. lazy, and hence lacking in self-respect, but also that the situation will generate problems: he will probably take to drink, which in turn will give rise to domestic violence. Moreover, as one man said: 'It shames men to accept anything from their wives. He does not want her to work because they will say that she is keeping him'.

However, it was not work per se that was denied wives, but rather employment outside the house and the ability to provide. Both these activities were associated with sexuality. The former was often explained in terms of a husband's jealousy (*los celos*) implying that 'going to work' potentially jeopardizes a woman's chastity. The latter was perceived as a manifestation of the husband not being man enough, thereby diminishing his respect in the eyes of others. There was also a general attitude that one must not expose or demonstrate publicly that one is in need or that the family is lacking in any way. The fact that there were few women selling produce on the local market was explained in these terms. It would be considered a public display of need and an affront to a husband's honour.

Finally, a woman's place is in the house, but the house is not considered a respectable one unless it is under the protective guard of an honoured man; of course not any man, but a man who is socially accepted as a guardian of her virtue, implying that women cannot fend for their own virtue. There is a local saying: 'A house that lacks a man lacks respect', which transcribed means: a woman that lacks a man lacks respect, and, by implication, can be considered publicly accessible, i.e. a prostitute. House, women, and respect go together as do public, prostitute, and shameless. Thus a woman who lives alone and works for her own upkeep would be suspect on several counts.

That wives are not to do paid work can therefore be seen as a direct reflection of the demands placed on men, as husbands. However, that does not mean that married women do not work nor find ways of generating income. They do, but mostly within the confines of the house, like selling refreshments or milk or selected household items from their door. Maria, however, had found other ways of making a little extra money. She worked as a washerwoman, receiving dirty clothes and linen from Juana who lived in the village centre. She did not dare tell her husband, and took great pains to conceal the arrangement from him and others.

---

[15] Women did not normally participate in agricultural chores either.

Her husband was commuting to Mexico City, and only returned on weekends. She was quite sure he had no idea about the difference between their own dirty linen and that of Juana. To her it would be shaming her husband's honour, not only to tell him that there was not enough money to keep the family going, but also that she had done something on her own initiative to solve the problem.

Such a division of labour is intrinsically tied to marriage[16] and by extension to parenthood. Marriage is not only the formal expression of this relation between providers and those provided for, marriage rests on the assumption of an exchange whereby women provide extended service in return for their upkeep. Underpinning the exchange are notions of her virtue as a contributing factor to her husband's honour. Women, however, expected their husbands to be unfaithful and accepted the meandering of their men as long as they were well treated. Being well treated implied above all two things: that they received the money needed for the upkeep of their children and that they were not abused.

In San Felipe, chastity (a term that is not used locally, although its meaning would be familiar) can perhaps best be glossed by the meanings attached to the term 'decente', conveying something about the proper conduct expected of a woman in terms of her deportment. The different aspects of chastity were signalled in various ways. Most importantly, they were expressed through women's daily conduct, in particular through the things that women refrained from doing – like paid work, casual visiting, loitering or gossiping – as well as those things that they were expected to do: preparing meals, doing housework, taking care of the children, or looking after domestic animals. Virtue was also tied to notions of not being selfish (an egoist), in particular not putting personal interests before those of one's children. However, ideas of women's virtue were most clearly expressed through a local discourse on suffering, specifically associated with motherhood.[17]

Suffering formed part of a moral discourse which is exclusive to women and serves to enhance a woman's virtue, making it visible – to herself and others. Although men were excluded from this moral community of suffering, they were necessary and conducive to its maintenance. The gist of the logic is that the more you suffer, the better you are, albeit within the limits of what is perceived as the morally right source of suffering. Not all suffering qualified as virtuous. The suffering involved in being abandoned by your children did not enhance a woman's public esteem. Nor would rape. Whereas the former was interpreted as a sign of having been a poor mother, rape was framed in terms of being a loose woman. Overall, perhaps, it seemed that the point was not necessarily to suffer, but to be able to frame your life experiences in terms of the kind of suffering that results from making sacrifices for the sake of others.

There were life experiences that clearly represented sources of suffering and fed into such discourses: maltreatment, being abandoned by a husband, having to fend for your children on your own, having to accept a husband's infidelity, not

---

[16] In line with local usage, "marriage" also covers consensual unions, which were the most common. Couples would often live together for several years before entering a civil or church marriage.

[17] For further elaboration of the relationship between suffering, virginity and motherhood see Melhuus 1992, 1997b.

being allowed to work, not receiving enough money for the upkeep of the children, toleration of jealous husbands. Yet, although many women were extremely mindful of their reputations, they did not necessarily find the acceptance they were seeking. Events might occur that impede proper conduct; most problematic would be situations that leave women to fend for their own virtue. Being abandoned by your husband, becoming pregnant without securing marriage, becoming a widow or even divorced, are all events that might in some way jeopardize the woman concerned. Not only would she be in a precarious economic situation, her virtue would also be at stake.

There are local terms to characterize these different types of women, e.g. *fracasada* (literally 'failed'), *abandonada* ('abandoned'), *viuda* (widow) and *divorciada*. The terms indicate not only the status of the women concerned but also the thrust of the statements made. The term *fracasada* is used to denote a woman who has given birth out of wedlock or to denote an unmarried girl's assumed sexual activity. Morally she has fallen from grace.[18] *Abandonada* is a term used to describe a wife who has been left by her husband. She has not necessarily failed, but she has definitely lost. *Divorciada* was a term rarely used; women told me they preferred to be abandoned rather than divorced. Although all these terms may seem derogatory, this does not imply that a woman so classified was considered shameless and without respect. This would depend on her conduct, on whether she knows how to treat people. Or as Ignacio's brother said: 'if she behaves'.

As I have mentioned, women are categorized into two kinds: 'la mujer decente' ('the decent woman'), 'que no le falta el respeto' ('who is not lacking in respect'), 'que tiene vergüenza' (who has shame), and those women lacking these qualities. Varying terms are used to denote the latter kind. The most common were: she has no shame, she is open, she does not maintain her distance, or she is 'loca' (loud and causing trouble). All these expressions have sexual connotations, alluding to the accessibility or availability of the woman. They are definitely negative. They also imply a voluntary aspect, that those women who go public are flaunting their sexuality and, as we would say, 'asking for it'. Although different people would put the emphasis on different expressions, there was a general consensus about what characterized an immoral woman. However, that does not imply that all are agreed in specific terms about who should be judged as immoral. Such questions are situationally and contextually determined; family loyalties,

---

[18] For an interesting discussion on honour and grace see Peristiany and Pitt-Rivers 1992. In his postscript Pitt-Rivers indicates the gender specificity of grace. He says: "Grace like honor, is not the same for both sexes. While masculine honor is a matter of precedence in the first place and the man of honor strives to establish his name in the forefront of his group, the honor of women is rather a matter of virtue and sexual purity. The distinction is clearly marked in Sicily under the titles of "Name" and "Blood". The first is active and positive ... The second is negative and passive, a matter of avoiding any action that might stain the reputation of the family. Male honor is something to be won, increased and defended against a rival; female honor is something to be conserved and protected from evil tongues of the envious" (1992: 226). The ideas of blood are interesting, not only because they tie into notions of (sexual) purity, but also because, like purity, blood "cannot be gained in any way, but can be lost by positive action: illicit sexual activity" (Peristiany and Pitt-Rivers 1992:13).

likes and dislikes etc., will all enter into any moral evaluation. Nevertheless, a woman's immoral behaviour is not primarily her personal concern; it has public ramifications, reflecting the honour of her family.

10.6 Issues of virtue: Ana's dilemma

Ana is a very social, outgoing person. She is a hard worker, always busy, moving about in the village with ease. In addition to taking care of herself and her children, she also looks after her mother who lives next door. Her father died many years ago. Quick to laugh, she never puts on airs and always has time for a chat with people she meets. She is careful about what she says and not prone to criticise without cause. As she says: she knows how to treat people. She is, nevertheless, outspoken and defiant, and does not tolerate what she sees as unjust behaviour. She is generous and also inquisitive, wistful and at times very lonely. She wishes things could be different. On the surface, she appears to be managing well and seems generally liked.

In one of my many conversations with Ana she said: 'San Felipe is terrible for women. There is nothing here for them to do. There is no work for women. If you want to do something you have to leave. Just look at Guadalupe [her daughter] who is not allowed to work [by her husband]. Women who stay in the village, they become housewives.'

With these words, Ana was not only giving her opinion about the local state of affairs, but also expressing her frustration over the course of her own life. Ana is one of the many women who have stayed in the village, but she is not (only) a housewife. She has found something to do, although at the age of 40 she is still struggling for respect and recognition from her fellow villagers, something they seem reluctant to grant her. Balancing on the limits of the acceptable, she is a critical reader of her own culture.

Briefly stated, this is Ana's dilemma:

A mother of five, she was abandoned by her husband, in a context where a woman's virtue is still linked to the presence of a man. This predicament, though unfortunate, was not uncommon. It was one shared by many women. However, being a woman on her own makes for a rather ambiguous situation. On the one hand, it leaves Ana vulnerable and open to criticism; on the other, it seems to create a space in which she can move about and thus test the limits of the moral order.

Ana was (is) a strikingly beautiful woman. She had married when she was fifteen. Actually, true to custom, she 'was robbed', as they say locally, and went to live with her husband, Jorge, in his natal village. Her parents were extremely displeased and would not have anything to do with her or her husband. They were only reconciled after she gave birth to her first child, Juan, and she asked them to be his godparents at the baptism.

The process of abandonment was gradual. It was, according to Ana, generated by her husband's work situation. He held a job that involved frequent transferrals. All the time her husband was moving about, Ana stayed with her in-laws, an arrangement that did not suit her very well. She was under constant surveillance by his brothers and sisters. She used the pretext of the return and ensuing problems with her sister-in-law to legitimate her move back to her natal village. In doing this, she was defying her in-laws and challenging her husband's honour. They claimed that her place was 'where your husband has left you', whereas she insisted that love was not dependent upon a place. They said that she would lose her husband if she moved.

Ana moved. And she did lose her husband. What really prompted him to leave her, the story does not tell; but Ana did tell me that he had settled elsewhere, and that he had other children (implying that he had another woman).

On returning home, Ana moved in with her mother. Having decided she had to fend for herself, she was determined to set up an enterprise. She took out a loan with the Ministry of Tourism, which was promoting local initiatives, to realize her plans to start a small restaurant. These were good times, the time of the renovation, as the villagers called it, and there were lots of construction workers in the area. Ana was very thrifty and her restaurant did well. Too well according to some.

One day on returning home she found a pile of salt on her doorstep. Throwing salt ('echar sal') is recognized as an act of witchcraft and a sign that someone wishes you harm. Ana immediately knew the reason for being subjected to such an act and could readily identify the culprits. They also had a restaurant and, according to Ana, they were losing customers. Although Ana said she did not believe in the efficacy of witchcraft, she nevertheless had a 'limpia' ('cleansing ritual') performed. Ana had become an object of envy and the victim of local witchcraft. She told me that she was in turn accused of having thrown salt in order to harm her competitors. She laughed, saying that this was a lie ('puras mentiras').

Ana was, however, not deterred, and after a while she expanded her business. She had decided she wanted to run a small hotel, and had three rooms built on the top of her house cum restaurant. She was happy. Not only was she managing to support herself and her children, but the granting of the loan in her name meant she was also recognized as an independent legal entity. This latter was received as a provocation by her in-laws. They were angry because she was in debt.

Although she felt lonely, for Ana to remarry was out of the question. Echoing the local sentiments, she claimed she could not do it because of the children. Ana's whole life revolved around catering for her children and securing their future. She wanted them to have an education and had sent the eldest children to school in Toluca. In order to be able to do this, she worked. It is significant that the work she opted for is a mere extension of family chores, of caring, of service done for the benefit of others. She stressed the work, but never the pay. Times were not as prosperous any more, and she openly complained of the suffering she had gone through for the sake of her children.

Children are important, not only because they confer motherhood, which is a central value, but also because they in a sense legitimise the mother. Ana is freer to move about in the company of her children. Without them she would be quite suspect. At the time I was there, only her youngest son was living at home. Ana felt the presence of children to be so important to her social survival that she dreamt about having another child, which in this case would be illegitimate.[19] She said: 'Quiero comprarme otro bebe para no estar sola' ('I want to buy myself another baby, so as not to be alone'). Ana often expressed feelings of loneliness. She does not have any intimate friends – friends she can trust ('amigas de confianza'). 'Whatever you say, the whole village will know about it. You cannot trust anyone. It's all pure gossip, gossip.'

Once, one of my neighbours, who I knew was an acquaintance of Ana (in fact it was Ana who introduced us), asked me how many children Ana had. I was puzzled by the question, since I knew (and she knew that I knew) that she knew the answer. I told her Ana had five children. The conversation continued in the same vein, of feigning ignorance, next with respect to the fact that Ana's husband had left her. Finally, she said: 'I would never have let my husband come and go as he pleases. That I should be there waiting whenever he comes looking ... never!' (Implied was that Ana made herself sexually available whenever her husband happened to appear.) Whereas others insinuated that Ana's last two children were not conceived by her husband, this woman was in fact accusing Ana of having illicit sex with her own husband.

Ana went to church regularly. She was active in church matters, participating in a group that helped run church affairs. She spent much of her free time on various fund raising activities. She was also a very close friend of the priest. He often came to visit her, and would chat with her into the evening about all and anything. This, however, gave rise to yet more insinuations. Ana was well aware of the gossip about her and the priest and indignantly told me what was rumoured. She worried about what people were saying about them and told the priest not to come so often: 'It is not for my sake, but for yours'. She had good reason for concern. The gossip also reached me. A woman I knew well told me that Ana had been caught in the very act, in bed with the priest. She insisted this was true, since the daughter of her neighbour, who works for the priest, had seen it with her own eyes.

Ana had also been active in school politics. When it was demanded that parents pay tuition fees, she led a 'no' campaign under the slogan 'we won't pay'. The president of the parents' association at the time (later a candidate in local elections) started to spread yet other rumours about her, saying she was doing this because she wanted to be president (of the association), and moreover, that she had children who were criminals.

Ana also told me about the time she was confronted by her oldest son, Juan, who was living at home again for a while. He said that people were saying that he was 'un mantenido', being kept by his mother. When she asked him who was responsible for this gossip, Juan said that, according to his sources, she was. She

[19] There is no space to delve also into the issues of illegitimate children. Suffice it to say that this is of major concern locally. If a daughter gets pregnant out of wedlock, parents would try to bring about a marriage. A woman would be concerned to have her child legitimized by its father, and a married man might also have an interest in recognizing his illegitimate child, although his wife would not.

denied being the source of this slander and was very much concerned about the reputation of her son. He was working as a driver and she was very explicit about the fact that he gave her money for his upkeep. She admitted to having interfered with his work once (refusing to let him drive when he was drunk), but on the whole he managed his own life. She nevertheless kept house for him, always preparing meals no matter what the hour, washing his clothes, cleaning his room etc. While Juan had felt his manhood questioned, Ana interpreted the event as a direct criticism of her, because she was working and had supported her children for many years.

For my purposes, the issue is not whether the rumours were true or false. Rather, the interesting question is what these incidents reveal about the local morality. At the heart of the matter is Ana's virtue and the acceptance or rejection of Ana as a morally good *woman*. A woman without a man – and in particular an abandoned woman – makes visible a paradox. On the one hand, claims to being a respectable woman imply being protected by a man. Ana should therefore remarry. But she cannot do that, because of the children. To remarry would be a selfish act, restoring her virtue (presumably) but at the same time it would be an abandonment of her children, and she would be considered a bad mother. Without a man, you have to fend for your own virtue, and this is impossible if defence of virtue is seen as a male prerogative. Ana gains her legitimacy through her children, but the community is not willing to grant her full membership.[20] Not only is the legitimacy of her children questioned, attacks at Ana are directed through her children, who are called criminals.

Framed in these terms, Ana's dilemma can be phrased differently. She is demanding respect for being a virtuous woman, i.e. a good mother with all that that entails locally. At the same time, she is obliged to reject the very same tradition of virtue in order to do what she is doing, i.e. working and maintaining her own household. Through her actions, Ana clearly demonstrates her independence, in particular her economic independence of men. She is not being provided for. She therefore precludes the possibility of being defined within the prevailing moral order, since effectively she is questioning with the necessity of that same order. However, at the same time, she is dependent on the community in her need to be acknowledged by them.

Ana seems to know what she is doing and is constantly aware of just how far she can go. A possible interpretation is that Ana is in fact doing something different for herself but within an overriding paradigm of doing things for others. And it is not as if her efforts go unnoticed. Others 'see' the difference and maybe even feel the tension Ana creates. She certainly does. By refusing to acknowledge that what she is doing is morally right, the villagers are refusing an alternative

---

[20] A notion of community evokes an idea of consensus. Therefore it is perhaps important to stress that individual people might have differing interests in Ana's virtue. Moreover, the community is also gendered; the threat Ana poses to men and women is not the same. Whereas women might see Ana as a potential lover for their husbands, men might see her as a threat to their roles as providers, and hence their masculinity.

definition of womanhood. But at the same time, they cannot claim wholeheartedly that Ana is morally wrong. They are caught in the dilemma, as is Ana.

10.7 A moral breach?

I have stated that a central trait of this moral order is that rules of conduct apply unequally to men and women: what is appropriate for men is not appropriate for women and vice versa. Central to this gender differentiation is a specific division of labour that directly structures the gender relation, tying ideas of manhood to a particular kind of work, i.e. that work which is seen as providing for the family. Women, to be virtuous, should be legally, economically and morally dependent on men. This very dependence, on the part of women, is a precondition for creating the independent, virtuous man. Hence men are, albeit in another sense of the word, dependent on women, if they are to continue as men within the conditions set by the same moral order. A single woman, successfully providing for herself (and her children) upsets this balance, and makes visible other viable ways of being. In moral terms, the problem is how such conduct is understood – and sanctioned – locally. Is the woman committing a moral breach – placing herself outside the moral community? Or is she just behaving badly, and should she be sanctioned accordingly within the moral community?

To come closer to an answer, it is at this point pertinent to re-examine Pitt-Rivers' assertion that 'once the sexual division of labour breaks down women become men and where this occurs there can be neither honour nor shame' (1974:70; see also Melhuus 2001a). What he is suggesting is that honour and shame as relevant moral categories lose their grip once specific gendered categories of work (or chores) are transcended or become gender-neutral. In other words, the dissociation of gender and work opens up a totally different social field, making possible a situation where women can fend for themselves, as caretakers of their own interests. This claim not only supports the argument that the sexual division of labour and a moral code of honour and shame are intrinsically linked. It also implicitly assumes that the breakdown of the same sexual division of labour will lead to a change in gender relations ('women become men') and hence in what it means to be a good man or woman. Such a breakdown will necessarily entail a change in the symbolic and moral connotations of sexuality, which in turn imply a change in moral evaluations and ultimately a shift in the power relations between men and women. In Pitt-Rivers' argument there is an implicit assumption that this shift will take a specific direction: it is women who will take over men's work (and not vice versa).

For a woman to behave like a man (that is, do what men do) implies at least two things: she would have to forfeit her shame (and accept being shameless), and she would have to forfeit the grasp that women have on men's honour. In other words, she must accept that female virtue is no longer tied to a woman's sexuality and, moreover, that her sexuality is of no concern to anyone but herself. As a consequence, she must cede the specific power (influence) that women have over men. However, for such concessions to have any impact whatsoever, they need to find some public acknowledgement, otherwise they will remain mere private points of view. Moral evaluations are significant only insofar as they are inscribed in the ongoing processes of everyday life, their meanings created in the relations between people. Thus we are back to empirical realities and social processes where such changes can be documented.

What the example of Ana shows is that the interdependence of men and women does not rest on just one factor, but on a combination of factors. Concomitantly, the inappropriateness of Ana's behaviour cannot be derived from a single breach of conduct. It is not each incident in itself which counts; it is the aggregate of different behaviours which becomes critical. They all converge and are in turn subsumed under the local notion of virtue. Recognition of her virtue or acknowledgement of her respectability are two things which Ana cannot give herself; it has to come from others. And there are obviously more ways than one of drawing attention to a lack of virtue. The varying responses to Ana all point in the same direction: she lives by herself, without the protection of a man; her children are not only illegitimate, but also criminal; she has illicit sex with her own husband; she uses her restaurant to seduce the priest. She is in effect a dubious woman, one without shame.

In their reactions to Ana's activities the community has the choice between two alternatives: either to question the prevailing ideas about women (and men) or to question Ana. As the best way to avoid talking about something is to talk about something else, they opt for the latter. The overriding cultural attributes of womanhood are motherhood and mothering. This forms the basis for Ana's self-reflection and also the frame of reference for levelling criticisms against her. She is obviously a mother; the trick is to establish her as a bad one.

Being a woman (on her own), Ana does not have many alternatives when it comes to defending her virtue. She cannot (yet) successfully appeal to an alternative morality, for example one stressing the equality of men and women, insofar as this morality does not predominate locally.[21] Nor can she openly fight for it, although women, who are the object of slander, do have recourse to one form of public response. They can, if accused of being a prostitute (or bedding the priest), and if they know the source of the accusation, protest by accosting the person openly and publicly. Locally such actions go under the terms 'reclamar' or 'demandar'. Though not very common, they do occur. Although well aware of which people were spreading rumours about her, Ana preferred to remain silent. Partly, this had to do with pride ('orgullo') and partly, I think, it had to do with Ana's not wanting to succumb to public opinion – or be part of a public spectacle. For her, these were her private concerns.

What perhaps saves Ana is that she is after all a victim, an *abandonada* and that she does know how to treat people. Treading carefully, she can only convince by constantly behaving well (and thereby proving the others wrong). She has not chosen her position as a woman without a man. Her husband left her. Yet the

[21] And it is important to stress that things are different in other areas of Mexico; and the processes at work elsewhere will inevitably affect San Felipe.

message is clear. She has not suffered as much as she should. Once abandoned the correct thing for Ana to do, according to her own statements, would have been to wait in silent, yet visible, suffering for her husband, crying and hoping that he would send money. She chose to do something different in deciding to manage on her own. Not only that, but it seems that the context in terms of which she attempts to establish her claims to suffering, and hence to being a good woman, is in part rejected. Her suffering is either not enough or perhaps not of the right kind. Moreover, the situation gives rise to a doubt: it might well be that she prefers it that way.

The people of the community cannot take away Ana's motherhood, nor can they annul her loan. Though attempts have been made to influence her business, these have been unsuccessful. Given this situation, to grant Ana her virtue would imply giving her everything, and thereby creating a new woman: an economic and legally independent and virtuous woman. This would imply creating a new man and thereby changing the very structure of the gender relation. However, what occurs is exactly the opposite.

Ana's behaviour is interpreted and evaluated within the prevailing morality, with one exception. Paradoxically, the only institution that has recognised Ana as an economically independent *person* is the bank. This act is significant, the implications of which have not been absorbed. By granting Ana a loan, the bank blatantly defies local mores, but it seems that neither Ana nor her surroundings have explored fully the meanings of that transaction.

Ana's strategy has proved culturally viable. Her claims to virtue lie in extracting credit for her good intentions. Caught up in processes of change, she may possibly also represent current trends. However, whether these processes will ultimately deprive the notions of honour and shame of their local, gendered meanings, or whether they will resurface with other connotations, only time will tell. Whether they will, as active moral concepts, become obsolete is doubtful, although their gendered and public connotations may well be transformed. In any case, such changes in moral evaluations will necessarily depend on a series of factors, of which the overall economic situation will be one. It is, as we (and they) know, possible to make a virtue of necessity.

With women increasingly entering the labour market, changes in the division of labour are already occurring. Moreover, with the active involvement of outside agencies (such as a bank, Ministry of Tourism) engaging directly with women, in a sense irrespective of gender, new standards for conduct are set. However, the implications for local meanings of gender remain to be seen (for a different example, see Villarreal 1996). Whatever the case, confrontation of values tied to ideas of moral worth will continue to permeate everyday life in San Felipe. Even if we accept that meaning is ultimately created in the relations between people, there is always the possibility that the meanings created are ambiguous and perhaps differently apprehended by the parties involved, as in this case by Ana and the others. The 'result' of the moral negotiations is not quite a continuation of the tradition of virtue as practiced within the community, nor is it a full transition to an acknowledgement of dignity or equality, as set by an alternative moral code.

However, it is this very ambiguity that gives room for manoeuvre and lays the basis for change.

References

Archetti, E. (1991), 'Argentinian Tango: Male sexual ideology and morality' in Reidar Grønhaug, Gunnar Haaland and Georg Henriksen (eds.). *The Ecology of Choice and Symbol. Essays in honour of Fredrik Barth*, Alma Mater, Bergen

Asano-Tamanoi, M. (1987), 'Shame, family and state in Catalonia and Japan' in David Gilmore (ed.): *Honor and Shame and the Unity of the Mediterranean*, American Anthropologist 22 (special publication)

Baroja, J. C. (1974), 'Honour and shame: A historical account of several conflicts' in J.G. Peristiany (ed.): *Honour and Shame. The Values of Mediterranean Society*, University of Chicago Press, Chicago

Berger, P., Berger, B. and Kellner, H. (1977 [1974]), *The Homeless Mind. Modernization and Consciousness*, Penguin Books, Harmondsworth

Bourdieu, P. (1974 [1966]), 'The sentiment of honour in Kabyle Society' in J.G. Peristiany (ed.): *Honour and Shame. The Values of Mediterranean Society*, University of Chicago Press, Chicago

Brandes, S. (1987), 'Reflections on Honor and Shame' in David Gilmore (ed.): *Honor and Shame and the Unity of the Mediterranean*, American Anthropologist 22 (special publication)

Clarke, E. (1979 [1957]), *My Mother Who Fathered Me. A study of the family in three selected communities in Jamaica*, George Allen and Unwin, London

Delaney, C. (1987), 'Seeds of honour, fields of shame' in David Gilmore (ed): *Honor and Shame and the Unity of the Mediterranean*, American Anthropologist 22 (special publication)

Dumont, L. (1980 [1970]), *Homo hierachicus. The caste system and its implications*, University of Chicago Press, Chicago

Edel, M. and Edel, A. (1959), *Anthropology and Ethics*, Charles C. Thomas, Illinois

Eidheim, H. (1981), *Grand Bay. Lokalorganisering i en vestindisk landsby*, Occasional Papers 3, Institute of social anthropology, University of Oslo

Evens, T.M.S. (1982), 'Two concepts of "society as a moral system": Evens Pritchard heterodoxy' in Man 17: 205-218

Gilmore, D. (1982), 'Anthropology of the Mediterranean Area' in *Annual Review of Anthropology* 11:175-205

Gilmore, D. (ed.) (1987), *Honor and Shame and the Unity of the Mediterranean*, American Anthropologist 22 (special publication)

Goddard, V. (1987), 'Honour and shame: the control of women's sexuality and group identity in Naples' in Pat Caplan (ed.): *The Cultural Construction of Sexuality*, Tavistock Publications, London

Goddard, V. (1996), *Gender, Family and Work in Naples*, Berg, Oxford

Guttman, M. C. (1996), *The Meanings of Macho. Being a Man in Mexico City*, University of California Press, Berkeley

Herzfeld, M. (1980), 'Honour and Shame: Problems in the comparative analysis of moral systems' in Man 15: 339-51

Johnson, L. L. and Lipsett-Rivera, S. (eds.) (1998), *The Faces of Honor. Sex, shame and violence in colonial Latin America*, University of New Mexico Press, Albuquerque

Lancaster, R. (1988), 'Subject honor and object shame: the construction of male homosexuality and stigma in Nicaragua' in Ethnology 27 (2): 111-125

Lever, A. (1986), 'Honour as a red herring' in Critique of Anthropology 6 (3): 83-106

Levine, S. E. and Correa C. S. & Uribe F. M. (1986), 'The Marital Morality of Mexican Women: An urban study' in Journal of Anthropological Research 42 (2): 183-202

Levine, S. E. (1993), *Dolor y alegría: Women and Social Change in Urban Mexico*, University of Wisconsin Press, Madison

Lewis, O. (1959), *Five Families. Mexican case studies in the culture of poverty*, Basic Books, New York

Lewis, O. (1961), *The Children of Sánchez. Autobiography of a Mexican Family*, Random House, New York (Spanish edition)

Lewis, O. (1965), *Los hijos de Sánchez*, Editorial Joaquin Mortiz, Mexico City

Lewis, O. (1964), *Pedro Martinez. A Mexican peasant and his family*, Secker and Warburg, London

Lippset-Rivera, S. (1998), 'A Slap in the Face of Honor. Social transgression and women in late colonial Mexico' in Lyman L. Johnson and Sonya Lipsett-Rivera (eds.): *The Faces of Honor. Sex, shame and violence in colonial Latin America*, University of New Mexico Press, Albuquerque

Martinez-Alier, V. (1974), *Marriage, Class and Colour in Nineteenth-century Cuba. A study of racial attitudes and sexual values in slave society*, Cambridge University Press, London

Melhuus, M. (1990), 'A shame to honour – a shame to suffer' in Ethnos 55 (I -II): 5-25

Melhuus, M. (1992), *'Todos tenemos madre. Diós también.' Morality Meaning and Change in a Mexican Context*, D.Phil thesis, Department of social anthropology, University of Oslo

Melhuus, M. (1997a), 'Exploring the work of a compassionate ethnographer. The case of Oscar Lewis' in Social Anthropology 5 (1): 35-54

Melhuus, M. (1997b), 'The troubles of virtue: values of violence and suffering in a Mexican context' in Signe Howell (ed.): *The Ethnography of Moralities*, Routledge, London

Melhuus, M. (1998), 'Configuring gender: Male and female in Mexican heterosexual and homosexual relations' in Ethnos 63 (3): 335-382

Melhuus, M. (2001a), 'The power of penetration – the value of virginity: male and female in Mexican heterosexual and homosexual relations' in Cathrine Alès and Cécile Barraud (eds.): *Sexe relatif ou sexe absolu?* Editions de la Maison des sciences de l'homme, Paris

Melhuus, M. (2001b), 'Hvilken skam uten ære? eller: finnes den skamløse æren?' in Trygve Wyller (ed.): *Skam. Perspektiver på skam, ære og skamløshet i det moderne*, Fagbokforlaget, Bergen

Melhuus, M. and Stølen K. A. (1996), 'Introduction' in Marit Melhuus and Kristi Anne Stølen (eds.): *Machos, Mistresses, Madonnas. Contesting the Power of Latin American Gender Imagery*, Verso, London

Peristiany, J.G. and Pitt-Rivers J. (1974 [1966]), *Honour and Shame. The Values of Mediterranean Society*, University of Chicago Press (Midway Reprint), Chicago

Peristiany, J.G. and Pitt-Rivers J. (eds.) (1992), *Honor and Grace in Anthropology*, Cambridge University Press, Cambridge

Peristiany, J.G. and Pitt-Rivers J. (1992), 'Introduction' in Peristiany, J.G. and Julian Pitt-Rivers (eds.) 1992: *Honor and Grace in Anthropology*, Cambridge University Press, Cambridge

Pitt-Rivers, J. (1992), 'Postscript' in Peristiany, J.G. and Julian Pitt-Rivers (eds.) (1992): *Honor and Grace in Anthropology*, Cambridge University Press, Cambridge

Pitt-Rivers, J. (1974), 'Honour and Social Status' in Peristiany, J.G. and Pitt-Rivers, Julian: *Honour and Shame. The Values of Mediterranean Society*, University of Chicago Press (Midway Reprint), Chicago

Piña-Cabral, J. (1989), 'The Mediterranean as a category of regional comparison: a critical view' in Current Anthropology 30 (3): 339-405

Prieur, A. (1998), *Mema's House, Mexico City. On transvestites, queens, and machos*, University of Chicago Press, Chicago

Rigdon, S. (1988), *The Culture Facade. Art, Science, and Politics in the Work of Oscar Lewis*, University of Illinois Press, Urbana

Pitt-Rivers, J. (1974 [1966]), 'Honour and Social Status' in J.G. Peristiany (ed.): *Honour and Shame. The Values of Mediterranean Society*

Rivière, P. G. (1967), 'The honour of Sánchez' in Man 2: 569-83

Schneider, J. (1971), 'Of vigilance and virgins: Honor, shame and access to resources in Mediterranean Societies', Ethnology 10: 1-24

Seed, P. (1988a), 'Marriage promises and the value of a woman's testimony in colonial Mexico' in Signs: Journal of Women in Culture and Society, 13(2): 253-276

Seed, P. (1988b), *To love, honor and obey in Colonial Mexico. Conflicts over Marriage Choice, 1574-1821*, Stanford University Press, Stanford

Stølen, K. A. (1996), *The Decency of Inequality. Gender, power and social change on the Argentine prairie*, Oslo, Scandinavian University Press

Villarreal, M. (1994), *Wielding and Yielding: Power, subordination and gender identity in the context of a Mexican development project*. PhD thesis, Wageningen University,The Netherlands

Villarreal, M. (1996), 'Power and self-identity: the beekeepers of Ayuquila' in Marit Melhuus and Kristi Anne Stølen (eds.): *Machos, Mistresses, Madonnas. Contesting the Power of Latin American Gender Imagery*, Verso, London

Wikan, U. (1984), 'Shame and Honour: A contestable pair?' in *Man* 19: 635-52

Wilson, P.J. (1973), *Crab Antics. The Social Anthropology of English-Speaking Negro Societies of the Caribbean*, Yale University Press, New Haven

Wyatt-Brown, B. (1982), *Southern Honor. Ethics and Behavior in the Old South*, Oxford University Press, Oxford

Wyller, T. (ed.) (2001), *Skam. Perspektiver på skam, ære og skamløshet i det moderne*, Fagbokforlaget, Bergen

Index

9781138258464